Procter was born in Trinidad at the end of the last war, and returned to England with his parents via a wartime convoy. On arriving in Liverpool, they stayed at the family farm in Northamptonshire, before leaving there for the Sudan and a house on the banks of the Nile, living there for five years until 1949. The family moved to Uganda, with Procter returning to boarding school in Sussex and later Essex. He read Mechanical Sciences (Engineering) at Cambridge, subsequently joining manufacturing industry in the Midlands. In 1969, containerisation was in its infancy and Procter moved to London for a position as a project engineer in among the old United Kingdom shipping fraternity. In 1975, he left for two years in Cape Town to help with the transition from the old mail boat service to container shipping. There followed many years of travel advising on initiating and completing shipping projects worldwide.

Although the author and publisher have made every effort to ensure that the information in this book was correct at press time, the author and publisher do not assume and hereby disclaim any liability to any party for any loss, damage, or disruption caused by errors or omissions, whether such errors or omissions result from negligence, accident, or any other cause.

Letters Home

Procter Hutchinson

Letters Home

Vanguard Press

VANGUARD PAPERBACK

© Copyright 2023
Procter Hutchinson

The right of Procter Hutchinson to be identified as author of this work has been asserted by them in accordance with the Copyright, Designs and Patents Act 1988.

All Rights Reserved

No reproduction, copy or transmission of this publication may be made without written permission.
No paragraph of this publication may be reproduced, copied or transmitted save with the written permission of the publisher, or in accordance with the provisions
of the Copyright Act 1956 (as amended).

Any person who commits any unauthorised act in relation to this publication may be liable to criminal prosecution and civil claims for damages.

A CIP catalogue record for this title is available from the British Library.

ISBN 978 1 80016 547 2

*Vanguard Press is an imprint of
Pegasus Elliot Mackenzie Publishers Ltd.*
www.pegasuspublishers.com

First Published in 2023

**Vanguard Press
Sheraton House Castle Park
Cambridge England**

Printed & Bound in Great Britain

Contents

Foreword.. 9
12 May 1996 — A day up country in Andalucia.. 10
11 June '96 — Russia after the fall of the wall... 13
11th July '96 — A project in sleepy Dhofar, Oman................................... 14
7th October '96 — First acquaintances in Salalah, Oman......................... 18
19th October '96 — Signing the new port concession for Salalah............ 19
6th November '96 — The Bait Saeed will not trouble us.......................... 21
15th December '96 — Containers and now dhows, camels and fish,
    in and around Muscat.. 23
5 January 1997 — Sailing Netherlands style... 29
5th March '97 — Holiday and friends in Cape Town................................ 30
11th March '97 — The lovely old Reina Christina..................................... 33
27th March '97 — Dubai revisited.. 35
26th April 1997 — Back in New York to fight the engineers and Charlotte........ 39
26th April — Back to New York for another engineer fight..................... 41
28th April '97 — World tour... 47
7th May '97 — World Tour — cancelled!... 48
20th May '97 — Iberia — The airline most likely to improve 1997.......... 54
5th July '97 — Cow tipping.. 58
1st Jun '97 — Rumania... 63
1st Aug '97 — Jack... 64
1st August '97 — University.. 69
4 August 1997 — Helevoetsluis... 70
11 August 1997 — Yachting... 70
3rd Sept 97 — Some time to spare on a brief visit to Algeciras................ 72
3rd Sept. '97 — Diana's death.. 75
10th September '97 — Oman.. 75
16 September '97 — Letter to Beijing friend... 76
18th Oct. '97 — Camel tour.. 77
19th October '97 — The English tea room... 86
25th November '97 — St. Petersberg.. 90
19th January '98 — Muscat... 94
19th January '98 — Damen shipyard.. 95
23rd January '98 — Ramadan... 96
29th January '98 — Rub Al Kali... 97
7th March '98 — Patricia in Oman... 99
6th March '98 — American friends.. 102
1st March '98 — Southern Russia.. 108
31st March '98 — Skopje.. 118
1st April '98 — Czech Airlines — Coach Class April.............................. 120
1st April '98 — Skopje & Sofia.. 120
6th April '98 — Answer phones... 122
5th June '98 — Oman.. 123
7th June '98 — Internecine strife... 126
23rd June '98 — England.. 127

8th July '98 — Oman	127
8th July '98 — London museums	128
8th July '98 — Mugsayl blow holes	130
8 July '98 — Grave mounds	136
1st Aug '98 — Khor Rouri or Sum Haram	138
2nd September '98 — Georgia	141
4th October '98 — Beirut	148
5th November '98 — Oman	150
29th November, 1998 — The Casino Hotel	151
30th November '98 — Oman	153
12th December '98 — Finland	154
22nd January '99 — Wimps	157
31st January '99 — Anti-gravity	158
5th February '99 — Cochin	171
21st February '99 — GM Foods	173
7th March '99 — Moodies	174
17th March '99 — Mumbai	176
20th March '99 — Italy	178
23rd March '99 — India	179
23rd March '99 — Above Iran	182
2nd April '99 — Things general…	184
29th April '99 — Poland	185
2nd May '99 — Poland	188
19th May '99 — The Malabar Coast	189
20th August '99 — Holland	197
22nd August '99 — India part two	206
12th September '99 — India part 3	210
17th September '99 — Oman	217
22nd September '99 — William letter	218
22 September 1999 — Dhofar	219
Date: 10/11/99 — Jebel Akhdar	220
16th October '99 — Ghubrah Bowl II	228
22nd November 2003 — Shiel Bet, Gujerat	236

Foreword

Over the years I have kept my distant family abreast and with some idea of what passes for a career in other countries. My mother and father started the concept when they were separated by seas and continents as they were travellers too. They started life with a whirlwind romance in England shortly moving to India and then Trinidad where I and my sister were born. From that beginning we were all lucky to see many parts of the more obscure world. These letters back to my family kept me amused writing them and I think them in reading them. Being an engineer brings a slightly different take on life which I hope, you the reader, will enjoy too. The places I went to professionally allowed some exploration, some concern and some downright fright. Keeping a journal, by way of letters, is better even than photographs and much to be encouraged for later life when you might wonder where you spent those weeks and months.

12 May 1996 — A day up country in Andalucia

Algeciras — Sunday, and I am waiting for my colleagues to show up or else I will go to the restaurant alone.

I have spent the day driving inland among the mountains and cork forests. The scenery is wild and deserted, and after the rains this last winter, wonderfully green and vibrant with wild flowers. I was advised to go to Castella de la Frontier, and after a false start, found myself on the right by-road winding its way among the oak trees, gaining height slowly until topping a rise. I found myself looking up at a castle on hill well above me and in the middle of nowhere.

You really wonder what drove them to build these places, and they didn't build them very well, either. When you think of Scottish or English castles, you think of something pretty substantial, but the Moors made do with something more temporary. I suspect the order to go and defend and control a chunk of wilder Spain was not an upward career move. More by way of two hours detention than the class prize for good behaviour. I can imagine Abdul, and possibly Mrs Abdul, slogging their way through the cork forest looking for a likely hill to invest, Mrs Abdul grumbling about how much nicer it was in Constantinople before Abdul forgot to bow seven times before the Caliph — or whatever you got sent to Spain for.

Since it was unlikely that anyone, least of all the building inspectorate, would bother to come and look over the castle upon completion, work could be begun and completed with unseemly haste. Some of the battlements of this particular edifice were only about eight feet above the adjacent piece of flat land. Drawing your bow one side of the arrow slit, you might find the point of the arrow already resting on the tin hat of your enemy the other side. The wall thickness was such that you could be warned by the sound of the attacking force sneezing on the outside of it while getting to work with the sappers.

The internals of the castle, unsullied by anything you might call renovation, still had a pub and the odd bod living in a cottage or two. I shot most of a 36-frame film. Well above arrow range, Mrs Abdul had insisted on an attractive arched gazebo, I suppose you would call it. With a fine view across the surrounding wilderness, it must have been a wonderful place to entertain the other expatriate wives, if there were any.

My colleagues failed to show, so must have got involved with the locals. I had hoped they might come back to the hotel and accompany me to a restaurant outside the hotel, not having the will or fortitude to go by myself. As it was, I dined alone on a steak the likes of which I have not had since being taken to a dreadful steak bar in St. Petersburg. The Reina Christina is renowned for its culinary efforts, but I suppose I shall go to bed on an elegant sufficiency rather than the excesses I have been accustomed to. The Spanish eat!

11 June '96 — Russia after the fall of the wall

I am somewhere over the Gulf of Finland — I think it is — on my way back from St. Petersburg to Amsterdam with all the other idiots who earn their living from thirty thousand feet. I've been in Russia with a party of likeminded masochists beating our heads against the brick walls trying to make some progress with a plan to take over the management of the container terminal. I'm pretty convinced about most of my colleagues, but the German contingent includes one and he might hold us up a bit. His boss, who used to be a roadie for Sting and others, says that after you have been in St. P. for a couple of years, you're not necessarily crazy, just a bit "special". This one is a bit special!

Alex

Later: Alex, in the operations office of a business, importing used Ladas from the UK and selling them to Russian taxi drivers. We were gathered in the bar of the St. Petersburg Europa Hotel recovering from a day with the Russians and the dilatory translators. I was taking calls from various parts of the world for my projects and Alex asked if I had always done a lot of travelling.

"Alex," I said. "I was born in Trinidad."

Alex turned round and called out, "Barman! More beer, this is going to be a long one."

Later and over another gulf, this time the Persian one. I got back to The Hague last night and caught the flight to Oman his afternoon. We have to land at Dhahran to let off the really lucky contingent of Saudi expats — glad it's not me, six years in Saudi was enough. Oman is another matter and even South Yemen could be better, I suppose. There is supposed to be a major port development in Aden but everyone I ask about it is maintaining or receiving radio silence. The investors are a group of Yemeni expats in Saudi from the Hadramaut and they are trying to attract users, but it would seem we are doing better than they are. I am on my way to Salalah again to complete a report on the conventional port. The government have asked us to take it over, as well as construct a new container terminal, so I am working on the handling rates of lads humping sacks in and out of dhows instead of all the hi-tech stuff I've been playing with these last several years. A lot more fun.

My involvement with Salalah again is much to the distress of my transatlantic detractors. My immediate superior would like me more involved but explained, quite rightly, that if he forced the issue the US would just try to see it fail. Nice to be appreciated. Trouble is, I find it difficult to be accommodating to those I regard as being empty suits. Nasty arrogant Brit! Anyhow, it's great pleasure to be down here. I think Oman is the last place in the Middle East to be worth being in. I was not impressed by Dubai last time I was through.

11th July '96 — A project in sleepy Dhofar, Oman

I am sitting here in my hotel in Salalah, and if all goes according to plan, once back in civilisation, I plug this thing in and off it goes down the wire. We shall see! I have just flown down here with two Danes who both started life at sea before the mast. I am continually being confronted by my own ignorance and it gets wearing. I am supposed to be shepherding these people round the port to get their assistance on the marine aspects of the place. I am off in a moment to listen to old sea faring stories and maybe a few ideas on how to run a tug operation. Perhaps after a few beers it will all become much clearer.

Aboard the pilot launch

I am here with the mariners to see whether they think they can get a hundred and twenty-five thousand tons of ship alongside without moving the tectonic plates. They reckon it will be all right. The weather was in our favour — the sort of day when wild storms and huge waves are inconceivable — about thirty C with a very light breeze and glorious sunshine.

Later: two Danish mariners and one Dutchman visited Salalah to assess the port for big ship calls. The gentleman in dark glasses was a member of the A P Moeller board and learnt his trade in the Baltic on sailing vessels 'before the mast'.

I was in Russia last week, helping to put up a bid to run the container terminal in St. Petersburg — slow job. The site is so cluttered with defunct equipment it is difficult to decide what is of use and what isn't. We walked

Navigation issues on the pilot launch

through the working container stack and found a line of boxes with the moss growing round them and weeds growing through the corner castings where they had also flowered, seeded and died! It's not as if they did not have the gear and the space to put them to one side, but where they are they can still point to them as the uncontrollable cause of all their inefficiencies. We had a team of five so the evenings passed off well enough, but the days are hard work.

A Russian railhead somewhere

I should be in the office next week, but Spain may insist on a visit. This is not because they listen to what I say or do what I ask, it's just that they feel more comfortable with the strength of numbers. The best was when I asked who and how the design got changed and they said, "You were at that meeting." I very possibly was, but since they only translate the bits I either won't disagree with or those that they need a fall guy for…

7th October '96 — First acquaintances in Salalah, Oman

Much later: I am sat here a little overheated with a few minutes to kill before my flights back to Muscat. Before me is the hotel swimming pool with the hotel to my left. To my right is a grove of coconut palms, and just visible and very audible, the Indian Ocean monsoon surf is breaking on the beach. For shorts and an open shirt, the temperature is perfect, but I have a flight to catch.

The last two days have been spent in the port talking to the heads of each department and their subordinates. After the contract was signed, they all returned again to the question — what happens to me? Perfectly understandable and I have been trying to allay their fears a bit, telling them about assessment, training courses and reemploying as many as possible of the local Omanis. The Indian labour and mechanics will probably be reduced, but we will still need the skills. What I didn't tell them was that if they thought they were going to turn up late and drink tea on the assessment or training course, they would not last very long. Now the question is who is going to do all this. I think this has to be the honeymoon period. They have been tremendously helpful and hospitable, both officially and on a personal basis.

Salalah is a small town of a hundred and fifty thousand or so, with schools, mosques, a shopping centre of sorts, hospital, government and the Wali's, yes that's Wali, offices as well as a palace or two. Right beside the sea is the old part of the town and its suq in amongst the coconut palms and going down to the beach road. The road and the promenade get washed away every other monsoon. To the east is a preserved area of ruins, a pre-Islamic graveyard (I think) and a typical Middle Eastern city tell which is as yet un-excavated. Driving into town the other day, we passed through a prehistoric burial ground of some hundreds of small tumuli. I was very excited with my discovery from seeing the same in Bahrain. I bought a book which includes some Omani prehistory, so I hope to find out more. They turned out to be anthills.

Bird life is abundant: glossy ibis, great white heron, grey heron, squacco heron, sunbirds, flamingos, osprey, shrikes, weaverbirds, lone brown goose and what looked like a flight of avocet. They came winging across the harbour, pure white until abreast of me and then the black of their backs. I must find out if they occur here — if not, more research.

In my hotel room back in Muscat, waiting for a lift back to the office. I have been writing after my notes on the first bit of the project I am dealing with today and there is so much to do that our people in the US have not even, as far as I can make out, turned their minds to. I must try and bring it effectively to my leader's notice; he will be no problem if I can provide the ammunition he needs to motivate the others.

19th October '96 — Signing the new port concession for Salalah

On Tuesday, I go to Spain and then either UK or Holland, from there to St. Petersburg and from there to Oman again. I am afraid that is still not the end of it, but it pays the bills. The last visit to Oman was hard work in terms of schedules but most enjoyable for all that. We were called to attend the signing ceremony for the new terminal, but I will attempt to attach that story to this — we are at the leading edge here (holding on by the synapses). We were all flown down to the port in a Royal Boeing 747 and met at the aircraft steps by a fleet of Mercedes, definitely how I prefer to travel.

The reception for the signing of the concession

I'm going to be here in England over the weekend, work Monday at home and then leave for Spain. My logistics are worthy of a treatise, as I brought the car over for a week's leave but that didn't happen, so at some stage I have to organise a trip back into the right airport in England to pick up the car and drive it back to Holland. My interview with my boss to discuss all this got lost somewhere in another travel change. We were in Oman together but were so involved we never even thought about talking to each other about anything other than what was happening there.

Been meaning to finish this but got waylaid by mad Spaniards. Got back from Algeciras yesterday and have spent today loading a builders' skip and doing a bit of papering and telephone rewiring.

6th November '96 — The Bait Saeed will not trouble us

The airport at Salalah and I am on my way North again after four days with the Al Kharra and their neighbours — well, not quite! The quotation above was not from Thesiger but from my friend, Saeed al Makhtari, who collared me one lunch time to lobby for the site of his cold store and fish processing plant. It is on leased ground and the government have foreclosed, as he is slap in the way of the new terminal. I am not sure exactly what he wants except massive compensation and a stay of execution until the end of the next lobster season. Since he didn't work the last season and it is rumoured the business is broke, I think we are dealing with some smoke and mirrors here.

That aside, he has been most hospitable running me round to see his various influential friends and arranging for me to see the most awful villas for accommodating our staff. They were built quite recently for rent to the locals coming to Salalah for the Khareef — I think it is called — the monsoon holiday season. It seems to be the wrong time of year as it is absolutely beautiful here now and the place is empty of holidaying Omanis. The villas themselves are, I suppose, all right except, in common with much Arab architecture, they pay no attention to the outside at all — it might as well not be there. The curtains are always drawn, and the villas are so close you would not see much anyhow. To make matters worse, they have concreted over the whole area. I thought of the pre-fabs up on the hill above the port with the mountains and the sea cliffs. I know where I would prefer to live.

And come to that, Saeed took me up on the cliffs last night to show me the battle ground where the Omanis defeated the Portuguese and threw them out of Oman. Apparently, the Portuguese attacked from the sea and were defeated at the bridgehead. To get there they had just climbed vertical cliffs some a hundred and fifty feet high and I suggested that this being the case they could expect to be defeated — lost on my companion! Nice guy, but I think he is a little larger than life. We went to see the place he would like to build a new cold store down by the beach. I thought we couldn't get stuck in the sand, four-wheel drive in the skilled hands of the desert dweller. Wrong! I was wondering whether I was going to embarrass him by getting his jeep out, but we managed it and trundled back to the tarmac. But a very nice gentleman and I'm looking forward to hearing what George has to say about him and the business. I have instructions to phone him when I am back, and he has promised to entertain me properly in the desert — hope it comes off.

(Note, 2014; Saeed was at some pains to tell me that the Bait Saeed would not present problems in the development of the port. This rather passed over my head at the time, but came back later when we got into hiring local staff. Each tribe and sub-tribe were of the opinion that they had been cheated, not least by our Omani HR manager. I still have to hand the analysis of the thirty-four major tribes and four hundred and seventy sub-tribes (families really) divided into desert, city and mountain dwellers, how many applicants from each and whether they were employed. The Sheikhs would show up in Jack's office demanding a greater share of the jobs for their youngsters and a few other things too. The Bait Saeed felt they had a claim to the port land itself, but the government dealt with that.

On the subject of accommodation for our labour, we were offered the old leper colony, never actually used as such. I decided that we had no need of the sort of publicity which placed an American company billeting their labour in an old leper colony.)

I thought today that it would be wise to come back whether I need to or not, just to throttle back the rumour mill. All sorts of stories get swapped around over the coffee and it does not do us any good.

Hassan, the chief engineer, was nice enough to say that they would like me to stay as they knew me and didn't want any other people coming in and confusing the issue. "When are you coming back?"

I had to say that I was not responsible for that.

Last night, I had dinner with the British Council manager for Salalah. Nice chap, started life as an engineer and migrated into teaching via the travel industry. The restaurant was the subject of entertainment by the Polish "Charisma Band" ("If you missed them last time don't miss them this time" — a rather odd injunction, I thought). The lead singer had been to the BC asking if she might take an exam in English. It would appear she took a shine to my companion, as every second song was dedicated to John, the British Council, teachers etc. John's wife was holed up in Al Ain, earning a salary, but he resisted all blandishments. The songs seemed to have been transcribed by a dyslexic listening to a Walkman with tired batteries. On top of that, the lady's accent, with affected American overtones, meant that I followed one word in forty. However, "Uh! Teacher, leave those kids alone" came through clear enough, partly because the tune was familiar from South Africa in '76, when it was banned as being the call to arms of the black students protesting against being taught in Afrikaans when they wanted English. Funny world!

15th December '96 — Containers and now dhows, camels and fish, in and around Muscat

My hotel room in Muscat, after a day spent in the country with George and Sonia. George runs a trucking company and is also our agent here in Oman — Sonia is his very energetic wife. I have been here for a week and Rob — just regaining consciousness on the sofa — for the last few days. Rob is off to Paris tonight, so has checked out and is using my room. We are dropping him off at the airport and collecting the next visitor off the incoming flight at the same time. Tomorrow I am off with the new arrival to Salalah to show him around for a one-day trip, back here for another day and then back to Holland.

I arrived a week ago to present our report on managing the whole port for the government, as opposed to just the container terminal. Writing the report was a bit of a tour de force since I've never run a conventional port, so it was time for a bit of intelligent guess work. I hope it was intelligent enough. The minister seemed happy with our proposals so we can proceed to the next stage.

Work being over on Thursday, we were called to attend the Caledonian Ball where everything except caber tossing was on the menu — ably supported by Scotophiliac Omanis. These appeared as pipers, drummers and dancers, together with an enthusiastic Sikh dressed in kilt, sporran, skidoon (spelling??) and turban. He looked rather fine, if a touch eccentric. Not half as eccentric as the Dutch oil driller with the Scots girlfriend wearing eye shadow — no, not the girlfriend, the driller. He was built like a brick outhouse, so not the best person to quiz about his makeup habits.

The following day, we were taken out for a gentle afternoon foray up a wadi with running water still there from the monsoon rains. Muscat is situated where the mountain range approaches the sea. Driving west, the coastal plain opens out into something almost as flat as Holland but is composed of alluvium, all the way from sand to pebbles and stones up to six inches across. My geological education should tell me what sort of erosion this is, but it doesn't. I can only assume that flash flooding must have something to do with its variety of particle size. The plain is covered thinly with thorn trees growing at a spacing of around twenty or thirty metres. Presumably being any closer is precluded by the availability of water, but does that mean the root system goes out ten to fifteen metres from a thorn tree of only three metres across and the same high? I suppose so. I have seen roots of grasses growing on dunes, exposed by the wind, of maybe 7 metres long.

The mountains rise quite suddenly from the plain with the odd date gardens in at their feet where the water emerges. We were making for a split in the hills where the level ground of the plain ran into what might have been a fjord at one time, with the plan to turn back at its head to follow another narrower valley back towards the plain again. We turned off the metalled road and were soon following a narrow valley with a gravel bottom winding between the water and gravel banks in the stream, Sonia giving instructions to George as to which route to take and when to engage four-wheel drive. George patiently explained that their vehicle was permanently in four-wheel drive!

We stopped beside the stream and got out beside the car for a picnic lunch and wander round. There was a lone figure sitting on a bluff which turned out to be a bedu with his goats when he got up, and calling the flock, picked his way down the rocks with his old breach loading rifle slung horizontally at his hip. They all seem to carry them this way, as opposed to vertically, where an accidental discharge might do less damage to the goats.

He walked past us, smiling a little toothlessly, and greeted us, "As-salaam alaykum."

We replied in kind, and he toddled off after his goats.

I left the others to walk up the levee to the other side of the stream for a view down the valley. The stream had brought on the grasses and the reeds, and you could hear a frog in the still desert air and the others talking among themselves. They were packing up so, reluctantly, I found my way back to level ground and across the stream again.

Driving on down the valley, it began to widen out and with the reduced speed of the water came a higher proportion of sand and smaller stones to drive over. Inevitably, we found the stuck Mazda up to the wheel arches, so stopped to do the honourable thing and pull them out. I once left the beach in Jeddah after I had pulled out five cars and tired of the novelty. This one came out easily enough so that they could retreat and take another run at it. We didn't stop to watch.

I have to tell you about Juliano. Italian, as you might have guessed, he is a seller of container cranes based in a town close to Milan. He lives in the square opposite the cathedral and the house of the bishop I have an invitation to visit (which I would love to follow up). He is not often there as his business (and, I think, inclinations) demand a travel schedule to rival tennis stars. You might imagine a business-suited, slightly overweight character of conservative habits. Juliano affects shoulder-length hair, a face that has been, as they say, 'lived in', soft shoes, open shirts and jeans. He turned up for dinner before the flight the other evening wearing what I took to be his usual business attire, for which he apologised with the excuse that the loose silk shirt, t-shirt and jeans were necessary for the disco he was due to attend with his friends once he got to Dubai — at one o'clock in the morning. As George said, "He likes to party"! and he is closer to sixty than fifty! He has been working the coverts of Omani sponsors with all the skill of his race. The French believe they are the only Europeans to understand the Arabs, which I think is rubbish. If you had to make comparisons; the Arabs understand the French are devious, they trust the English more but enjoy the Italian's company — well, that's my view.

As for the Americans, they are envious of their international stature and a bit impressed — and if the balloon goes up, they can get into the USA quicker than elsewhere. Anyhow, Juliano wants us to buy his cranes for the new port, but since I am not involved, I can relax a bit. The problem is that they have a horrible reputation for late deliveries and general Italian unreliability, but that is for our American brothers to say — I'm so glad.

And so to the American brothers, who, with typical arrogance, have completed their short list of crane manufacturers, and despite all advice, have informed their unsuccessful bidders that they are not on it. This without consulting or advising the Omanis, whose money is being spent, of their reasons. George's phone has been red hot with aggravated sponsors ringing up to ask why their pet manufacturer has been excluded. The engineers are down from the US next week to explain themselves!

Sunday was a holiday for the prophet's birthday and George and Sonia took us out again to see the hot springs in the mountains and two mud and stone forts built to protect the date gardens in the hills. The hot springs are of fresh water emerging from the rocks well below the summits of the mountains but also well above the coastal plain. The water is pleasant to drink, though I only tasted it, and not sulphurous as one would expect. I have a book on the geology of Oman — must read it! Below the springs, the water forms a river watering the date gardens via the falaj (gadwal) as it descends the hill. They have built pathways and seating for the inevitable crowds that arrive to enjoy the cool and for the children to swim and play in the river, which spoils the atmosphere a bit, but nonetheless it was a pleasant spot.

From there, we drove on to Nakl, where there is a fort just completing restoration. The architect selected an outcrop of rocks to build his fort on so that it stood a little above the surrounding village. When we first arrived, there was an Indian at the gate who could not give us access, but in due course an elderly Omani turned up, and after some Scots-Arabic from Sonia, let us in for "five minutes". We were delighted. Inside they were still working on the restoration, but being just about complete, we were able to wander all over the storerooms and living areas and the battlements. The mud plastering is a lovely mellow pinky-brown with teak or thorn wood doors inset and windows with iron bars to set it off. The geometrical shapes, blue skies and green of the date palms will hopefully produce something for my camera.

Date gardens from Nakl Fort

The next fort was larger and with commodious upper rooms, with the most wonderful cool breeze through the open shutters. Down in the dungeons, they had excavated a complex water system distributed outside to the falaj, which led to the date gardens with water still running. To walk through and imagine how it might have been lived in and used no doubt within living memory…

From there, we returned to the modern day, stopping for lunch at a new hotel on the beach. Dreadful food, but I believe there is an inverse correlation — the better the view, the worse the food, and the view was beautiful. Apart from the gardens and the beach, there were several rocks,

The author

islands, I suppose, off-shore, with sea birds and brilliant turquoise water. An osprey wheeled above the cliffs.

I must get some supper and despatch this into the ether, or is that aether?

5 January 1997 — Sailing Netherlands style

My letter writing of late has been neglected. There seems to have been so much written work in the office that the urge to write has all been used up on that. Last year, I put together two long papers, proposals for port management, as well as a lot of other stuff of a similar nature. This year looks like being more action than thought, but we shall see.

I have just come back from a drive down to the boat to see that she is still there after a period of my absence. She is caught fast in the ice, didn't stir when I got aboard, and all about, the ice is four inches thick or more. The Haringvliet, our immediate sailing water, is frozen over from bank to bank, a matter of a mile or so. Out in the middle, people were skating, and one brave soul was trying out his wind-surfer sail but without great success.

The sun had come out briefly, but by the time I got down there the biting wind had the place to itself under a grey sky, so I didn't stay long. Yesterday the whole of the Netherlands was gripped by the Elftesteden Toch. This is the Dutch skating marathon, two hundred kilometres, that they run if the ice is thick enough on the canals. The last time was eleven years ago and that is something like the frequency. The Dutch are mad on skating; they have the World and European in-door speed champion, and he is defending his title next weekend. Elftesteden means eleven cities but actually it's a couple of cities and the rest are villages up in the North, Friesland. We have not been up there yet, but will wait for the summer, I think. The weather has been bitter here — minus sixteen C — with an easterly wind directly from Murmansk or the like. Because of that, there has been very little snow while in the UK. With the opportunity for picking up water vapour over the North Sea, the snow has brought the Eastern seaboard to a halt. I came back from the UK via the Channel Tunnel on the 2nd and by then the roads were clear, so I had a very good run as most others had stayed at home.

5th March '97 — Holiday and friends in Cape Town

We are here in Cape Town enjoying excellent weather, company and food. We have just got back from Hermanus, a resort of sorts to the South towards Cape Agulhas, an hour or two's drive from Cape Town across the Cape flats and then up into the hills above Somerset West. Hermanus used to be a very small village with some fishermen and the odd artist and drop-out. The trendies have moved in, and it is now a select area with some superlative real estate, and the odd drop-out has turned to with a bit of plumbing and leather crafty work. We stopped for a drink and some soup in the "Burgundy" restaurant where our order, devoid of main course, was regarded with some disdain. It took so long to bring the soup that they had to bring more bread to eat with it. Refreshed, we took a walk along the coastal path and found some Dassies (rock hyrax — related to elephants apparently and the Afrikaans name means little badger) to photograph as well as the dramatic ocean scenery and surrounding mountains. Patricia bought T-shirts and pictures for the boys, and we got slightly hi-jacked by an artist chappie who was so pleasant it would have been difficult to get out of buying something. Fortunately, he had something pleasant. He was full of chat about the Duchess of Harwood, who, it seemed, had been mixing with the hoi-poloi. She was the daughter of an Australian trumpeter and I happened to sit behind them on a flight to Singapore in 1969. He was on his way to a bit of operatic impresario-ing in Bombay and I didn't know who I was chatting to until they left the flight.

Fishing boats Hermanus South Africa

Back in The Hague now — the 5th — and off to Denmark tomorrow for a couple of days, back here for Saturday night, to Spain on Sunday, back for Monday night and then to Oman for ten days or so. Once back, I will have to be in Spain again and then there is the possibility of a trip to the US. It all keeps the miles programme topped up.

I got back from SA last Monday morning after a weekend out in the country. Our friends suggested we stay a night at a hotel they use quite frequently. It was an old water mill and now has several Cape Dutch style cottages each with two double rooms scattered around the grounds and a super kitchen. The exchange rate is so in favour everything is about half price to us, so the night plus dinner and full breakfast cost us very little indeed. We drove about two hours from Cape Town up onto the plateaux known as the Little Karoo. The road travels through a wonderful range of scenery, the rolling wine lands of the Cape, the scarp and then into the plain with mountains still above. The weather during our whole stay was sunny, the one drawback being the wind. The South Easter was in full flood at times and coming back we saw the effects of a bush fire still raging above Somerset West driven by the wind.

Old Dutch vernacular architecture

While out at McGregor, where the hotel is, we drove up to the top of a pass leading to another hamlet. A dirt road winding into the hills where they grow… the South African flower, can't think of the name… (Ah! Proteas) commercially. You are not allowed to pick them in the wild. As we gained height, the flowers began to appear, and stopping at the top, we were able to watch the Cape sugar birds and the sun-birds chasing each other around the shrubs; an absolutely beautiful morning.

The Cape has changed very little from when we lived there. Even the security aspect seems much the same, unlike Johannesburg. There has been a huge amount of development in the coloured areas, and you now see that the wealth has reached a few of them — they drive cars! The whole impression is one of a burgeoning economy; however, that is said not to be the case. The problem for the whites is finding jobs, particularly for graduates and school leavers. Affirmative Action, the preferential employment of those "historically disadvantaged", means that it is not always the best for the job that gets it, and they say that academic standards have been eroded on the pretext that, because of historical disadvantage, they cannot be expected to pass the same exams — tricky logic when you are employing doctors. The minister for education also laid off, on good terms, fifty thousand teachers — there is now a huge shortage, and the beneficiaries are setting up private schools to fill the gap with their redundancy money. However, if you want to convert your North European assets to Rand, you can buy a palace in Newlands or Constantia, the places to live.

I came back to a desk full of paper and silly political stuff I could well do without. It seemed like a good idea to turn round and go back again. My favourite bête noire who retained some very strange consultants for the Oman project will retire in March and guess who he is going to work for — the very strange consultants. Since I predicted exactly this eighteen months ago, it had at least the murky pleasure of a 'told you so'.

While in CT, I had a stream of faxes from the office to keep me engaged and Patricia exasperated. I have a problem in Algeciras which is proving intractable, so spent a bit of time on that and think I know what to do as a result, but I was less than amused by the reaction of the manager down there, who is demanding my presence there. It's one of those things you wish would solve itself and go away. Add to that a letter from our partners which required a very starchy reply to put me in a better mood…

11th March '97 — The lovely old Reina Christina

The Reina Christina was built by a British railways engineer around 1900. He must have done a good job, as the building has not had a lick of paint in years but is in good condition. The extended eaves, of a colonial tropical aspect, have kept the weather off the stucco and the teak windows

I am somewhere over North Europe — wonderful, is it not? I've been in Aarhus debating the use of port facilities with a pleasant group of Danes and am now on my way back home for a day before heading off for Spain. Last week I got back from Cape Town. I am now in the Reina Christina in Algeciras. It used to be a smart hotel, along with other colonial establishments. One 'gort orf' the B&I or P&O steamer on your way to India and did Spain for a week, picking up the next vessel through. It used to have steps down to the beach and its own golf course, but my employers came along and put up a container terminal which thoroughly wrecked the position. The poor Reina has now come down in the world and entertains the bottom end of the UK tours industry. Bingo, fancy-dress, Trivial Pursuits get public display by turns each night of the week. Must go and find a drink and something to eat. Tomorrow, I must do battle with the locals and our consulting engineer. The latter affects a wig which could have come from one of the cheaper makes of doll, being dead straight and very nylon. He would perhaps look almost presentable without it. I fear the wig affects what he keeps protected below it…

That was the end of the plan — the contractor wanted to take us to lunch in a restaurant, but we elected for Il Palmita, my favourite pub — olives in garlic, roast salted almonds, beer in glasses kept in the freezer so that it comes with snow on the outside, Spanish ham and goat cheese by the plate full, octopus in a spiced sauce and country bread. Very healthy but… there is always the airline meal to give a miss to.

I came away from the meeting finding that I seemed to have won my point with the consulting engineer, but the result is I have to do some more work on my calculations to give him the parameters instead of the other way about.

I must get ready to go to Belgium tomorrow and thence to West Meon for Easter week.

27th March '97 — Dubai revisited

This is Dubai airport and the incoming KLM aircraft has just crossed my field of view when it should have been sitting on the tarmac fully fettled and awaiting our boarding of it. Well, it looks as though we are running somewhat late. So long as I am not seated next to the garrulous lady in the departure lounge, I shall be reasonably all right. Friendly soul but not interactive — it seems to me that boredom should be both given and received by both sides. This flight will eventually depart sometime before sunrise, I suppose. I checked out of my room at midday and since then have been in a meeting and wandering around with my gear in someone else's room and no opportunity for a lie down. It is now 0335!

We have been sitting in our hotel and interviewing people for jobs in Salalah. Not a very edifying business. Most of them we know already as long-time employees in Dubai. I said to the Managing Director of the new company in Salalah that we would have done well if we could have picked them up when they were all ten years younger. Our American colleague was telling us what you could and could not ask in an interview, age is one, pregnant another, health yet another, etc. These people are really looking at retirement and it is hardly fair to take them out of their current positions for what we have in mind. We did see two who would be really valuable to us, and talking to several of them, we got confirmed some serious misgivings about our two set of consultants and their designs. I hate this part of the business.

On Friday, I was able to arrange an old friend to pick up two of us and take us firstly for breakfast and thence to the sailing club we used to be members of. We sat there and enjoyed the sun and the view of the boats, and in due course a collection of other old friends turned up, quite fortuitously. I had taken Bill with me, an engineer from Sealand, and felt guilty that we were all mumbling about old times and older friends, but he expressed himself well satisfied with the day, saying in all his travelling he had never had a day as good. I went and viewed our old boat, still there after all these years and looking better below the waterline — the owner had hauled her out — but a lot more weathered above. Diane suggested a swim which I declined pleading the cold — I was sitting in a sweater and cotton slacks so the indications were against immersion (I have just realised I don't have a spell check; will have to type more accurately). We ate a light lunch and later returned to the hotel to pick up Jack and find dinner.

Dubai Creek

Dubai has changed very considerably over the intervening eight years. Trusting that the hotels were much as before, we took a taxi to the Sheraton, a hotel I quite like, with architecture and interior decor surprisingly undated. Inside, we found the porter and asked for his view on the establishment's restaurants. We chose the seafood place, but found it not open for another half hour. The lady from the Japanese restaurant alongside stepped forwards and said, "We're open," so we went in there instead. We had had Japanese a few nights previously in Muscat and not very satisfactorily, so we were very happy to find ourselves well looked after — you can get fussy, I suppose. My diet over the last few weeks has been almost exclusively protein with some detrimental effect on the waistline. I have put in place the "eat less of what you like" policy and am trying to observe the scheme. Trouble is that after a lifetime of eating until I was full with no ill effects, there is a little voice saying that it will be all right to eat the rest of the plateful. The dietary trouble started with our signing ceremonies. Our sponsor took us to lunch on Monday, we had the formal dinner on Monday night, lunch on Tuesday with the Japanese agent, dinner that night with the Chinese and dinner the following night with our sponsor and banker — and there were others before all that.

Back to Muscat for a bit:

Muscat residential quarter

The ruler, Sultan Qaboos, decreed that buildings were to be painted any colour you like, to paraphrase Henry Ford, as long as it is white. It was told that he would take on the disguise of a taxi driver and take to the streets to gauge the opinions of his subjects. The McDonalds golden arches were cut down to head height so as to be less obnoxious.

The Ministry of Communications asked for a presentation from the consultants on the progress of the project. We had been hearing rumblings of dissatisfaction and the Minister arrived "loaded for bear" as the Americans say. The consultant chosen by our engineer in the US stepped forward to do his piece and got to the bit where he was relating the steps so far and found a one-month hiatus, which he thought was the fault of the ministry. The ministry, on the other hand, are very critical of the way he has been running the bidding process, not least because there have been a hundred and twenty changes to the bid documents and four addenda. The minister came out of his tree. As one of our American colleagues remarked afterwards, our guy didn't know enough to lie down. He tried to argue his case. The minister was apoplectic. Very, very sorry, Your Excellency!

We all sat round like kids in class, hugely relieved that it wasn't us that were under attack.

So, what else did we do? We had dinner at the Japanese crane manufacturer's agent's mansion to celebrate their order in circumstances of some luxury. The house or the parts we saw are solely for entertaining, I would guess. There must be somewhere you could throw yourself into a chair without damaging several yards of silk upholstery. The rooms were high, wide, and handsome, with mouldings in the Louis whatsit style and vitrines everywhere with priceless copies of priceless real stuff displayed for the connoisseur. He must have had an expansive and no doubt expensive interior decorator. The Japanese were everywhere, bowing and scraping and generally fixing everything, including a re-run of the previous day's television coverage of our signing ceremony. Champagne was served without popping corks — you cannot expect too much alcoholic exhibitionism in a Muslim house — and we moved into the dining room for lunch — twenty of us.

The five front of house staff did their bit while a very competent French-type chef did his bit round the back. Our host, about thirty-five and pretty fit, sat at the head of the table and helped dispose of the South African and French wine. The table settings were the best of plate, with a very fine damask tablecloth with gold embroidery and associated napery. Before lunch, we were taken on to the roof to admire the view out over the bay and an azure sea. The servants' quarters had a roof garden to which Rob remarked that one might not want to live there — you'd have to mow the roof. We wrapped that up when someone pointed out that we were due at the Chinese ambassador's place in three hours to eat dinner.

We were and that was a different kettle of fish. Still with the communist flag flying, but nevertheless a few capitalist comforts, together with the most plutocratic sequence of laden dishes of this and that — mostly that, as it was not the type of Chinese food that is light upon the digestion. Our host, the Ambassador, was an urbane gentleman with good English; conversely, the chief executive of the crane builders had only very recently left the paddy field. By the end of the meal, there was more food on him than on the plates, and when the more slippery parts of some beast defeated his chopsticks he brought his face down to plate elevation and hoovered from there. Smiled a lot through a positive gallery of snaggle teeth and bargained with our crane engineer over a few million dollars off the price to get the next set of quay cranes. Quite a character!

26th April 1997 — Back in New York to fight the engineers and Charlotte

What happened to weekends? We are due at the consultant's offices at 0900 for another meeting, which hopefully won't go beyond lunch time. We got to Charlotte very late as there was a lot of traffic, apparently exacerbated, according to the captain, by the local requirement for thirty-five miles separation between aircraft. How they do it down there, he said. In Europe, the airports are closer than that… We were stacked half an hour from landing, and I couldn't see any other aircraft and got to wondering whether they hadn't told us the wheels wouldn't come down and we were using up fuel…!

We got down eventually and found our way to the Park Hotel, a more than half decent hostelry with friendly staff and rooms big enough to swing several large cats at the same time. This one in New York, by contrast, is a wholly American invention called a suites hotel. This means I have a kitchen, two bathrooms, a living room and a bedroom — and zero service and worn carpets because nobody refurbished it in twenty years. However, this is a hundred and fifty US$ a night, instead of the three hundred and fifty US$ where the Omanis are staying and the hundred and thirty US$ in Charlotte.

Anyhow, back to Charlotte and the next day when we took the hotel car to the office. Last time I was there it was still unfinished, and people were moving in from the old office. It is now finished, and a lot of people have moved out again, having lost their jobs. The atmosphere is a bit like a turkey farm before Christmas. Corporate America! Apparently more cuts are expected, and everyone is manoeuvring away from the daylight in case they are noticed. Some have a French aristocrat view of life, or expected lack of it, making jokes about the tumbrel and its driver, others, like the one we met by chance in the hotel, mutter darkly about college fees and how much his lawyers can get in a lawsuit. He was told to fly into Charlotte, meet his boss for dinner, but not go near the office and not to let people know he was there! We met with most of the people we had gone to see but the level of progress was depressing. Apparently, we need more people working rather than debating.

The flight back was full, and they were being difficult with carryon luggage. We got ours stowed safely but then the arguments started with the crew about how big this bag was or how far did it stick out. My neighbour had quantities of stuff wedged under the seat in front which the steward spilt ginger ale all over. He was offhand, she was abusive (and larger than her seat) and wanted everyone else to get involved. Behind, a very well-dressed woman talked non-stop to a student, and vice versa, so I don't know how they managed to communicate. The well-dressed lady's daddy was a New York Cadillac agent, thus the smart gear. We came into land flying the length of Manhattan Island — the Empire State, the Chrysler building, the Statue of Liberty (which, by the way, was refurbished four years ago by Bovis, the British company — well, I suppose if the French gave it to them in the first place...) and all their huge bridges. We left the plane with considerable relief for a remarkably fast drive into the city.

The Rockefeller Centre, 5th Avenue N.Y.

Having washed up, we set out for dinner, walking all the way up to Broadway, theatre land and a suitably chi-chi restaurant where the waiter really actually said "foist" instead of "first". The restaurant specialised in steak, so I was able to have a decent sirloin with some fat on it. The restaurant's ambience was saved from being close to that of a slaughterhouse by the wooden decor and the walls covered with photographs of the stars of stage and screen from nineteen footsack as they say now in South Africa (footsack = get out of here in Africaans, and may be used to dogs, beggars, servants, and in times of stress, your children). Fat is an evil word in the US, but if you walk through the streets, you can see how it got its bad name.

26th April — Back to New York for another engineer fight

This morning we went to the consultants' offices to meet them and the Omanis again. We had heard that they wanted to discuss some new ideas and it was a breath of fresh air. At last, we have a rational discussion and the makings of a good layout. It has taken months to get them to listen. We can now chalk up some progress. We got away from them after twelve so dropped the papers at the hotel and set out to walk to our lunch, stopping on the way for the Sikhs' parade. John's wife, Elaine, asked another bystander the reason for the parade — "In New York you don't need a reason for a parade!" There were schools and local organisation banners and a couple of bands that didn't look very Sikh at all — short gym-type skirts and drum majorette headdresses.

New York marching season!

Apparently, you need bands for your parade even if they have nothing to do with your particular ethical or ethnic venture. They hire them in. There was one that should have been charged under the false descriptions act. However, there were a myriad of orange turbans, orange banners and orange flags to convince you.

    I have never eaten in a "diner". A bit like the old Civic Restaurant in Cambridge put up after the war, or during, to feed the masses. We were just beyond oil cloth on the tables but not much. We have eaten in some fairly dire places in New York, all at my colleague John's suggestion — no style but we are working on him. Leaving there we progressed to Fifth Avenue and walked all the way up past the Rockefeller Centre, the brand name shops, Cartier, Saks, etc., photographing the architecture and enjoying the warm spring sunshine. I wanted a photo of the library, a rather fine neo-classical building with lions out front and a banner advertising the Tyndall Bible on loan from the British Library, but had to wait, it seemed, ages for the sun to come from behind a cloud.

New York public library

After that, it seemed to be out all the time. I think I have rather too many shots of New York canyon architecture, but we will see. As I look out of the window opposite me, I can see right across the roof tops to the World Trade Centre and all the skyscrapers of downtown Manhattan. Funny thing about New York roof tops, every available space seems to be taken up with round wooden water tanks. The design is standard, built like a barrel with vertical staves compressed with circular steel straps spaced closer at the bottom to withstand the pressure, overall a conical lid and anything from three metres in diameter down. They stand on trestles and pylons, waiting… I thought they were a legacy from the fifties, but I saw two brand new ones the other day. I asked our consulting engineer, a New Yorker and long-time resident of mid-town NY, about them. I don't think he had even noticed them (believe they are for firefighting).

The building right opposite me, turn of the century, I suppose, is fairly typical of the cheaper old commercial structures. Brick and terra-cotta elevations with no architectural merit whatsoever but approximately a hundred and ten life-size foxes' heads, as you might see above the fireplace in an English country pub, adorning each storey. I wondered if the owner years ago rode to hounds; but maybe they are wolves. Interspersed among the dilapidated relics of the last century are the refurbished ones and the impressive pieces of corporate egotism, all half-silvered glass and vertical lines. Each one attempts to outdo the next in height and opulence. The last century produced the incredible embellishments of gilded copper, aluminium and stone detail that looks big from the ground but must be vast on close acquaintance. My favourite, with others I am sure, is the Chrysler Building, which seems to have survived the worst excesses of aerials that hang about the Empire State, making it look like a construction site. The Rockefeller Centre has a wonderfully clean tower above it — and flower beds below filled with azaleas. We wandered as far as Central Park and though we walked round it for a long time, later inspection of the map showed we had seen about a tenth of it. Poser's paradise.

Roller blades are the thing in New York for exercising, hanging out, commuting to work and impressing other people. Obviously you don't buy a pair and walk out to try them out — you have to practice in secret first. This must be the case, as only perfect and future perfect can be seen on the roads and pavements. Central Park is the venue for the really accomplished who dash to and fro like demented swallows or pirouette above twiddling wheels making artistic movements with the arms. Very impressive! I have no doubt that if I lived here, I would have to get a set — and practice on the carpet for a long time. To watch them swooping among the yellow taxis is nerve shattering.

Roller blading N.Y.

I've been reading the biography of Thesiger that William gave me — a great book. The contrast between his life and this lot is something else. He would not approve of us building a container terminal in Salalah — though he was a bit scathing about Salalah anyway.

Some places in New York you could be in another land. If you move one block between 7th Avenue and 8th, the whole ethnic scene changes completely; you become a foreigner — a bit unnerving, too. Cross back to 7th or 6th and there you are, back in the Northern hemisphere again — strange. The twelve tribes of Israel were out and about quite a lot. Chaps with brass crowns and loud voices haranguing the crowds about their destiny. I was trying to make out what this consisted of, but it got lost in the

Central Park

rhetoric somewhere. Anyhow, there were a few more lads standing around with staves and leather belts round various parts of their anatomy, looking tough, and rather dumb, to give the impression that destiny was all about fixing something for the brothers, even if no one knew what or how. The brothers surely — oh! I'm sorry and the sisters — need things fixing. The poverty of this place is a bit like Bombay, except there are more arms and legs to go round than in Bombay. I must get this away before we leave for San Francisco.

28th April '97 — World tour

The first opportunity I have had to write to you sitting on the flight to Charlotte. The last few days we have been in New York, meeting the consulting engineers on the Oman project. It could have been better. The Under Secretary from the Ministry of Communications was there with his engineer and the plan was to assess the civils bids for the new quay and buildings. The bids had come in well, being for the most part below the budget, but the difficult bit was that the Chinese have offered at a twenty-five percent discount to the next bracket of three. These are the ones experienced in the area, and not the Chinese. So, what to do?

We had expected the consultants to have prepared a detailed assessment of the bids, but when we got into the meeting all they could manage was to wring their hands over the difficulty of making a decision in such awkward circumstances. This was not the plan, and the Omanis made their unhappiness more than plain! Never having been much in sympathy with the choice of consultants in the first place, it was difficult not to smirk, but we have to live with what we have until complete disaster strikes, so we tried to help out. I think this made it worse, as the Omanis then asked why all the ideas and action was coming from the client's side of the table instead of the consultants'.

They had hoped to get the bidders to New York this week, but that failed as the Chinese could not get visas. They will now get them all to Muscat the first week of May to go through their offers. I think we will end up with the Chinese, but it will mean considerable reduced confidence in the delivery date and the quality. Our advice from our contacts (not the consultants, who don't seem to have any) is that they can do a good job if you can get them to send the engineers who speak English and are competent, but it seems they have another set without either asset.

They are working in Kuwait at present. I knew someone vaguely in the consulting engineers in London, who gave me a name. So, we rang him up for a chat. The Omanis suggested putting him on the speaker so we could all hear. I got the individual I wanted, introduced myself, said he was on the speaker and asked if he felt able to comment on the Chinese.

"Not on the speaker, I can't."

Not a good story! However, we had better reports from Hong Kong but that is, to an extent, their home territory. A lot of work to do yet!

7th May '97 — World Tour — cancelled!

We are now in San Francisco, having been up to Seattle for a couple of days to see a terminal in operation. We also went to Tacoma which used to be the Sea-Land flagship terminal. What a dump! We found old equipment and piles of what might come in useful someday all over the place. They are not spending any money they don't have to on the structure of the business — eating the seed corn, to my mind. There is to be a new series of cuts in the US and possibly elsewhere in the next week or so, as goes the rumour mill, so morale is once again at boot level. For a variety of political reasons, they tried to stop this trip, but it looks as though we shall continue but we have to check on Monday. The tickets are non-refundable, so it will cost more to turn it in than to continue, but logic is now a forty-fourth consideration. Seattle, close to Canada, was a pleasant change from the urban chaos we have been existing in. It is still a large city, but you can see the green, and of course, the mountains. Our hotel was in the old docks area, and was I to have stepped from my window, I would have been in the water. Right next to the hotel was the berth for the cruise ships that ply the Alaskan coast, and one came and went while we were there. She left to the accompaniment of the tug with all her fire hoses running. Approaching by air, we could see the tops of Mt. Hood and Rainier above the clouds — volcanic and therefore roughly conical and snow covered. Rainier stands above Seattle, a bit like Fujiyama but not nearly so regular.

We did our duty and went down to the container terminal and watched the systems at work preparing for the vessel arrival the next day. I took an evening off and ate in the hotel so as to get to bed in reasonable time, but what with time zone differences and trying to stay in contact, it was not that early. The next day we saw the ship working and found no one in the office — no problems, so the computer seemed to be just getting on with its job.

We got back here — San Francisco — after seeing Tacoma terminal and driving back to Seattle airport. We found a makeshift stall in the airport concourse which announced that it was not the Chinese that are the enemy but the British. We had to go over and find out what it was about, and I think the chap had failed to read the date of the history book — all about the Brits ruling thirty-five percent of the world's dry land and so forth. I told him I felt a lot better having not realised before that we were all powerful — he took it all in good humour. Back in SF, we were picked up by the stretch limo and driven all over town by the driver, who was lost, eventually arriving at our next hotel. This one is in the manner of the great turn of the century hotels and well looked after as well.

Hotel San Francisco

Last night was proms night — the dances celebrating graduation? — and the hotel was full of svelte urbane young ladies on the arms of their spotty teenage dates. Funny how girls manage to look mature when boys of the same age... well... often don't! Just by the way, for those that saw the American drama *Hotel*, it was shot in the one we were saying in. Much better than New York!

Well, here I am back in Rotterdam and still not seen the mysterious Orient. Politics raised its ugly head and after an enormous amount of bickering on Mt. Olympus, it was decided that two mortals had to return to base to assuage the anger of one side of the Pantheon. Our side lost! Quite ridiculous, since it cost more to turn round than to go on. The excuse was that there were too many people devoted to this project, but that is hogwash. As it is, I shall be back here working on the same thing, but with the exception of a hand-holding trip to Spain. I shall go down at the end of next week, come back to England for the weekend and then leave for Oman on the Monday. As you may imagine, San Francisco via the far East to Oman is much the same as via Holland. What really happened was that our company was building software to control port operations and they wanted us to use it in Oman. We spent time in Charlotte with the staff and the consultants and concluded it was hopeless. At a wrap up meeting with the man in charge, I said so, and he was not happy, while our team was relieved that we could move on. Charlotte did not want me or anyone else spreading despondency in Hong Kong, our next stop, so I was recalled to avoid embarrassment (and truth). It never did work.

My solution for the problem in Algeciras worked, I am told, so all they have to do now is follow it through. Bit relieved, as I didn't have much more to offer if it failed.

San Francisco is built on hills. The result is the switchback road contour you see in the films, with the car chases over the bumps beside the cable car. I wondered why you don't see the same sort of roads in other cities built on hills and concluded that the older cities used roads that wound up the steep parts, otherwise horses wouldn't make it. But was the horse not a feature of early SF? Certainly, the cable car is a magnificent piece of engineering. The cable runs in a slot below the road and the driver of the tram-like vehicle has a hand actuated clamp which grips it when he wants to move off. The cable moves continuously, driven by electric motors in

Yachting and Alcatraz Island

winding houses and even goes round corners in the road. How they do it beats me. We got on one and the driver, starting off, fished out a hooked rod which he used to pull the cable up into the clamp mechanism below the road surface. The cars are all varnished wood in turn of the century décor, with wooden benches and steps, or a running board, on the side with a notice saying, "only two standees". Sunday we took the boat trip round the bay, up to the Golden Gate bridge and back past Alcatraz, the bay bridge to Fisherman's Wharf.

The waterfront development in Cape Town is likened to this, but the SA ability to keep things absolutely spick and span is not present in America. I think it is a matter of priorities, as there is plenty of cheap labour in both places. The urban poverty in the US keeps nagging at you. Ten million people visit Fisherman's Wharf each year according to the guide on the boat. It was a chilly, windy day, but the sun was out. I shot a full thirty-six film with the film in the cassette throughout. I was not amused and then did the same again with the next film. I could have chucked the camera in the bay.

We lunched in China Town, badly in my case as I had ordered the chicken — boiled! In the evening, we went out to eat at a restaurant where there was supposed to be music. The pianist failed to show but we were entertained by a very pleasant Brit waitress from Blackheath and the redoubtable Rob, who for some reason was flying that night. Returning to the hotel, we took the lift up twenty-four floors on the outside of the building to the Crystal Room overlooking the whole of SF, a wonderful sight.

Got in this morning at eleven a.m. local or 0200 my time, caught the train to the Hague, had a shower and went to the office. I am now feeling a bit fragile so will to bed.

Golden Gate Bridge

20th May '97 — Iberia — The airline most likely to improve 1997

Iberia was voted today, by travellers with no choice, as the airline most likely to improve in 1997 — or '98 or '99 or 2000... The only way is upwards. Last night, I left the office at 1600 for the fifty-minute drive to Schipol. Leave aside the fact that Schipol traffic was in chaos for some reason, and I got there an hour and ten before the flight, checked in, went to the lounge and thence to the gate. At 2300 I was back in the flat again after listening to Spanish storytelling for the best part of five hours. The flight is delayed...the flight is further delayed...an Iberia representative will be here soon to tell you about your connecting flight...soon...you should be all right for your connecting flight, everything is delayed in Barcelona... the crew are out of their hours, we'll find another crew... the crew are tired... there are no hotels for the crew and if they don't rest they will not be able to fly tomorrow... there was a football game in Barcelona... there is a football game in Amsterdam so no hotels for anybody... we might fly at 0830 tomorrow... we will fly at 0830 tomorrow... if the captain had been one of our decent ones he would have (ignored the IATA rules?) flown anyway.

Well, we flew at 0900 and my connecting flight out of here to Malaga is at 1625, getting in at 1800, so I will get to the office for my 1000 meeting at 1930. I suggested to our local manager that we meet anyhow since the consultant will have to stay overnight. Very difficult — we'll delay your departure tomorrow. So I get into Gatwick at 2300 — thanks very much! So here I am in Barcelona airport, using up the next four hours before my next flight. The one ray of sunshine is that I have found a secluded corner with three desks and chairs behind a glass screen and with power for my laptop. With a modem connection, I could be almost cheerful.

One result of enforced incarceration in airports is that the finer end of the duty-free business gets to insinuate itself into your psyche. (Poor you! Stuck in this airport. Nothing to do — have a look at my shelves — no need to buy anything, of course, but travellers like you often do. Of course, being in an airport you're obviously, well, you know, affluent, like all those other people. And they're buying things — DUTY-FREE. Sorry, didn't mean to shout… Yeah! You're right, and I do need a gizmo with detachable widget… been thinking about it, putting it off, really, for ages. THAT MUCH! But it is duty-FREE… AMEX. That'll do nicely, sir! You better believe it will.) I unpacked all the rubbish from my laptop bag, including the laptop, and repacked it on the lady's desk, asking her to throw the old bag away — off of which the handle had broken — and wondered how much I could swing onto my expense account. Anyhow, the ensuing further hours of wandering around trying to find another flight left me appreciative of the new case, which holds everything without a struggle and also doesn't create such a sensation of pins-and-needles in the shoulder and nether arm bits as the last one.

(That was 1997; the bag is still in use seventeen years later, having done more than its fair share of air miles. It is no longer black leather but grey.)

I booked a taxi for the morning from the KLM limousine service and then went to find my car and drive home. I should not have poured the rest of the milk away — no tea and no cereal for breakfast. The incredible romance of travel! I have just discovered there was an Alitalia flight out of here at 1225 which, had they tried last night, they might have got me on. I have asked our secretary not to book me Iberia again — this is not the first time.

It occurred to me that, while talking about other things, I don't think I ever told you we went to two Broadway shows while in NY — *Annie* and *The King and I*. The latter put me in mind of sitting in the sitting room at Mother's, listening to the record player. They had chopped the plot around quite a bit to allow teams of people to leap about the stage in glittering costume to achieve the "spectacle" to be expected of a Broadway musical. It was pleasantly diversionary — not words used in the hoarding quotes of the critical acclaim received. *Annie* was probably music by Tate, words by Lyle. I am reminded of an overheard conversation in a queue somewhere…"I watched *4 Weddings and a Funeral* again the other night and realised that it was not as deeply relevant as I thought the first time…" Uh…! In my day we went to *Last Year in Marienbad* four times and still had no idea why they made it, what it was about or why we went more than once anyway.

There was one really excellent piece in *Annie*. The wide boy, Rooster, sees the opportunity to make a fast buck and he, his evil bird, and the mistress of the orphanage sing "Easy Street" — brilliant. Apparently, the show has run for twenty years — can that be right? It may not run very much longer. The little girl that plays Annie is a replacement for the last one whose performance was dropping off, according to the management. In true US fashion, the parents of the one let go plus the agent and a hundred unemployed lawyers are going after the company in the courts for wrongful dismissal, loss of earnings, mental distress, affront, affray, grievous bodily harm, and anything else they can think of. Half the seats were said to be empty because the populace had voted with their feet.

We were there because these were the only cheap returned seats available in the evening. The returned seats business is set up in the centre of Times Square — which is triangular traffic, not a square — in a couple of red portacabins. They open at 1000 and you need to get there half an hour ahead to join the queue. You then pass the time watching the resident half-wits, dodging roller bladers and eating leaden bagels washed down with weaker than weak coffee. The result is half price tickets at, say, twenty-five Sterling — worth the wait.

Yesterday was interesting. My boss, together with his boss and his boss's boss, left for Muscat on Tuesday in the company jet on a VIP visit. The plan had been to see the ministers, and if the Sultan's schedule allowed, have an audience with the Sultan. Our chief executive counts himself among the world leaders ("Today megalomania — tomorrow the world", fits quite well) now and finds it difficult to fit in heads of state from the smaller economies. So, when the Sultan's men said 1930, our CEO says, "Sorry I'm out of here at 1600 — got to be in Rome for dinner." In an extremely difficult lunch with the ministers, my boss took the blame on himself rather than let the situation deteriorate further. However, later in the day, my boss rings me to warn of something about to get some attention. The Minister of Communications hates the consulting engineer 'with a passion' and blames it on us to an extent, because we brought him and his company in. Our CEO asks how we got to the stage of recommending a consultant in the first place and that was explained in terms of needing continuity, since we had picked them to do our initial studies.

"But who picked them anyway?" my boss's boss replies, such and such who is now working for the consultants having left our company. If the CEO discovers they bid twice the competition and still got the work, the fat will be truly in the fire. I sat in the offices of these consultants in New York with such and such a year or so back, and after ten minutes, thought to myself, "Am I being stitched up or what?" so perhaps there is some justice in the world.

Well, I will take a cruise round the airport for bit. The flight left to time, and I made it to Algeciras at 2000 to find three people sitting around waiting for me. We sallied out to the terminal to take a look at work in progress, discussed options and retired to a place to eat tapas and generally chew the fat in Spanish. They are pretty good at translating from time to time to keep me at least informed of which way the conversation has turned in the last half hour. As is usual in Spain, the evening was passed wandering from one tapas bar to another, eating and drinking. At the third or fourth, I started making going noises, which finally took effect at the sixth or seventh. They don't pay me enough for this!

I got back to the hotel by taxi at one in the morning. I have changed hotels; my usual kennel being full, I patronised a new place overlooking the yacht harbour of Sotogrande. Very pleasant, only had no real opportunity to enjoy it bar a walk among the yachts waiting for a taxi this a.m.

Back in the office, we got down to the consultant's design and I have cut about eighty thousand US$ off it — so the trip was worth it. He will keep on solving problems that don't exist — and he gets all unhappy when I point it out. He has gone away to organise with the contractor.

My rescheduled flight out of Gibraltar was for 1410, so I got there with an hour to spare despite the border queue. The Spaniards are still making it difficult to get in and out of Gib. Bring back Walter and singe the King of Spain's beard. The line of cars going in stretched right back through La Linea — some half a mile or so. The taxi dropped me at the border, and I walked across, which took ten minutes or so. I checked in and went to the business lounge, wondering why there were so many people waiting. An aircraft was outside and very soon it started boarding, so I went to check it wasn't mine to find it was the earlier flight delayed. I asked the BA person in the business lounge if she could get me on it, and good as gold, she did. What a delightful difference from Iberia — no broken English and no broken promises. Feeling quite, quite jingoistic — go for it, Walter! Sat here in business class somewhere above the Bay of Biscay and feeling a lot better. Yes, sir! No, sir! Three bags full, sir! What I cannot understand is why in America, the egalitarian society, they are so, so subservient, though it is less than skin deep.

Had a couple of days at home with time to discuss the furnishing of the last rooms of the Lessingham House development project. I can now start back at the beginning again, or maybe do a few of those nice jobs I have had to put aside in favour of more domestically necessary bits and pieces. I flew down here — Oman — last night and am in the new office they have set up here. A great improvement on camping out in someone else's patch, though they were very good to us.

5th July '97 — Cow tipping

Dear Family,

I have been wanting to sit down and write for ages, but time has not been on my side. The amount of work to be done with the resources available would be a lot if progress wasn't quite so viscous, but what with local politics, company politics and consulting engineers… However, that is why they pay us all this money and if it was easy, they wouldn't need us (what money and who needs us?). I spent most of this trip in Salalah and it will have to continue that way if only because we cannot keep the files in two places — as we discovered. John Fewer, the operations manager, has moved to Salalah and left a selection of stuff in Muscat — the wrong selection. We made progress none the less and have put some things in train, done a bit of delegation — hopefully not circular delegation — and sorted one or two decisions.

We have had two additions to the team with us, Arnie Garcia and Bruce Henderson. The former, a Spanish American from Algeciras, is here to sort out the old port's equipment, throw out the rubbish and fix the rest. I thought he wasn't going to last the pace. He was being so negative about just about everything until the other day he was up one of the cranes and was nearly knocked off it by an errant ship. The ship ploughed into the quay, making a dent in the bow six foot high and quay-shaped, and took out the power supply to Arnie's precious cranes. Arnie told me that, at the time, he was up the crane with two Indian fitters.

"Ever seen a ship hit the quay? No? Well, turn round now and you will do."

They were made by Stoddard and Pitt in the UK and are, according to Arnie, as good as new, having survived this corrosive atmosphere without any ill effects. By contrast, the Japanese job alongside is a rusting heap, according to Arnie. Anyhow, Arnie came down off the crane with something real to do, and since then he seems to have got the wind behind him, organising the Omanis and the Indians and getting the cranes powered up again so that they can work the dhows loading cement for the Horn of Africa (Why do cows have horns? …Because they aren't fitted with bells).

Bruce came here from the US to help us out with the buying of equipment. We were somewhat negative about the trip ourselves, but Bruce turned out to be a real asset, open to discussion and doing some work himself. He was good company as well, so we made the most of him while he was here.

I took him up the hill above the port to have a look around and on the way back, we found an aged Omani just coming out of his house. He was carrying his rifle slung over his shoulder with the barrel pointing at anything in front of him, like a handbag, and Bruce said, "He's got a gun… Must be going camel tipping."

"Camel tipping?" says I.

"Like cow tipping. Never head of cow tipping? Well, cows sleep standing up. Right? What you do is, go out at night with your mates, find a sleeping cow, shoulder charge it and if you get it right, it falls over — Cow Tipping! The farmers don't like it very much and one fired a gun over our heads."

Well, I suppose life in North Carolina can get quiet at times, demanding drastic measures to liven it up.

Stodhart & Pitt Cranes – made in Bristol

Mirbat Fort

Last Friday, we took the Patrol I had on hire and headed northeast for Mirbat, about seventy km up the coast. The Patrol came to me after the Toyota Landcruiser had gone off to have its clutch seen to. I thought it was some weird sort of automatic. You put your foot on the accelerator and the engine gained revs without the car moving faster. It got worse very quickly — partly because I was demonstrating the symptoms to my passengers — and I thought I wasn't going to make the hotel for lunch. Anyway, Budget produced a Patrol with only seven thousand km on the clock and coil springs all round — dream machine. Mirbat is there because of the fishing and not a lot else. The houses run down to the beach and there is a small artificial harbour for the boats. The old houses are made of what looks like coral blocks, but I think is the local stone, which has slightly better structural properties than a Victoria sponge cake. I jumped out of the car to investigate a ruin with the old gate standing slightly ajar. Inside the place was pretty much a shell but some of the rooms were still standing, very small and grubby and the roof didn't look very safe.

(Mirbat was the site of a famous SAS battle with insurgents in the seventies.)

Mirbat residential quarter

1st Jun '97 — Rumania

P.S. at some length!

I think we are over Rumania or somewhere… ia like that. We have just crossed over what has to be the Danube, as there are no other rivers as large this side of the Nile. Below, the country has changed from obviously flat river flood plain with large regular fields to the more broken outlines of hill country agriculture. The music has changed from Brahms' First Symphony to Mendelsohn's 4th. I didn't know I knew it — "De-Der-De, De-Der-De, De Derrr Derdlerder" etc. I am sure you recognise it! Really quite mountainous below now — eventually on this trip you get to the Black Sea — Oh! There it is now. One time we flew over a big new container terminal and then made a pass at Istanbul, flying right round it on the point of the wing with a superb view of the Grand Mosque — I think it is called — below us. It would be nice to do it again.

Last evening, I went out to check on the boat and Keith came with me. We fired up the engine and motored round to Hellevoetsluis for a light supper and then back. She seemed to be really dragging, either with a polythene bag round the keel or just the weed. I do hope to get her out of the water and cleaned down soon, if only I can stay long enough in Holland to organise it. I will be in Oman for a fortnight or a little more and then back for two weeks in the office, followed by a week at home. Looking forward to that! Keith is not that good at boats. He went up to the foredeck to get a clear view for his mobile phone and nearly fell off on the way back. Our efforts at making fast were, at best, clumsy, however the boat was there when we got back, so the cat's-cradle of lines did its work. Keith had had a very bad week in the office — trying to sell a product we don't actually have. This results in lots of pain and anguish when the prospective customer starts asking the difficult questions — like, "Where can I see it?". Just passing over the Dardanelles, I think. Istanbul must be on the other side of the aircraft. We are now over Turkey.

I have found a shop in Muscat that will digitalise thirty-five mm slides and give you them on a floppy with .JPG files. I have picked out some for the office so I can produce them on my laptop to show what the place looks like; might add some drawings too. Hope it works out — could be impressive! Must type a missive to Richard in Bangkok. He has an email address but hasn't worked how to do more than read it. His reply came as a fax written with a ball-point pen! I shall pull his leg unmercifully.

1st Aug '97 — Jack

I am in the kitchen of Jack Helton, our GM, in Muscat. My suite is across the hall downstairs and the rest of this Arab-style property is Jack's Oman home. His other home is in Amarillo, Texas, where he has a ranch of five or six hundred acres run by one of his sons and his father of eighty-six. Jack was in Russia for four years where I first met him on a trip to Novorassyisk — no, I first met him in Anchorage, Alaska but very briefly. The trip to Novorassyisk was the coldest I have ever been, including winter holidays at Cransley. I spent the last two weeks down south in Salalah and things are at last moving in a professional fashion. We have new people joining in September; the reclamation is really underway, as the dredger arrived early this week and started sucking and spitting yesterday, and the quarry is kicking out five thousand tons of stone a day for the dykes and sea walls. The Brits are on site now and what a change from the Greeks and Yankees. Sorry to be so xenophobic, but the difference is really palpable — or is it just more comfortable? I don't think so, as my American colleagues find the same. We have had so much politics and dissembling to date, it is a tonic to find someone who knows how and gets on with the job.

Jack's House Salalah

Somewhat by mistake I sent off the last missive unfinished. It was in the outbox and the s/w said if it is there it must be to go — so it went. I had got as far as Mirbat and the ruins there.

We drove out to the seashore, where a small fishing boat had been wrecked last year, and watched the monsoon waves roaring ashore, round the accommodation, across the fore deck and spending themselves on the beach. I wondered whether the crew had managed to walk ashore in the morning or whether they had decided to swim for it.

Wrecked fishing boat in Dhofar

I read once in a yachting magazine the advice to only abandon ship when you are standing on the truck of the mast with the water round your waist. Then is the time. I hope they followed the advice.

We left Mirbat back the way we had come, and after about twenty km, found a dirt road going up a bluff into the mountains and the mist. I suggested a diversion and we took off to see how far we could get. It was on our map, and we thought we could probably circle round and re-join our route later. The track was of stones and clay, and with the monsoon rain, quite slippery, running in zigzags up quite a steep incline.

Over the course of the day, despite brave talk, I decided that my colleagues were not actually the greatest of off-road drivers. John could not pick a line, just driving along the track as he saw it, dropping into all the holes and knocking paint off the chassis and sump — but slowly. Arnie, unused to a stick shift, took us up the hill in second with the engine complaining (but only slightly, as the Patrol has a long stroke very flexible engine) until we got to the steeper part.

"Arnie," says I. "How about first gear?" We stop and Arnie searches for gears, any gears, and then finds something; the wheels spin and we are going backwards to the place where the road ends and the precipice begins. We stop and John suggests the advantages of four-wheel drive. I have my hand on the door handle. More searching through the gear box options and then we leap forward up the hill.

Arnie!

In half a kilometre, we go from brown desert to Kodak green hills and valleys, all the same vivid emerald green, grass, trees, bushes and wet. A few cows, a house or two and we find a Jebali sitting beside the road with his battery, flagging us for a lift. We picked him up and he sat down beside me after stowing the battery in the back. His English was pretty good, and he asked us where we were from. I said Mina Raysut, the Arabic name for the port, to which he said "Ah! Sea-Land! 30-year contract — big ships next year." He went on to complain about the road and suggested Sea-Land might like, or rather should, build a new one for them. Arnie got going on the 'these people are all the same route' so I countered by explaining the economy of Sheikhs and tribes and said that if Sea-Land wanted to be the big Sheikh, there were some things that go with the territory so far as these people are concerned. Not sure I had it right, but I was getting fed up with all the criticism.

Eventually, we dropped our Jebali and joined the tarmac again to return down the mountain to re-join the main road. On the way, we passed a place we had been to in the morning — Wadi Thabat, which appears in Thesiger's books, according to Ahmed, but more of that later. Arnie was still driving and on the coast road again we came across groups of camels grazing. They have no respect for traffic whatsoever, and being the right height, go straight through the windscreen if you hit them — even the Omanis slow down for them. Not so Arnie! I made my resolutions.

That was the last trip. I was back in Rotterdam for a week, then to West Meon where William, Andrew and I set about the pond, as I told you on the phone. I have just about recovered. We also prepared a new base for the oil tanks, as they are now at the stage where a replacement is essential if we are not to have a flood of oil down the Cross or into the kitchen. The cost of the new tanks is about what I paid originally for the whole heating system.

The pond looks very attractive, and once I have bedded in the stones around the edge, it will be delightful. Andrew used it for a swimming pool after I left, as there is nothing in it until we have finished the edging — can't think when that will be, next summer, I suppose. They are leaving for Holland on Sunday and Patricia is dropping Andrew and a school friend at Calais to catch the first train of their European saga. They will have to be in the Hague for Andrew's results and whatever he does from there, and then they can set off again to be back at the end of August.

I got back here two weeks ago and have been in Salalah since then.

The world famous Mughsayl blow holes in the Khareef

One Friday, we drove south towards the Yemen border, along the coast road to Mugsayl, and then inland a bit to climb to around four thousand feet where you could be in the East African savannah.

Coast road down to the Yemen border

We found remnants of the Dhofar war in the hills, gun emplacements and ammunition boxes and wondered what it was like fortifying a hill in forty-five C, building a rampart of rocks and stones and digging a trench behind them with a pickaxe and spade. The views were for the most part obscured by the monsoon haze and rain at times, but we followed a track off towards the border (Jack thinks we might have been across it and John was very nervous) and the sun broke through for us. We parked the car above a two hundred foot drop into the tropical woods below us and sat and watched the swifts from above. Eventually we had to drive away, as Jack had a flight to catch — and John was getting more nervous!

Another day we were taken by the locals to Wadi Thabat. As I said earlier, we had been there before but had not known to drive up the valley further to where it narrows and there is a lake with waterfowl. The hills above are clothed in trees and greenery. Jack and I decided that we just had to walk up into the hills one day and camp — tantalising sometimes when you cannot get on do these things there and then. I will send this off now — have a wonderful time in Australia and I do hope the weather was good in Ireland. Not heard from Ollie lately, but haven't written either — sorry, Ollie. I will get this printed and sent from Holland.

1st August '97 — University

Not sure how far I will get with this but will see. I am in the lounge at Muscat airport waiting for the flight to Amsterdam. I've been here just over the fortnight I think, losing count a bit, and am now on my way home, or rather to Holland, where I am expecting to be joined by Mum in due course. She is going to drive over dropping Andrew and his travelling companion off at Calais, where they will start their train tour of Europe — or part of it. They have to be back in the Hague for A's results, which come out on the 14th August. I am afraid I don't hold out a lot of hope in this regard, largely because A does not seem to, either. I hope the fates are merciful and he gets enough to get started on a university course — what's done is done, I guess.

Later: well, he made it to Cardiff and Civil Engineering!

Had some good ventures in the South, up into the mountains. I will print my family letter and add it to this later — once I get close to a printer. There is a party of Dutch with kids in the lounge; one has, at last, bit its tongue or banged its head or whatever it was trying to do for the last half hour.

Had lunch today with the training people we retained to assess the Omanis we have on the workforce of the conventional port. Yeeessss! They are… despondent about the prospect of employing our troupe of clowns in a state-of-the-art container terminal (not my words — it's a bog-standard container terminal). The equipment driver instructor could not understand why one fork truck driver always went the long way round to pick up or drop off the next load until the driver nearly ran him over. The instructor realised the driver couldn't see him. He was blind in his right eye and only made left hand turns.

4 August 1997 — Helevoetsluis

Just back to the office and have been able to find the new rubber buttons for my laptop mouse. The old mouse was getting geriatric. Much use and finger acid had turned it into something closer to blue-tac than mouse, so that your finger became attached to the thing. I got in yesterday morning and threw myself into doing absolutely nothing all day — and got very bored. The world championship athletics was on from Athens and not a lot else. It's nice to be in the office — well, almost.

I think I will inveigle Mum into a trip or two to the boat to do some clearing up in the evenings, and then perhaps we can sail on the weekend if the weather is anything like it is today — sunny and dry with a light breeze. I have to reassemble the bilge pump. You need either two people or one orang-utang. When you undo the bolts from the cockpit beside the tiller the nuts fall off into the bilge two inches away as the crow flies but twelve feet away via the companionway and head down the quarter berth. Very good design!

11 August 1997 — Yachting

Time flies — had a great weekend on the boat. So great that I got to feeling like fixing things and then got to feeling like buying bigger and better — even managed to get Mum to the point of wondering if boats are cheaper in UK how we could get one over here. I informed her, airily, that there were people who did nothing else but boat deliveries. I don't think we will get to doing it but it's a nice daydream. We went down on Saturday morning to find the deck filthy with spider guano and dust from this or that refinery. There must be something that kills spiders, but I've not found it yet. They are incredibly robust, and cunning, too. You think you've squashed them or thrown them overboard and there they are, hand over hand up the rigging or swinging from a thread, hauling themselves back on board to scuttle down a crevice and wait for you to turn your back before running out another cobweb. I'm sure I saw one wearing an eyepatch, a wooden leg and carrying a cutlass. Missed the parrot.

Thank you for your various postcards — South Georgia looks terrific. Andrew and comrade are in Venice and threatening to arrive back here on Wednesday. I think the rail pass has been a great learning experience for the two of them — something to the effect of travelling with parents is a joyful diversion, travelling with yourself is a trifle more complex. Their results are in on the 14th, so we wait with bated breath. I hope that he has got enough to get him to the next stage, but the omens are not rosy according to A and his teachers — well, it would not be the first time.

Must now work — well, coffee first, then work. I should really have been in Spain this week but can't somehow get motivated. I have to leave for Oman for four days on the 21st and will be back for when William is here — wish you could be here as well, but there it is. Suffice to say, it pleases me enormously that you are, if not always contented, out in the world seeing what it has to offer and making the best of your opportunities. I felt badly that I saw so little of Mother and Father in their last years, but I console myself that they understood — for the most part, at least.

3rd Sept 97 — Some time to spare on a brief visit to Algeciras.

Gibraltar Rock

I am just waiting for our… well, he came — our Omani Marine Operations Manager and we went for a bit of lunch and a taxi to Gibraltar. I am now in Gatwick with a flight in, ostensibly, ten minutes with no gate and therefore no aircraft. I hope we get home before midnight, though I am not optimistic.

We were expecting to do a lot of sailing, but Saturday turned out wet and windy and we thought Sunday would be the same. However, it dawned with high cloud and not a breath of wind, so we got ourselves organised and I phoned a Dutch colleague with a message about his next job. He asked if I had heard about " Lady Di." I thought it was another weak joke, so said no patiently and he told me the unthinkable. Now it appears the driver was drunk and driving at a hundred and twenty mph in a city. We have had the villains stolen from under our noses and it now appears as the most stupid avoidable accident instead of a crime — which for some reason was more acceptable to me at any rate. The plaudits rain down, would it that she had been around to hear them. I have wondered if I wrote down two, perhaps three, columns, headed one hundred percent facts and one hundred percent hearsay, how little would appear in the first. How little we really know about these people and how much is what is portrayed by a press, with only its circulation figures to stand before in judgement.

Our day was turned suddenly silent, and we went about preparations in silence, followed by a long silent drive to the boat. The wind had got up by the time we arrived, so we set just the number one jib and reached across the Haringvliet to the far side, and set about beating east up the estuary between the channel buoys and away from the sea. With only the jib set, no boat sails that well, but we made reasonable progress with the crew sat on the weather deck and Andrew and I working the ship as it were. William was explaining fish genetics to Sam, who has the pleasant habit of being a good listener — he can come again! We ate lunch on our knees in the sunshine — or is that off our knees — and then I decided we might risk a reefed main, but as William got the ties off, I realised that the galley slave was pouring boiling water into cups on the draining board. This is officially frowned upon by the upper deck as it is dangerous, but then the upper deck has to make sure the galley is not inconvenienced by lists to port or starboard.

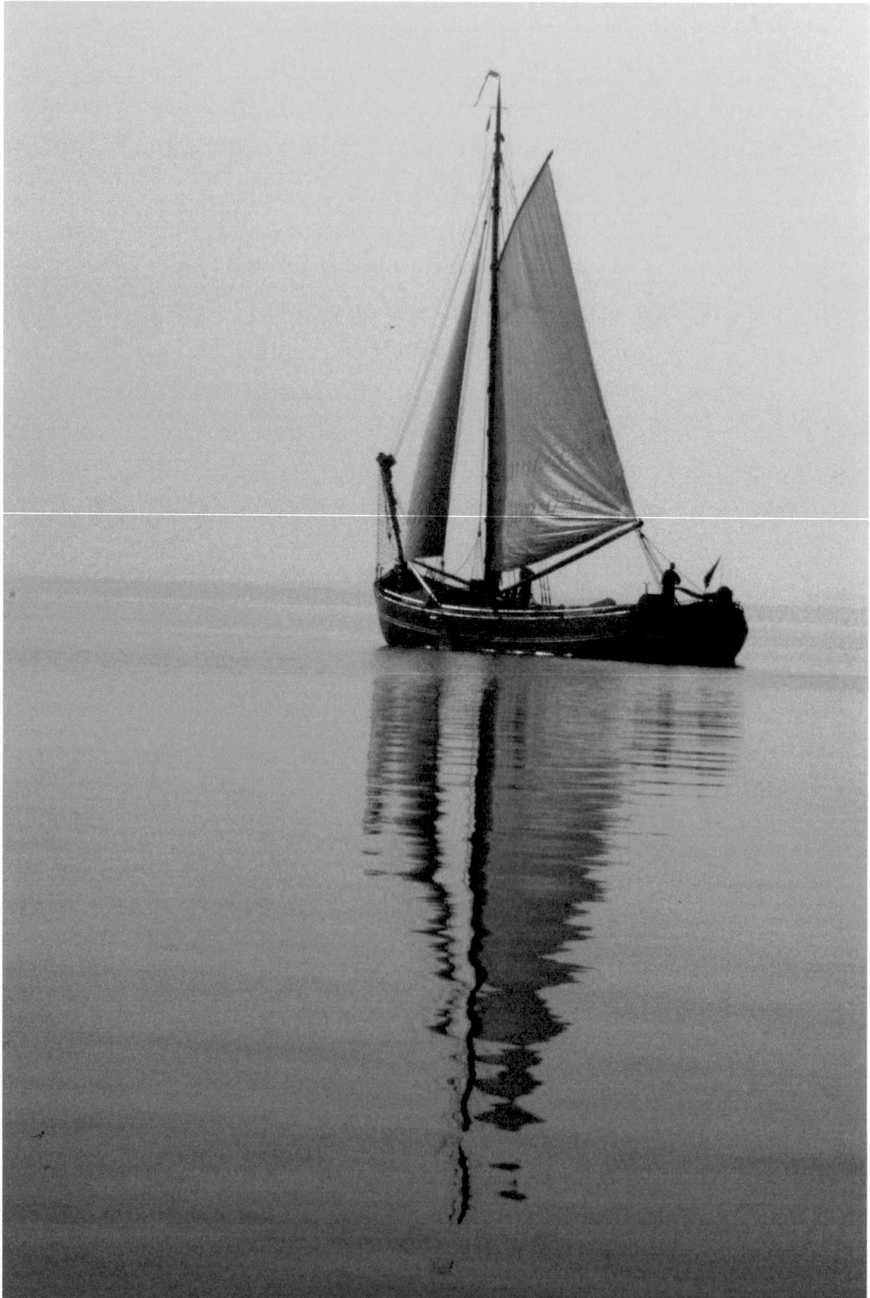

We scrapped the reefed main idea and stuck with the jib, which was just as well as the wind freshened up a bit to become quite lively.

3rd Sept. '97 — Diana's death

I am leaving for Oman on Monday and will be away a fortnight. It is difficult to write of very much.

No decision yet on whether I will come back to go with A to Cardiff. I should really stay in Oman longer, but we will see what he decides. Thank you for the card — do they really live in a tree house? I always wanted to live in a tree house… don't think it would go down too well with the galley slave. It is difficult to write of very much. The news is grinding on (death of Princess Diana) and I wonder where to take my mind. I always seem to end up in a cul-de-sac with it. Why? How? And to what end and why I am I feeling so cheated? I think that it is really being cheated out of someone I felt — for whatever reason — gave the establishment and some dreadful Tories a run for their money to the benefit of the disadvantaged. I must get this away

10th September '97 — Oman

Work on dredging the new port has started. Boskalis, the contractor, lost a barge ashore in the monsoon just south of Salalah last week with all the long delivery spares for their dredger, so they were asking the ministry to help them get a helicopter from the forces to go and look for it. Meantime, they are air freighting the bits they can get.

I got back from Oman last weekend and will be in Spain Monday with an Omani trainee, and back to Oman in a week from then. Salalah at this time of year is cool and very foggy, with rain in the mountains, which are quite as green as the photos. It is a good project to be on; the only disadvantage is that I cannot spend more time there, as things tend to slip. The CEO's venture did us no good at all and I think the chickens have come home to roost. Relations with the Ministry are proving very difficult at the moment, and they are heavily into the Japanese. They have a "free" adviser, Dr Kuda, who is there solely to increase Japanese influence by whatever method is most appropriate, and it is sickening to watch the Omanis fall for it. They will have to learn. It is also sickening having to sort out the mess that Charlotte left us and get tarred with the same brush. Every time we try to put something right, the comedian Charlotte hired as consultant wants more money for a redesign and the Ministry says they absolutely accept that what we are saying is right, but was it not Sea-Land that got it wrong in the first place? However, the dredger is dredging, and huge quantities of mud and stone are building up the container stack area hour by hour — impressive to watch.

16 September '97 — Letter to Beijing friend

Are you still down there underneath me, or somewhere else? Got back from Salalah yesterday, straight to the office and on to a Mongolian barbecue. The Mongolians failed to turn up, but the barbecue did and very good it was. I was talking to Scandinavian — Heyerdahl type — about polyethylene plants when it all seemed awfully boring, and bed called.

Feeling a little less jaundiced this a.m. Had a good few days in Salalah. I walked into the port director's office and a crew of Bedu — straight out of Thesiger — were parked on his sofa. I apologised for interrupting and asked if they were his family, which they were, so I was introduced to them. The younger ones were looking for work, but I could not quite see them sitting in clean overalls driving a crane and entering numbers to a computer screen. We shall see!

Flew out over the port and had a good view of the dredging and other construction. Turning north, we flew up the coast, looking down at the town and then flew inland over the jebal. At this time of year, it appears deep emerald-green, while the coastal areas are largely desert, so you get the contrast suddenly changing at the foot of the hills and then in fifteen kilometres the green begins to fade swiftly into desert dunes. Amazing! Must work a bit.

Dhofar from the air

18th Oct. '97 — Camel tour

Back in Muscat after a weekend of fun and frolics with the weather and a disparate crew of friends and acquaintances. George is our agent in Oman, Sonia is his wife, and they had friends from Scotland staying: Brian, Thelma — normal enough — son, Keith, and his girlfriend, Stacey, and son, David, all three of them… different. Keith was, I thought, possibly mute, but he did manage the odd caustic comment, generally aimed at his father, after he became comfortable with the crew of strangers he found forced upon him. Even for sixteen/seventeen, his narcissism was positively extortionate, and faintly revolting. His girlfriend, Stacey, was rather sweet, would put up with anything, greeting discomfort and calamity with suitably blue language for the occasion. David was, I thought, if not the village idiot, at least severely simple, but then I discovered it was not him, it was me. His Scots accent was so thick that the stream of grunts and whistles were, in fact, words if you had had the time for your synapses to accustom themselves. Regrettably, mine did accustom themselves and I was then able to discern why Stacey had so many different recipes for disposing of him. There is no edit feature between brain and vocal cords. Any thought is instantly translated into words — any thought…

Also present, Jack and his son, Cary — thirty-five? — visiting from the US. Sonia is in charge of Cub Scouts and is the fear of all parents, but the Cubs are such fun for the kids that they insist on going — which means the parents have to face Sonia.

As you may imagine, some of the children are as spoilt as their parents, arrive in chauffeur-driven cars and have their gear put in the tent for them and their camp chairs set up for them etc., etc. Sonia sends the drivers away and then makes the children get on themselves — some hardly know how to clean their teeth. Parents who arrive to collect offspring and hoot without getting from their cars need not expect to see their children until they show up in front of Sonia — contrite. As a result, Sonia is well capable of getting us on the road with a stream of instructions — all rapid-fire Scots. We were to go east and camp one night, walk up an interesting wadi and then head south to the Wahiba sands, where we were to meet a Bedu who would guide us into the sands to camp again the next morning — camel trip.

The first night was old ground, as Jack and I had driven that way a month back, promising ourselves we would come back to camp there some time. The road out from Muscat to Quriyat is paved, but then becomes graded for the next eighty km or so before reaching Sur. We stopped about halfway along the graded section on a rise above a beach and camped, with more gear than you would have thought possible. We stopped around midday and was it hot. No wind and humid. Once the shelter was up and all the stuff extracted from the three four-wheel drives — each one of them full — we collapsed in the sea, which was warmer than at Salalah but still pleasant. Some went snorkelling and I thought of the Red Sea, where you would not suggest snorkelling in such boring water.

East of Muscat on the beach

As the sun dropped, so did the temperature. George cooked over a fire and we sat round watching the sea and the few birds that put in an appearance — whimbrel (?), osprey, heron, terns, and I thought I saw one as large as a Caspian with an orange beak, flamingo, duck, Egyptian vulture besides gulls on their way home going east. Out to sea, the odd dhow on passage to India, Pakistan, or perhaps south to Salalah and Mukalla. The next morning, we had thought to do the wadi and then break camp, but some were a bit jaundiced after night exercises. It had poured with rain before dinner, and we had taken the hint from the thunder and lightning and put tarpaulins over the shade netting. After I had managed a shower under one corner, washing off the salt, it had all cleared up and we could get on with dinner. I had decided to sleep out while the others had all put up tents to sleep in, which they regretted later.

It was delightful beside the fire on a stretcher bed, the ones with the legs you stick into the side frames, until about two in the morning. The wind got up and flogged the tarpaulin to and fro, so three of us got up and tamed it, but Cary couldn't get back to sleep and I could see him sitting watching the sun get up.

We ate breakfast, cleared up, packed and set off for the wadi. It is a deep cleft in the mountainside where it comes right down to the sea. There is a village perched on the rocks, and a lake impounded behind a shingle bank with green grass growing on its banks, and a football field where there is no point in growing things, as they would get swept away in the floods. It must be the only natural grass football field in the whole of Oman.

We parked the cars between the lake and the date gardens and took the ferry across the water to the other side, where the path up the wadi starts. The ferry is manned by three little boys and crosses with the aid of a rope fore and aft, attached to the staging at each end. The rope is only just long enough, so you cannot bring the boat alongside, but you must board over the bow or the stern. We managed without losing anyone.

On the other side, the path wound across more grass and then entered groves of bananas and date palms watered with a falaj system, small canals — gadwals in the Sudan — carrying the water from higher up and distributing on a flood irrigation system. Now they have cement to build them from, but you can see the old ones out in the desert formed of dry stone walling, proofed, I suppose, with clay, though they did use some sort of lime for proofing water cisterns. The walls of the wadi rise vertically hundreds of feet above the bed, meaning that we were in shade, but at times there was no breeze whatever. The water runs over a rocky bed with boulders, for the most part piano-sized, but we saw one place where a chunk

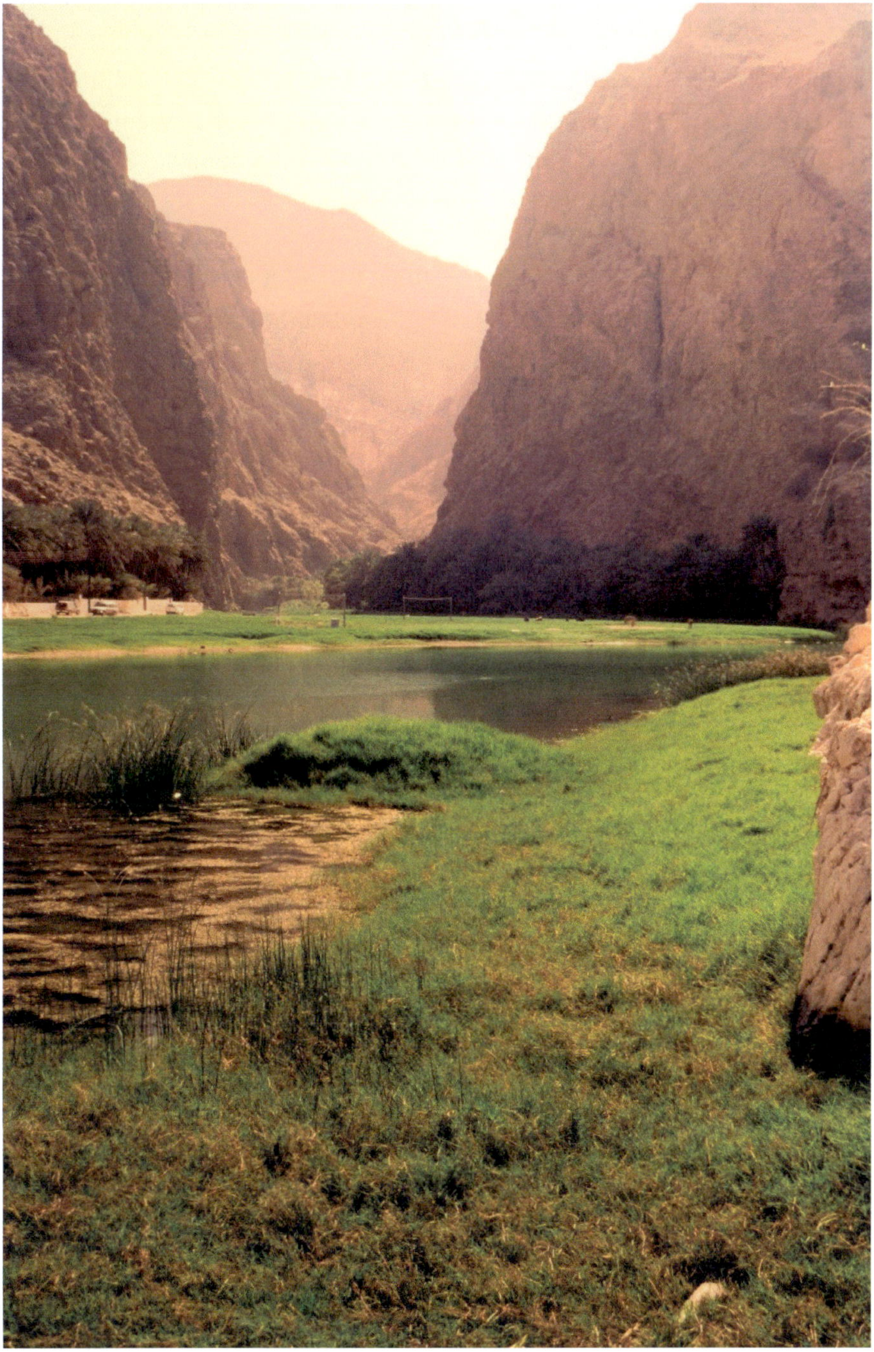

the size of a small house had fallen off the mountain and all but blocked the bed. The path had difficulty in finding a route along the side, but for the most part there were ledges giving a reasonable footing, and from time to time, concrete steps and bridges had been added for our convenience. The water itself was clear and quite cool, with fish in places and masses of reeds where they could find a place for their roots.

The goal was the top of navigation, as it were, after which the head is walled in from all sides. There is a pool there which you can swim through until you reach a wall with a hole in it. Through the hole is a cave with an open roof and a waterfall for the adventurous to swim to, mostly under water. I did not get that far.

The clouds were gathering on the mountains above us, and the thunder rolled around our ears. Jack and I stayed put while the others carried on, rather foolishly I thought, into the pool to swim. There were others there too who were a lot less mobile than any of our party. Jack and I sat there until David came back by himself and we agreed I would take him down, as if it came to evacuating, he would be the most difficult. I marched him back down the wadi to a constant stream of incomprehensible inconsequential Scottish commentary. By the time I got back to the ferry, the others had caught us up without any dramas and it was not until this evening that I thought that I had been most probably right. John and his wife, on another trip but in a similar area, had been cut off by flash floods on the main road.

We left the wadi and headed east again for Sur and the hotel for a bit of civilisation before going into the sands — and a loo. There were three games of cricket going on in Sur, probably amusing ninety percent of the Indian population. While sitting in the hotel restaurant, looking out at the sea, one of the players in his whites walked out onto the rocks, not to fish, as I had supposed, but to relieve himself of some unwanted waste matter. Upon completion, he used the available salt water to wash his rear end, got to his feet, adjusted his dress, practised a couple of swings with his bowling arm and walked back to the game.

We had to reach Al Suwali at 1600 to meet our guide, but we were a little late because of the sandstorm. In the Sudan, they were called haboobs, and I can remember once seeing one approach; this was the same. Once in it, it was like a London peasouper. However, we found our guide, and after a short game of charades to find out what we were supposed to do, we set off in line astern through the village and out into the desert dunes. We knew this because it was on the map and we had seen pictures, while out of the windows of the truck we could have been in Wapping. Said was quite happy that we could follow him, as was evidenced by his speed over the sand.

We had only gone a couple of kilometres off the macadam when Brian came to a halt on a slight incline in soft sand. Said missed his lights and turned around, driving on his balloon tyres across the open desert. We got out to push and it then became apparent that Brian had firstly failed to engage four-wheel drive and then had selected neutral, so that while we were heaving and pushing and the engine was turning, no one had noticed that none of the wheels was going round. Once in gear — no problem!

The drive through the dust continued, with wind whipping past us; every now and then it would clear a bit and we could see a bush go by and then we were just trying to keep up with the lights in front. At last, we slowed and turned up a slope running across the face of a dune, but we realised we had lost George. Back down the slope, followed by Said, who set off to search for George, while we sat with the headlights burning, wondering how far George would go before he stopped. One way and another, two sets of heads came back through the dust and the night and we were able to all drive up the slope to the Bedu tents, or rather shelters.

We parked the cars and got out to see what was what. Said called us over to the further of the two shelters, throwing mats on the floor for us to sit on. I was in first and found myself confronted by his family: granny, wife, three daughters, three sons and a baby. I left my shoes at the door and sat on the mat next to Granny, who was spinning black goat hair. Everyone said 'as-salaam alaykum' a lot of times, and then dates and coffee were brought for us while we watched the storm rage outside. Said said it would last only an hour. The goats came to see us and were shooed away, and we tried to communicate a bit with our hosts.

The very beautiful family were all too shy to even smile at us. Big brown liquid eyes gazing at us in the half light. It was decided (I could have slept there and then on the mat) that what with the children and the storm, it was better to find our way back and put up for the night at the government guest house in Al Quabil. My Arabic is such as to be best kept for greetings, but it had to be dragged out to embarrass itself in order to establish some sort of agreement about the night and the morrow. That done, we were on our way again back the way we had come, but as Said had said it would, the sky was already beginning to clear.

We reached the main road, ensured Said would be there the following day at 0900, and then set off for the guesthouse — full! However, there was a hotel at Ibra that had rooms and we got going again, reluctantly leaving the lights of the guest house, and its restaurant, behind us. At Ibra, we found the rather unlikely Ibra Motel and sent in a party to investigate. They returned with encouraging news, so we all checked in there for the night — not at all bad. The restaurant next door produced supper of a sort, and we went to bed.

The next morning, the sun was out, not a breath of wind and no dust so our Bedu had been right; it was a short-lived storm. Back at Al Wasil, Said was waiting for us in his Toyota pick-up and led back to just short of where we were the previous night. Driving across the sayl outside the village, we passed the remains of an ancient city sticking up above the outcropping rock in the dry riverbed. Dark grey gravel turned to red sand where the dunes encroached on the flood plain, moving westwards at ten metres a year.

The crisp morning air was such a contrast from the night before — we could see for miles, particularly where the track rose up above the valleys between the lines of dunes running south to the sea. The desert is well covered with camel thorn, tussocky grass and ghaf trees such as you would think of it more as savannah than desert. We stopped under a thorn tree where two or three camels were standing hobbled, and Said got down from his truck. Other Bedouin appeared and began to marshal a few more camels until we had enough for those keen on riding them. I confess I was less than enthusiastic all along, and even more so when one of them began to groan and grunt, baring his teeth at his master. The Bedouin signalled the camels to couch by dragging the head ropes down to towards the ground, the animals getting down on their hunkers with a great deal of complaining. They started to load up, picking riders according to the camel until it came to George.

Said's face cracked up as he walked over to him and said, "You — etnain gemal (two camels)."

George said he knew he was too heavy and retired happily to sit under the shade netting. Thelma and Narcissus also declined, but the rest of us were getting up on rearing beast, one by one. My first mount was the most recalcitrant of the lot, groaning and baring its teeth, and once I was up, weaving around at the end of its head rope, banging into the others and generally creating mayhem.

Said came over and examined its foreleg and then dragged its head down so that it couched, and I hopped off — with some relief. The next animal was much more docile, and we got along quite well. The one tethered behind me liked to walk with its head on a level with my thigh so I had ample opportunity to look him over from close up. I could get quite attached to a camel.

We set off. Just ahead of me was young David, and his mouth didn't stop for the whole trip, apart from a period of about a minute when I prevailed upon him to shut up. We were high up the side of a dune, and you could hear just the desert silence, broken by the pad of the camels' feet. It was bliss for a few moments, but someone had to burble — not just David. Actually, the poor lad was adopted about four years ago and is apparently much improved from his former self. I felt quite mean when I was told.

We were out about an hour and never really out of sight of the cars. The animals moved slowly at the pace of the camel men walking barefoot on sand I couldn't bear for more than a few seconds on my bare feet. The rocking and the thin blanket over the wooden saddle frame combined to wear through the thin skin of us pampered by sitting in air-conditioned four-wheel drives. I believe the Bedu can ride a galloping camel kneeling on the saddle. I didn't try galloping and I didn't try kneeling, but I did take a lot of photos and change a film.

Back at the cars, we sat about under the netting between two cars drinking water, eating candy bars and trying to converse with Said. I discovered he had eighteen camels, six of which were females and six babies. Later, I asked Jack, who has a farm in Texas, whether he thought he could make a living for himself and a family of eight from eighteen camels. He said that, given the lifestyle, there might be a possibility, but the thought of dispatching goat every morning would get to him at finish.

The return to Muscat was pretty pedestrian by comparison, though it runs through some impressive mountain ranges and steep-sided wadis. We got back to George's house to drop off Stacey, and then back to Jack's to get something to eat and shower. Cary was leaving for the US that evening, so back to George and Sonia's for a barbecue and thence to the airport.

I am in Jack's kitchen and Ellaine, another company wife, has just walked in and handed me *Looking for Dilmun* in hard back. Erv gave me a copy years ago and it contributed so much to my enjoyment of this part of the world that I keep forcing it on other people — hope they enjoy it.

19th October '97 — The English tea room

I am on the flight from Salalah to Muscat. Next to me is a chap who really ought to be on his camel, but seems to have strayed onto an aircraft. A good-looking man, fine featured and as thin as a racing snake. Designed for deserts and not a lot to eat and drink.

The other day, I wanted to take some photographs early one morning and took our new terminal manager's fiancée with me. It being a Thursday, a late breakfast at the English Tea Room was a possibility. The ETR is an establishment in one of the hotels, run by several ladies, mostly connected with the army, baking very fine cakes and serving under-the-counter bacon sandwiches. The family owning the hotel are a bit more fundamental, but I digress.

Ellen and I toured the site, and then set off for town via the fishing beach. They were just bringing in the catch, so we wandered in among the boats to see what they had: big fish, and down the beach, a shark about five feet long. I asked one picturesque individual who had just bought his lunch if a photo was possible. It wasn't, so we restricted ourselves to the fish, until three chaps siting on a pile of nets offered their services as artist's models. This seemed to break the ice a bit and a blonde Dutch lady wandering around was not quite so threatening. We set off back, but on the way to the car were accosted again by some old boys sitting under an awning, welcoming us, and offering Arabic coffee. They threw a blanket on a pile of nets, and we sat down to be served coffee in the little handleless cups and pass the time of day.

The tug master from the port walked over to join us — I didn't recognise him out of his khaki uniform — and another fisherman with a bit of English engaged Ellen in conversation. She turned to me, and in Dutch, explained what he was saying. I suggested English might get us further, and for some time, she couldn't make out what I was wittering about. She had an invitation to go fishing one morning which I have no doubt she will find a way of taking up.

That afternoon, we finished work about four and went to the Holiday Inn for lunch. You might imagine from the name some typical international Holiday Inn-type hotel, but they would have beaten you to it. Somehow or other, they have contrived to eliminate all HI-type ambience. They are always burning incense in the hall so that sometimes you choke on it. The level of service is friendly but hugely inefficient, and I can personally vouch for the coffee shop menu as having remained unchanged since my first visit in 1998 — if it works, why fix it?

Anyhow, it has a great pool and access to the beach, so we sat around there and debated tomorrow's entertainment, which was to a sortie up the coast to a recommended beach. Later, we took a walk along the beach and came back to watch the hotel barbecue going up in smoke. Apparently, overzealous application of the fire lighter caught the thatched roof above the grill. We decided to eat elsewhere.

Next day, we loaded into Joost's Toyota Landcruiser and set off north to Mirbat and then to take the dirt road a further twenty or so kilometres to said beach. There was some muttering about the siren calls of the Holiday

Inn pool, with cold beers and showers, but we soldiered on, hitting the dirt road rather literally.

Joost, being a good Dutchman, is an aggressive driver, without a shred of wimpish defensive driving in him, but the corrugations slowed him down and we wound off along a series of interlaced half-tracks among the rocky hills and outcrops. We could see the sea not far away, but we really began to wonder why we had come all this way when there are pretty good beaches a lot closer to Salalah.

Saladah beach picnic

Our party consisted of self, Joost and fiancée, Ellen, and friend of Ellen, Kristiana. Joost and Ellen are Sea-Land, seconded to Salalah Port Services. Kristiana is a rather unlikely German lady who has taken a job in Salalah with the Dhofar Tourist Company to develop tourism. Uphill, we thought. Just how many camel trips can you sell in Europe or the US? She told us that, in tourism, you make the money on the return visits, as the first timers cost you so much money in advertising and attracting them. They don't get any return visits! After a good few false starts, we found a delightful beach, but it was already occupied by our consulting engineers and their friends. They were polite enough, but didn't press us to stay, so we took the hint and set off again and eventually arrived at a sandy bay that fulfilled everyone's expectations.

While the people we had just left had everything properly sorted — agricultural shade netting is wonderful — we were still at the beach umbrellas, mats, and everything in the sand stage. Having established camp, the time came to go in the sea — and get knocked down by the second wave, if not the first. Even Joost, who is built like a brick outhouse, went down. The German lady retired, injured, to smoke like a chimney and read a book. However, she had come armed with food from the hotel, so we did get something to eat beyond crisps.

I had driven the last piece on the way in and taken it a bit faster over the corrugations to even them out a bit. Joost drove us home at a similar speed but without putting a little variation for the low frequency undulations. With a seat belt on and one hand braced against the roof, it was not too bad. The beach was we decided worth the trip, curving shore with rocky headlands and silver sand in between and no one in sight in any direction. On the way back, we stopped to watch a school of dolphins working their way up the coast, chasing tuna or something. We saw what to me looked like tuna jumping out of the water. The others said it was the dolphins jumping and that they didn't eat tuna anyway, so I shut up (I still think they eat tuna).

One night that week, we dined in the local Omani style restaurant (Indian cooks, of course). Ahmed, our Marine Operations manager took us and we sat on the floor and ate what Omanis eat. The Saudis have very little by way of culinary heritage — rice and goat — but the Omanis, by contrast, have a rich variety of dishes borrowed or adapted from the whole of the Indian Ocean. I had a local fish, grilled whole and very fresh. The others were eating a spicy chicken dish. Ahmed was suddenly at ease with his new colleagues and sat at one end, expounding on Omani culture and replying to John's — Operations manager — questions about how you coped with two three or four wives and what they were prepared to put up with in return. Bit close to the bone, I thought, but Ahmed did not seem to mind. Apparently, not many Omanis have more than one wife, and if you do, according to the Koran each must be treated equally in material terms (never heard that in Saudi!). As to affections, these you cannot control, so if you like one more than another, so be it.

The work has been hectic. We are bidding for three different types of equipment and for tug and pilot services, as well as computer systems. We cannot get our computer bod down here until March at the earliest and we should have had him in September. As well as all the above, we have all the other pieces of the puzzle to play with. The civil works has been stymied for two months, as they have not worked out how to establish a firm base for the quay wall. It is founded on a rock mattress which is placed in a dredged trench, but the trench keeps filling up with slurry — it is seventeen metres under water — which is a poor sort of porridge to put our quay wall on. They say they will start construction this week, but didn't I hear that before…?

25th November '97 — St. Petersberg

Gustav Mahler — I mean to write down the composers I should follow up from listening to them on aircraft — but somehow it never happens. I was impressed by Pier Gynt and Rachmaninov's piano concerto No. 2 just now. I had failed to realise I even knew them, but you get exposed to them in lifts and places where they sing. In the Nevski Palace Hotel in St. Petersburg — Austrian managers — they used to feel compelled to play Strauss waltzes — all day.

We were waiting for someone in the foyer one day and I said to Rob, "Do they have to play them all the time?"

Complain, he says, so I wander off to the reception and ask if they have any other CDs and am assailed by half a dozen Russian staff begging me to complete the user groans form. I did and this last time, no Strauss — I'm almost sorry.

So, this is thirty thousand ft over Germany, I guess, on my way back to Oman. What joy to escape from the Rotterdam office. I was in a meeting shortly after I got back last time, which was solely devoted to cost cutting — a whole day of cost cutting, which generally means putting people out of work. We have put so many out that there are very few left now to do the work, which means only half of it gets done. As someone said to me (Oh! Prague — ten km high) we are no longer playing to win, but not to lose. It will be a pleasure to get back to Oman, where we are in the growth phase — the advantage of being in projects. The disadvantage is that, if you have to make something happen, you upset people in the process; however, you also make very good friends among your enemies!

I was in Russia two weeks back, looking at ports there — again. This time to Ust Luga on the Estonian border. We drove a couple of hours to get there. St. Petersburg extends some distance in suburbs of massive apartment buildings, and then quite suddenly nothing but pine forests, with a break now and then for a field of a hundred acres or so of stubble, and then more pine forests. Where there are villages, they are small, of fifty houses at the most, strung out along the road, each one with a bit of ground around it for the crop of potatoes and cabbages. There are some new ones going up, but for the most part they are single storey, of timber construction painted a grim green or maybe blue with little signs of life.

As we got further from St. Petersburg, the villages got fewer still, until we were in unending pine forest. Eventually, the lead car drove into a town and pulled up at an office building where we all disembarked for discussions — all in Russian, so I tried to make sense of the drawings. Leaving there, we were guided to the telecommunications building, again in a forest, where the worldwide STC fibre optic net reaches Russia. It was like a scene from 007 with a shortage of Aston Martins. We made lots of impressed noises and then departed to look at the port development — or lack of it.

Ust Luga, I guess Wurst Luga is the other one and probably couldn't be much Wurst. The place is a Baltic beach with a Baltic wasteland of pine forest behind it. The nearest civilisation is fifty km away through the woods. I saw no wolves, but I bet they are there somewhere waiting for unsuspecting terminal engineers to step out of line. We arrived at this cold, wet stretch of Baltic beach with a crane, a pile driver, and four trucks carting in some fill, and behind: more forest. The labour for the port came from the nearest town — fifty-three kilometres away.

They were doing a bit of construction by way of piling and dredging and very pleased with themselves for the progress they have made since Feb. I would think they should have a coal berth there in another two or three years. The container berth they are talking of could be a bit longer. However, nice, enthusiastic people who did not seem to be as crooked as the usual we meet there. I was with a couple of our people I have met before, and it was very pleasant to see them again. We didn't think this was the answer to our immediate problems and headed back to St. Petersburg, deeply grateful they had not invited us to eat with them — or rather, drink vodka with them.

The Russians regard investment capital as well, vodka? You drink it and feel better or less worse. The plan seems to be that you have some roubles in the bank, and you get hold of a contractor, tell him you want to build a port and you have enough to start with a couple of piles. He goes off, gets the piles and maybe drives them, then you all wait around until some more money appears in the bank account when you buy a few more piles, etc. As to paying interest on the money in the meantime — why would you want to do that! They didn't seem to have a word for interest.

Back in St. Petersburg, we treated ourselves to dinner at the Canadian Steak House, being Richard, Maciek and self. Richard is American and ended up in Russia as the result of arriving three days late for his induction course in the American military Arabic.

"Sorry, you're too late, we've done the alphabet. Come back in three months"

Richard asked what else they had on the menu, and ended up studying Russian. Maciek is Australian Polish and speaks Russian as result. He was in the Russian Far East, running the port of Vostochny, and then joined us in Moscow. A really nice Aussie.

That was lunch. Luckily, the Napa Valley had experienced the cooling effects of fog from San Francisco Bay that year. The vintage I was drinking could not have been the same otherwise. The North Sea halibut was in good form as well. I wonder how they are doing down the back among the peasantry.

Hereabouts, we have Verdi to amuse us, lamentably introduced by an American soprano. Broken Italian would be so much more appropriate. Anyhow, back to Russia and St. Petersburg. We took ourselves the next day to the timber terminal, where stacks of sawn lumber interspersed themselves with containers. On the quay, they had a couple of East German-made cranes that looked like great spiders sitting astride the quay, trying to distribute their weight in such a way as not to collapse the whole structure. We deduced that this wouldn't serve our long term aims either and set off for the berth that brought me to St. Petersburg originally to find it all but complete — embarrassing! We wandered around, wondering that they had

LETTERS HOME

PROCTER HUTCHINSON

SIZE:	(234X156)
ISBN:	9781800165472
CAT:	AUTOBIOGRAPHY: GENERAL / BIOGRAPHY: GENERAL / MEMOIRS
PRICE:	£22.99 / $24.99
EXTENT:	248
FORMAT:	PAPERBACK
RIGHTS:	PEGASUS PUBLISHERS
TERRITORY:	WORLD
IMPRINT:	VANGUARD PRESS

About the book

Like many others in my business, I lived and travelled a lot away from home. Keeping in touch meant writing letters before the advent of internet connectivity. I wrote about the places, the cultures and the people I met, hoping to keep my family aware of the other side of my life apart from the business of planning my projects and seeing them through to completion. My mother kept most of those handwritten letters, composed as much as journals, and I kept some of the others in arcane text software which few will remember now. So here are some of them from a diversity of countries between China and Alaska. As an engineer, my profession may intrude from time to time, but mostly they are about matters of interest, I hope.

About the author

Procter was born in Trinidad at the end of the last war, and returned to England with his parents via a wartime convoy. On arriving in Liverpool, they stayed at the family farm in Northamptonshire, before leaving there for the Sudan and a house on the banks of the Nile, living there for five years until 1949. The family moved to Uganda, with Procter returning to boarding school in Sussex and later Essex. He read Mechanical Sciences (Engineering) at Cambridge, subsequently joining manufacturing industry in the Midlands. In 1969, containerisation was in its infancy and Procter moved to London for a position as a project engineer in among the old United Kingdom shipping fraternity. In 1975, he left for two years in Cape Town to help with the transition from the old mail boat service to container shipping. There followed many years of travel advising on initiating and completing shipping projects worldwide.

Pegasus Elliot MacKenzie Publishers Ltd.
Tel: 01223 370012, E-mail: editors@pegasuspublishers.com,
www.pegasuspublishers.com

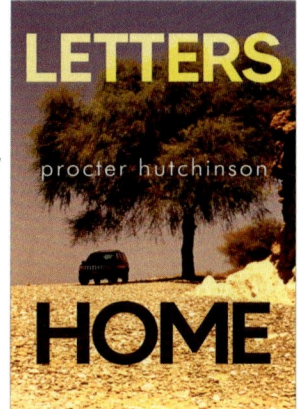

achieved so much. It has taken them five years and they haven't earned a sou yet on their investment, but they do have a berth. We have the cranes I bought for the project, but we are trying to sell them at any price. The — sorry, intermission while I listen to Der Rosenkavalier.

Ah! The cheese and the French red wine — apparently the aroma of the latter offers fine impressions of toasty wood. Well, I'll be jiggered, as they say in Chateau Cantermerle. I'd never have thought it.

Oh Yes! St. Petersburg — retiring to Daddis (sic) steak house for a recuperative steak — again — we decided that if we could put enough shipping lines together, we might have enough clout to get the original plan off the ground, but as I said, we are still trying to sell the cranes we need for the plan! I left Richard and Maciek to return to Rotterdam and some other problems.

The following week, I was in Bremen for a day, looking at another wild plan to build a container terminal. This time, we are being dragged into it by our partners Maersk Line, who persist in being rude about our liquidity. Last time we met over dinner, the Maersk man asked whether we really had our capital lined up for this particular multi-million-dollar project. I said I couldn't understand their worries; after all, we had paid for dinner, had we not! Maersk are largely owned by the Moeller family, who invest in shipping. We are owned by an American railroad, which is owned by Wall Street, and both of them regard investments in shipping as verging on the insane and investing outside the US as commercial suicide. Much better put your money into signalling and engines.

Bremen was a pleasant change. We met in offices overlooking the old — 1930s — dock area, virtually completely empty of ships and too big to accommodate a trendy shopping precinct. I wonder what they will do with it.

Back in Rotterdam and worrying over such diverse locations as Port Said and Kandla — the massacre in Luxor is of some concern professionally, but hopefully they are looking for more obvious targets than engineers going about their business. It would be pleasant to see Egypt again, but I doubt there would be much opportunity of sightseeing; more like site seeing, instead — more grotty ports.

19th January '98 — Muscat

I am at Abu Dhabi airport, waiting for us to get going again to Muscat. I shall be there for a month and Patricia is due out on the 28th to spend a fortnight with me. I do hope she enjoys it. It was lovely to see you last week and thank you for the excellent and memorable supper — did you find the missing bird? The chicken was from days of old, when birds tasted of chicken and were special, not KFC variety. The government is to phase out battery farming, it says, so maybe times are changing.

Back in Muscat and trying to get straight after being away for more than a month. The desk has had to be given away and it is becoming increasingly difficult to get any work done, as the office is too small. I am staying at Jack's house, which is always pleasant. We just ate dinner of baked potatoes and bacon, plus other bits and pieces — just as good as a hotel meal!

Ramadan is still on here, so the locals are not to be seen eating in the daytime — doesn't stop us, mercifully, so we repair to the hotels, which are allowed to serve "travellers" or back here. The Eid starts around the 27th so Patricia will be here for the local hols. When I got back to Muscat, Jack told me he had had a call from Patricia to say that a good friend of ours in the village had been killed in a car accident with a tractor. It is difficult to come to terms with the fact that he will not be there when I get back. Patricia was closer to them than I, and I feel badly that once again I can only talk down the phone. He left a wife and children at school.

I shall be here for the next few days and then down to Salalah for a couple of days and back here to meet P. The project is rolling along but there is a huge amount to do. Friends of ours from the Hague have in all likelihood accepted a job in Salalah, and the hope is that she and Patricia can house hunt for her together — if they can each coordinate the visas. The team is growing, and the members are all pretty good people, I think. This means that we are draining head office of good people, but they weren't fully appreciated there, so tough! This afternoon was spent with the architects — not before time, as we have put it aside — trying to get them a little closer to the financial ground. They have good designs for the labour lines, but a far cry from Namulonge, our old home in Uganda.

19th January '98 — Damen shipyard

Am on the road again at thirty thousand feet somewhere over Saudi, I guess. Yesterday I was in Holland, looking at tugboats being made, as we need to buy two for Oman. I've just thought of the wind-up toy every small boy used to have called Tugboat Annie, redolent of bath times — hot baths and perishing cold bathrooms. I didn't see any called that, but I saw some in the shed that were the size of a house up on blocks, having been hauled up the slipway to be fitted out. They build the hulls in Russia in a yard where they used to build submarines. The welding is perfect. Every beam and stringer is welded both sides, whether structural or not. The Dutch tried telling them it wasn't necessary, but it made no difference, they just carried on the same way. The finishing is perfect too. And all the detail is there, so they don't have to do any more to it after the grit blasting and painting the whole hull. The Dutch fit them out to yachty standard. I hope we get the chance to buy from them, but way things are now we will probably get cheap Japanese second hand. We went aboard one that was ready to sail for Abu Dhabi; they were just waiting for a favourable forecast and completing the victualling. The crew were stowing beer in the bunks and chicken in the freezer, as you do! As I wandered round the yard with all the tugs, I thought how nice it would be if they would offer to overhaul my yacht in Holland! They have in the group a yard that builds the luxury stuff — I picked mine, but they didn't offer to throw it in with the order.

Thursday, I had the chance to introduce some of our staff in Rotterdam to what we needed them to do for us by way of assistance in the purchasing process for the port. Like building a town, they said! If you stop to think what has to be done in the next six months — well, better not, actually. I could spend all the time in Muscat and still not have enough. We are getting four additional staff in February or March which will make a huge improvement — or will maintain the status quo…

Holland

I got up a bit earlier than I felt like this morning to go and check the boat over. A bitter wind and the sun getting up between the clouds and the lines of poplars; the boat, green with algae, looked very dejected. I really wondered whether the engine would start after a two-month absence, but the lights looked bright enough, and I turned it over with the crank to move some oil around and away she went, good as gold. Maybe this year we can get you over to sail her for once. I would enjoy that. I find that most times I am effectively single handed, which is rather hard work! I try to run the engine for fifteen minutes to get her thoroughly warmed, which drives the acids out of the oil, they say. A lot of the other boats were out of the water, and I really must get her out in the spring this year.

I am so impressed with your home. From being a very ordinary did-it-myself, it's now a proper place, which is a real pleasure to be in. You don't feel the need of a new challenge yet! I tell you I don't. I think I could tackle another, but it would have to be very different and a lot smaller. I think I would have to employ people to paper ceilings and plaster walls. Some things you grow out of. I have this bachelor pad concept of a barn somewhere facing a view of the South Downs with big stable doors all in one long line. A huge living room which starts at one end with a kitchen and dining area, followed by big sofas and a massive fireplace, followed by quarry tiled floors and fetching up with a workshop and forge at the far end. Somewhere some large speakers tuned specifically for Verdi, Puccini and the other guy what wrote La Boheme. Outside, an orchard with all sorts of old English apple varieties and a prolific damson tree, plus cherry plums to make jam. I would have to have a bunk room and showers for visitors somewhere — women on the bottom bunks and men on top, and no malarkey. I think I would probably sleep on a camp bed beside the forge. You can see why it has to be bachelor…

Well, must get this in the outbox. I will copy you a family one which you may not have got as a mail shot.

23rd January '98 — Ramadan

Good morning! Though I guess you are still in bed. It is Friday, so day off, though Jack, our general manager, was fool enough to start the day by reading emails. When I got down for breakfast, he was taking it out on the frying pan and muttering darkly to himself and less darkly to me. He has been with Sea-land for years and has seen all the good old boys come and go. Right now, we are trying to hire someone to come down here and work out of Rotterdam, but the chief snake has vetoed it, despite the individual concerned having accepted the job with great enthusiasm. You can imagine his level of motivation when he gets to work on Monday. For years, the company has been eating the seed corn and suddenly we are fresh out of people who know our business, so this guy cannot be released to follow his career — how do you like that for corporate morals.

Well! Well! I am sure it will look better in a week or two. I am staying at Jack's — general manager's — house rather than patronising the local hotels. He is on his own here, so I think appreciates the company. For me, it is a whole lot better than hotel life, which palls after a bit. Patricia will be here on the 28th for a fortnight — unless I can persuade her to stay longer — and we will stay here and then go down to Salalah for a day or two and stay in the Holiday Inn hotel down there for a few days. I need to look at my diary and find out when.

Today we are scheduled to go to a wadi for lunch, so must close this up in a moment and get packed. It is still Ramadan, so you don't see people out much during the day. The shops are full of Ramadan offers, sales, inducements etc. I had to buy a pair of Docksides, mine being (a) in the UK and (b) ten years old and with them came five raffle tickets for a BMW. I am sure they will arrange shipment to Holland for me — pity about all those disappointed people… A bitter east wind and a watery winter sun over the polders and people keep telling me I should ship the boat down here…

29th January '98 — Rub Al Kali

I am on my way to Salalah, somewhere just to the right of the Rub Al Kali or the Empty Quarter. The sun is out — there's news — and the view below is scorching. Just out of Muscat, you fly over the foothills of Jebel Akhdar, a fascinating geological exposee (can't type an acute accent) of crushed tectonic plates (sounds like nouvelle cuisine).

Just got back from a picnic on the beach. Three cars, which is fine, except you can't stop to look at the interesting things on the way because everyone needs to get somewhere else. The rock formations are incredible. The folding in Oman is caused by the Indian Ocean running up against the Arabian peninsula — tectonic plates and all — so the strata are all turned up on end, twisted, bent and turned back on themselves and then eroded so you can inspect the result. I suppose the same process is still continuing under our feet, where it's still hot and a bit toffee-like — quite a thought. Everyone professes to know all about how it happened, so I keep my mouth shut and wonder!

The beach we were at is the head of a fjord, a desert fjord, running back from the sea into a winding wadi full of Ghaf trees and boulders. Just before Christmas, some friends of our GM were cut off there when the road was washed out and had to get a lift home from a fisherman. The road has been bull-dozed back again… until the next time. Nit was no great shakes as a beach, but the road there followed a steep-sided wadi for a few kilometres with water running in the bottom; the aquifers are so full after the winter rains. The water, over the eons, has cut down through the ancient land surface, polishing the strata to reveal the convolutions of folding that occurred before it all cooled. I wonder what sort of consistency the rocks were when they were bent — must have been like red hot iron, only it would have to be hotter still.

I have had to admit that my grave mounds at the foot of the Jebel Harrar just behind Salalah are no more than ant hills. Last trip I went out to investigate with greater time to play with, and scraping the earth away, discovered what I had come to suspect — there were no particles bigger than what your average navy ant could carry up a one in four slope. Big ant hills though! This was a tremendous disappointment to your amateur archaeological sleuth and in future, I will leave it to the experts.

Our accountant, the Omani with the Cockney accent, was so foolish as to marry an English girl without getting state permission. He now has to legitimise the situation by applying for a retrospective licence. Not easy, and they are working him over in the usual way. He is getting little sympathy from his Indian boss, who in his turn is applying for a driving licence. He has been driving for thirty years, but has to have ten lessons before they will allow him to take a test, so each afternoon he is picked up by the Omani instructor in a tiny little red and white striped car — all L cars are striped — to be ushered round the streets, putting up with the instructor telling him which gear to use and trying to trick him into turning up one way streets backwards. Meantime, his shiny new BMW 5 series sits at home in the garage, being polished regularly by the hired help. The latter cooks an excellent curry, so will not speak loudly on the subject! I believe a crate of beer helped the transition from learner to licensed driver.

On my way back to Muscat after a tiring couple of days putting together the schedule; now we have at least a few of the fixed points established. The Ministry have been in cloud cuckoo land for a few months and have, at last, got reality into their thinking — we think. The fact that others float in and out of reality is just another aspect one is paid to deal with. Had a little problem yesterday with an email that was not overly polite about someone's ideas which got forwarded to the individual concerned by a quirk in the email software. I had no intention of publicly questioning him — quite the reverse — however, it might serve to get some honest debate going on the subject.

Patricia arrived last night, and I collected her from the airport in the Jeep Wrangler that the car-hire company had come up with by way of transport. She is looking forward to driving it! A four-litre engine with a little tin-can body on top and four-wheel drive! The next few days is the Eid holiday, so we are going to have some time together before work starts again next week.

7th March '98 — Patricia in Oman

It has been an unconscionably long time since I wrote, and phone calls have been a bit thin as well. One way and another, there has been little time over the last months for anything other than catching up with what should have been done a month previous.

The project in Oman has been all-absorbing, but this last trip I had Patricia with me, which made a huge difference and was great fun to boot. We will do it again in October, if not before. This next trip will be too short, as I have to be back to go to the Balkans (Skopje?) at the end of March to talk railheads. I know a bit about railheads from early days with Hornby — I hope it's enough.

We got back to UK a bit bleary on a Thursday morning and tried to make sense of the clock most of the day. Friday was better and then Friday afternoon and voice on the phone announced itself as belonging to the garage we bought the car from. How was the car doing, it asked. Not so bad, says I, bit of trouble with the clutch. Oh, says voice, would we be thinking of selling because voice had a client interested in our sort of car. Well, we was actually — partly because of the clutch (why did I say that) and yes we would come to see them tomorrow and talk about options. The long and the short of it was that Saturday ended up as change the car day — and big hole in bank balance day. We collect next week!

We had a great time together in Oman. I went ahead and Patricia followed a week later or so. I had been down to Salalah for a few days and got back to pick her up from the airport just prior to the Eid Al Fita holiday at the end of Ramadan. The lease car company had fixed me the only 4WD they had left a Jeep Wrangler. I was not at all sure what this apparition would engender by way of response from my gently nurtured spouse, but she jumped in with enthusiasm and could not get her away from the wheel. We meant to take photos of Patricia at the controls, but it got forgotten.

The Eid was a disappointment in some respects, in that it poured with rain, flooding all the roads around town. However, the Jeep came into its own and we saw a lot of Muscat and environs without going too far off the beaten track. My friends and colleagues took Patricia's arrival as an excuse for more than usual entertaining, so we did our best to keep pace with the schedule. We stayed with Jack, the general manager of the company, in his large, Omani-style house — four or five bathrooms, six bedrooms and plushy furnishings — looked after by Nila, the Filipino house keeper. Apart from us, we had a stream of business visitors and Jack's son Chad, so P. was kept busy while I was in the office with airport pickups and drops, shopping for the house and shopping for cooler clothes as the weather had turned suddenly a lot hotter than expected. She found the material shops and a seamstress with the aid of Sonia, wife of our agent, George, with astonishing results. Spare moments thereafter were devoted to similar activities, resulting in a stream of new shirts for me and skirts and dresses for P.

One evening, we went to the souk to buy spices for a friend of Patricia's and got involved with the shopkeeper and his staff in the mixing of Masala. As we walked in, the second assistant was spooning all sorts of sneeze-inducing powders into a brass scale: two of this light brown one, one of yellow, three of orange, etc. We asked what it was, and the chief Indian told us it was Masala for chicken. The Omani owner sat behind his till, collecting the money and smiling. Our turn came and Patricia filled out the list and then asked about the Masala again — only to be mixed in half kilo lots, but the thought occurred to have it split into four for the family, so this we did, each poly bag being taken down the passage by the third assistant to the shop with the sealing machine. I wondered what a kilo of spices was going to set us back, whether I had enough cash with me — converted three St. Pds., would you believe.

We flew down to Salalah together and spent three days there. I had business for two of them, but we took one to ourselves and drove north along the coast towards a small fishing town called Mirbat. About halfway there, we turned inland on a metalled road leading up a switchback into the hills, leaving the sand behind us and getting into scrub and thorn trees on steep hillsides.

Dhofar coastline

Nearing the top, there is a turn off the metalled road onto a dirt road leading slightly downwards, following the contours of the scarp back towards Salalah. It drops a couple of hundred feet to a valley floor, which is cut off by a cliff several hundred feet high from the coastal plain below.

During the monsoon, the water flows down the valley and cascades over the edge in spectacular waterfalls. Turning inland again, the valley floor is quite level and wooded on either side, and if you drive far enough, you get to a permanent lake with reeds and waterfowl. An elderly man and his wife were the only other occupants of the valley with their herd of goats together with camels and cows. The camels had all been recently giving birth to their young and all about were baby camels of varying ages. The youngest retained their Astrakhan coats, little woolly chaps with long legs and necks, some of them twins.

Towards Yemen

6th March '98 — American friends

Later — and how time flies: back to the last trip and the cast of characters who comprised it. Let's start with Jack! When he was a boy, they lived on a farm in Wheeler, Texas, and Mother sewed their sheets and underwear out of old flour sacks. He struggled out of that, driving a truck and studying nights at college, working his way up through the company and ending up in Alaska, building and supplying the North Slope. He joined Sea-Land there and progressed through a variety of jobs until he took over the Russian operation, which was where I met him after briefly doing so in Anchorage.

In Russia, we travelled to Novorossiysk together in a chartered turboprop. That was another crazy trip! Jack was expecting to retire, but this project and a wish to buy some more of Texas conspired to keep him at work for another year or two. He is a great host and made us all feel very much at home in his large, Omani-style house. He cooks Tex-Mex well, so long as you are into black-eyed peas, beans, cornbread and such — which we all were. He does Weenies in barbecue sauce, which are generally in a pan in the fridge to be eaten hot or cold according to taste or time allowing. (Weenies are cocktail sausages to the uninitiated). When he is not working, he is generally working, and since Mrs Helton is not around, that keeps him occupied without inconvenience to anyone else, and also keeps him away from the clutches of the large and stately American Ambassadress who we all think might like to get a clutch or two around him. He loves the country and getting out into it when he can, and he and I have had some good runs around Muscat and Salalah.

Chad, Jack's son, runs the ranch while Jack is away and has a girlfriend, Kelly, who is "coming along well" and was in charge in Chad's absence. My only contact was a rather frightened phone call. Chad and Patricia kept each other company while the rest of us were at work and taught each other different aspects of Western culture. Chad had never been outside the US before, and found the flight across the Atlantic and then changing in Heathrow quite a challenge. He couldn't sleep in HRW because of a fear he might miss the next flight. He arrived in Oman very diffident about a strange country and all these wild people his father had collected around him. It took him a few days to emerge and turned out to be a quite delightful, unassuming character with a nice sense of humour and an intelligent view of life from a chap with "truckin' in ma blud". I would have to leave Patricia to tell you about the stacked jeans, the cutting out horse called… "Babe"… how hip pockets "spoil the view" and all the other arcane details of life in the country in Texas.

The two of them drove around in the Jeep Wrangler, hitting the shops for mementoes and clothes and phoning me on the mobile when they got lost, looking for instructions.

Alan had been brought up by missionary parents in the Philippines and used to be able to talk Tugela — but you wouldn't guess it. He left college and migrated to Charlotte, North Carolina, to get a job with Sea-land. When you address a question to Alan, you have to allow processing time while he gets the answer ready for you. Being a bean counter, you make allowances, particularly being American mid-West. His wife was expecting him to be away for five days, but we needed him for longer — a fortnight — and I don't think they had been apart for that long before. Alan was more than a little amazed at the goings on around him, not least that he had to find his way through a whole lot of disciplines that he was not supposed to be trained for. The American education system is incredibly focused, and they grow up with frightening tunnel vision. I asked him how much longer in Oman and he would be unemployable back in Charlotte. Long pause, and "Yeah I guess you could be right." His boss complained that not only had we kept Alan too long, but when he had been out, there had been no one like Patricia running him around and providing home cooking of an evening. P. was showing them all round Muscat and doing airport runs — sometimes because the men didn't know the way.

Bruce, big American lad given to cow-tipping. Now, you might have heard about cow-tipping before, but our Texan Americans had not and thought it was a convoluted wind-up. We eventually sorted it out with a search on the Internet for cow-tipping — 1364 matches, from cow-tipping chat lines to virtual cow-tipping. Bruce and Patricia spent a morning sorting out the vagaries of transatlantic slang and such things as estates vs. station wagons. The last time Bruce was in Oman, I took him to the souk and while wandering down the lanes and alleys looked back to see he was still with me. He looked as though I was leading him through some dangerous wilderness and if he lost sight of me, he would never be seen again. He said this time that he had felt last time like a fish out of water. This time we couldn't keep him away from the souk and buying things for the girls and his wife. He went with P. one day to look for Omani dresses for his little girls and came back with embroidered bright scarlet dresses and equally gaudy shoes. I must ask him how they went down in ultra conservative Charlotte.

Marcel, big Dutch lad, quiet, always smiling and shy. He had not been to the Middle East before, so was eager to find out about the place approaching everything with a slightly amused incredulity. He obviously liked what he saw and the change from a rigid Rotterdam environment and wants to join the team on a permanent basis. I hope he does. We are steadily draining off anybody worth anything in Rotterdam and it is easily done.

Head office is all about cost cutting and attending your bosses' Rah! Rah! Sessions, which seem to concentrate on ensuring the bosses' share options pay out again this year, while the workers accept cuts in everything except responsibility and workload. Give it a couple of years and the unions will be back in force, in my view.

Bill, "what would Barbara say?". Barbara is Bill's wife and someone I would like to meet, from hearsay. Bill is a brilliant raconteur, so Barbara should be amused and relaxed, but I somehow doubt it. Unfortunately, I cannot remember which of Bill's stories was on show that night, but I do recall we were all metaphorically lying on the floor of the Intercontinental Hotel Coffee Shop, holding our sides.

Somewhere over Turkey in a BA 777, I first heard Handel's " Zadok the Priest" on the veranda of Robert Milburn's house on Makerere hill overlooking Kampala. The dogs were barking among the cooking fires behind the hill. In front the lights of the town, the darkness hiding the red pan-tile roofs and the greenery of the gardens. Today, at thirty thousand feet, I am listening to the same music, looking out at the wing (that bent upwards so dramatically on 'rotate') and wondering if you stood out on the wing in the bright sunlight whether the music was all-encompassing — a great ethereal resonance among the cloudscape. How could Handel have imagined that his music would be carried into the sky the way it is today — there's immortality.

Does "Pouilly Fume" mean smoked chicken? If I was only a wine buff, I would know that. The guy next door to me knows — I know he knows because he's been impressing himself, at least, with his studying of the bottle labels and the colour and the bouquet... and all that good stuff.

Ahmed was brought up in Salalah, the son of the old harbour master, Abdullah. He is a serious observer of Islam and won't join us for dinner if alcohol is to be served, and I respect him for that. It would be too easy to compromise your beliefs to fit in with your new employers. Salim, also serious Muslim, presented us all with a book introducing Islam. Salim is our Human Resources manager. I wonder how that fits with Islam! Ahmed is a very hard worker and keeps me on my toes with initiatives I haven't got around to thinking about — all the time. He used to have a small shipping agency dealing with dhows loading goats from Somalia and dried sardine from Aden, but he has sold out, as he felt it was compromising his professional employment in the port. One can whinge about the way business is done in the Middle East, but when you see this sort of ethics you have to rethink. We in the West have our own devious ways, but no attention is paid because they are our ways!

Here comes the chicken korma, but I note that there is rhubarb crumble to follow. They must have seen me coming. Why don't Indian restaurants serve rhubarb crumble?

So where did the title of this missive come from? It is a pity Patricia can't give you this live, as just watching her in action is enough to reduce you to tears. It's her story, but here goes! It so happened that Jack and I were breakfasting, and we get a call from Patricia to attend the front garden. Creeping out of the front door, we find the source of the noise that had been worrying Patricia that morning. There, in Jack's garden, was a guinea fowl, wandering around by the gate to the road, thinking about nesting in the hedge. We admired his/her smart regalia and went back to our breakfast. Later that day, Patricia raised the guinea fowl issue with Nila, Jack's Filipino housekeeper.

"Omani man come to take but he gone now. He say it European chicken."

"No! Nila, it is a guinea fowl." So, the guinea fowl stayed for a few more days until one morning, Nila goes out to see the Indian gardener.

"You catch that European chicken for Omani man."

"It not European chicken. What you think? That bird."

Patricia is watching and listening to this exchange of ornithological knowledge.

"That not bird. That guineapowl!" says Nila and stalks off triumphant.

Nila is a widow, but lives here in Jack's house and has her daughter for company working in a business here in Muscat. Her daughter won the local Filipino beauty contest recently, much to Nila's joy. Her daughter is called Jiamie (sic) from the credits of a British soap opera she enjoyed watching. It would appear that when they typed the credits, they spelt the name wrong, thus Jiamie! Nila likes to keep house and the place is cleaned thoroughly and the guests are force fed over breakfast. It would also be lunch as well, but she is off by the time we get back from the office.

England:

Day before yesterday, the Patricia and I took off to the New Forest and Beaulieu and Bucklers Hard. We had consummated the deal with the garage in Winchester and ended up the richer by one car and the poorer by one bank balance. Hopefully this car will not depreciate with quite the Cresta Run rapidity of the last one. We decided that, after doing kitchen research at the Southampton branch of "Never-Knowingly-Undersold", we needed a break in the country. We really passed by Beaulieu and must look another time, but we parked up at Bucklers Hard, paid our money and wandered off to see the museum and the houses set on either side of where they stored and worked the timber before bringing it down to the ways where the men-o-war were built.

There is an excellent model of how it might have looked as a working eighteenth century shipyard, a far cry from the one I saw in Holland a month or so back. They have used some of the cottages to create tableau of the pub and the ship wright's house and so on. The pub scene is accompanied by a soundtrack of actors laughing, quaffing ale and a lot of Eee! Arhhhggg! Shiver m' timbers type stuff. The life size characters look quite real in the soft light and are supposed to be modelled on known characters of the time whose CVs appear on the walls.

Outside, we walked down to the Master Shipbuilder Hotel which had, we thought, seen better days. My romantic thoughts of booking a night there for fun were doused by the vision of peeling paint and water-stained ceilings, a waste of a wonderful location for a hotel.

It began to rain, and we ran back to the car just before it tipped down. It is some time since I've driven in the New Forest, and it is so easy just to follow the main road and miss the country of heather, reed and bog, with the New Forest ponies wandering along the highways, uninterrupted by the twentieth century.

1st March '98 — Southern Russia

As tall people do, he looked down at me, smiling. He was holding a piece of card with the company logo on it, in red and black, and apologised for being late. He had a young man's smile on a face long, with ears set close to the head and cropped hair of a military style. His long nose, long by his own admission, gave him the air of an unhappy Saluki, but his ready smile belied that. He took me out to the car, where the driver awaited us with one eye on the police moving-on the traffic.

We took the road from the airport towards Moscow and discussed how we could use the time until George, the other member of this particular venture, should arrive. Vladislav agreed that we should investigate a rail yard that was on my list, and so we drove to the only one of a name similar to the one I was given in Holland. I knew that it was supposed to be equipped with some indifferent cranes and lacked pavement, so when we got there to find some sort of organisation, I began to think that we were in the wrong place. It was approached down a track between parked lorries and open drains. Men were working on the drains in the cold air, dressed in dirty padded cotton jackets and hats pulled over their heads and ears. They were shouting instructions at each other around the cast iron drain covers removed from the road surface, but did not seem to be progressing much.

Meeting out guide with rail/stack cranes

We stopped at a piece of wire stretched across the road and Vladislav negotiated entry with the man on the gate. It transpired that since there was a foreigner in the car there would also be a charge for entry — no foreigners, no charge. The yard was quite well ordered, though obviously congested, and I couldn't see any of our equipment around. We took a few photographs as evidence of having at least tried and left. The customs lady on the gate inspected our boot but evinced no interest in the contents so we were free to leave. There was no exit charge.

We passed the Kremlin walls on the way to the hotel. I will have time sometime to look at it properly, but for now I retain only an impression of immense ornate architecture and a confusion as to why they would want to retain it all inside a wall. Who were they defending themselves against? No doubt I shall discover. George arrived later that evening and we had a drink in the hotel bar, followed by dinner. The morning was to be an early start, so it was an early bed.

Vladislav and the driver picked us up next morning for the journey to the airport — one of the five around Moscow. It was an hour and a half's drive, I suppose, initially through the outskirts of Moscow and eventually getting into more and more rural areas. After leaving behind the blocks of flats, we were among the peasant houses with their small holdings, interspersed with woods of silver birch. The houses are all single storey, with boundary fences composed of anything they could lay hands on. Russia seems to have only blue or grey paint, so all the houses are of a similar shade. They are of timber, some with hugely ornate carved window surrounds to look like Georgian facades, but incongruous on a bungalow. The poorer properties have no embellishment and seem to have no means of heating, since no smoke comes from the chimneys. The cost of fuel must mean considerable hardship in winter. Every now and then we would stop to ask the way, and I became convinced that we were lost, and as the roads got narrower and more rutted, it seemed that no airport could be at the end of them. Eventually, we turned into a car park in front of a ramshackle building that had aeroplane things around it and got out, leaving our driver and the comfort of a Japanese car for the grubby cold confines of a Russian domestic airport.

Instead of corridors to departure gates, we walked through the hall and out of the other side into the cold air to another building, in front of which stood a desultory queue of passengers before a locked door. We joined the queue. In due course, the door opened, and we were admitted to an even dirtier shed, painted green and cream some years ago, where we awaited the flight to be called with our fellow passengers. I looked around at them and thought they looked insufficiently desperate to be on an Aeroflot flight at this time in the morning. Maybe the maintenance was not as bad as I imagined, and these people could travel in comfort and confidence. Maybe!

The flight was called, and we walked about half a kilometre across the snowy wastes to the waiting aircraft. I once took a flight in the US and the age of the plane was such as to put me in mind of a Southern Region commuter carriage preparing for take-off. This was something else again. The cabin was old twenty years ago, and nobody had fixed much in the interim. The seats fell this way and that, as the ratchets had worn away long since. The carpet was threadbare and not fixed down, and the seat structure similar to a hammock when you sat down in it. Last but not least, I wondered if the seat spacing could physically be any less. I wedged myself in and tried to get to sleep before take-off, so that I could perhaps avoid the trauma of wondering if, at full chat, the engines would or would not fly to bits.

Rising above Moscow, we achieved level flight and settled down to the two hours or so of increasing discomfort all the way to Anapa. George attempted to use his laptop but soon gave up, as the angle of his seat was such that he was forced into a reclining position,, and in any case, he could not easily get his fingers to the keyboard. I slept as much as I could. Things began to go wrong at Anapa. We had been told that we could not book the return flights from Moscow, and it must be done the other end, so Vladislav went off to do so, only to be told that he would have to go to the town office. This we did and were told that the flight was full, but that we could be waitlisted. Offers of pecuniary advantage were useless, as the lady concerned did not control the tickets. We saw the result of this process on the return flight when we had two standing passengers. The planned excursion to Odessa was beginning to look complicated. We talked about alternatives, the boat trip which was three hundred and twenty nautical miles and would take eighteen hours, the car journey that might take thirteen hours, and the return to Moscow, with a later flight to Kiev, followed by a thirteen-hour train journey. We left it all there and watched the scenery.

Since my last visit, the snow had melted and more of the country was in evidence. The fields, still bare after the winter, stretched between rows of poplars planted, I suppose, as wind breaks. The country is gently rolling and sparsely populated, but the soil is rich, looking as though anything might grow there. My Protestant farming upbringing reacted sharply to the amount of good land given over to growing grapes for champagne. If the country is so hard put to it, then there could be more contributory crops. Alongside the road, we saw at least some evidence of a returning economic effort. While no one was actually working, houses were in process of being built, piles of bricks and other materials were being fashioned into walls and roofs. Perhaps the spring would bring a new burst of creative energy.

Travelling through the towns, I was left with the feeling of the enormous task in front of the Russian people to recover from so many years of neglect. It is easy to see how a people can be so overcome by the work before them that they can deal only with the immediate. Perhaps small beginnings will achieve more than grandiose schemes. Certainly, the motive of possession is essential. With your own house in your own patch, there is something to fight for, something to pass on, to share. The tragedy of Bosnia, apart from the loss of life, is the workload they are putting upon themselves to rebuild for the present when they could be building for the future. The debt we owe to our forefathers in infrastructure and accommodation is too little apparent, from Georgian manor houses to Victorian sewage systems; we use them with little thought of the cost to our standard of living if they all had to be rebuilt for each generation.

Perhaps the international banking community should be thinking more in terms of the Russian citizen than the Russian city, as they are doing in India, where small rural businesses are the subject of economic assistance. Massive civil construction projects have their place, but the ordinary man's first priority is the house he lives in where the climate is so hostile. I think I will start the Free Paint Movement to provide pretty colours to the Russian working man! It would put the municipalities to shame and boost personal pride no end.

We had a new hotel in Novorossyisk — well, another one at any rate... Strangely, the decrepit bathroom and stunningly awful bedroom furniture and decor from the previous hotel were reiterated, broken tile for broken tile and gimcrack bed for gimcrack bed. How do they do it? We lunched off bread, cheese and sausage and sortied out upon the world to find the shipping agents who had offered to serve the line, once operational. They collected us from the hotel and drove us to their office, a room with two people playing computer games and piles of cartons of what looked like stationery. Not very auspicious, but things were to improve. It was agreed that they would arrange visits to the various authorities and facilities the next day.

We discussed the proposed trip to Odessa. I decided that I was not in for a midnight flight to Moscow, followed by an early flight to Kiev. From there, the train journey of twelve hours to Odessa, followed by a day's work and the same journey back. This sounded like something for younger bones, quite apart from the fact that I had to be back in Rotterdam to sort out the cranes for Rostok, preferably on Friday but essentially on Monday. I wished the others luck.

We returned to the hotel for dinner in the restaurant, as opposed to the coffee bar. Telling the difference was solely a matter of which floor you left the lift. We were served by a young lass of blonde hair and unhappy mien, who stood at the table, twisting her fingers around the pencil with which she was to write our choice of viands on her pad. It was hardly necessary since the actual choice was restricted to about three items. After the pantomime of having the menu translated, making choices for things that were nor there and finally settling on chicken, we asked for mineral water. That was only obtainable two floors down and we would have to go and get it ourselves. The meal came and we asked Vladislav to ask our waitress why she was so sad.

"I am not feeling well," she said, but did manage to smile at this unaccustomed concern for her wellbeing. As we paid the bill, George put down a tip of fifteen thousand roubles — about ten US$ — saying that no matter it was more than the bill itself, he would tip elsewhere at that level, so why not here. Vladislav pointed out that it represented a week's wage. She came back with the money from the kitchen, saying there had obviously been a mistake, but Vladislav said that no it was as intended and perhaps she would cheer up a bit. Her grin was worth ten dollars!

We had sat drinking coffee and after one more — that came in a bucket instead of the little cups previously — we went down to the bar. Another room not readily distinguishable from the other public rooms, it accommodated a bar and several low chairs and tables. A group were sitting at one table, and we took another in the corner. It seemed that the youth of Novorossiysk — such as had that sort of money — frequented the place of an evening together with the more professionally minded young ladies who turned up, swinging their shoulder bags and meeting any eyes that might indicate possible custom. One such stopped in the doorway, a striking figure in a short, almost bolero jacket and a lot of red hose, challenging the room to produce a customer. It didn't, so she sat down with her friends to go through the doings of the day with high pitched squeals as punctuation. Seeing business might need encouragement, the barman came over, and sotto voce, asked if we would like a lady at our table. Repulsed, he returned to cleaning his glasses to a clinical shine.

We had been told that there was a British delegation meeting the port so were on the lookout for the competition in one of only two hotels. Shortly, two Britishers arrived and sat opposite to us where we could only just not hear what they were saying. We sat chatting and trying to hear, but unrewarded, began to think of bed and in due course, fortuitously, departed. Before leaving, the girl in red legs and her friend had moved over to sit with these people (who later turned out to be a film crew), though apparently without profit, and their places at the other table were taken by two heavyset men in black leather jackets. At breakfast the next morning, Vladislav told us that he had heard a conversation through the wall of his room in which it transpired that one of the heavyset men had insulted the girl and another guest had found it necessary to knife him by way of improving his manners. We shall watch the company we keep more closely, I expect.

The next day was given over to visiting the port, the agents and a company offering container storage. The deputy port director was persuaded reluctantly to see us. He sat behind his desk for the first ten or so minutes, unsuccessfully trying to make a phone call. When he had finished with that, he turned his attention more particularly to being rude to us. Since he had just returned from an "all-expenses paid" trip to the US, courtesy of Sea-Land, this seemed lacking in grace. When asked about the details of his services and the container berth in particular, he invited us to look out of his window and see for ourselves. His view on our business was that it would be most inconvenient to find a place for us and that his scrap iron trade was too valuable to allow things like containers to get in its way. He sat like a toad with gold teeth, playing with three pencils on his blotter, reluctantly allowing us to draw his attention back to the matter in hand. George's Greek temperament was getting steadily more stretched, and the final straw was a discussion of possible rates. While offering us productivity that would cost us four thousand US$ a voyage in additional port time, he wished to obtain the same revenue as a North European port working at ten times the pace. George was in danger of telling the man his innermost feelings but restricted himself to an expression of extreme dissatisfaction. Toad nearly invited grievous bodily harm by remarking that George didn't look too unhappy. Afterwards, George was wagging his finger, saying that the man would regret the day and not be allowed to forget it.

We concluded later that we could not afford to expose ourselves to the risk of using the main port, particularly as they had in the past turned away two-vessels with not a box moved. There is another port known as the Geo Port which was ostensibly constructed for marine mining exploration. It's true purpose one can only guess at, but it would provide us with reliable facilities, if not allowing of any expansion, now that it's other function has ceased. That night, we left Novorossiysk to its own devices and caught a taxi to Krasnada. We expected it to take us up to three hours to get there, so we had dinner in the hotel, this time being served by the other waitress, who was hopeful of a similar gratuity, got George quietened down again and she got her tip.

George was at sea in the Mediterranean, South America and the Red Sea among other places and had a fund of stories of wild sailors and mad Egyptians. His imitation of Egyptians arguing was a classic. On the long taxi drive, we swapped tales and experiences and solved all the problems of business philosophy while Vladislav talked to the taxi driver in Russian. George's home was the island of Lesbos, unspoilt by tourism, as the Colonel's Junta regarded them all as communist so spent no money on the place to develop it. His father was a potter and he started work at eight years old, delivering chickens around the neighbourhood. Close to their house was a museum, and since he spoke English, he was often asked to assist foreigners visiting the place. He learnt quite a lot about the history of the island and astounded his audience from time to time. He said he would like me to come to Lesbos to visit "his island". He is a fanatical fisherman, along with his father, and when he was called up for national service and given a patrol boat to play with, he ensured that they had a crew of professional fishermen. He never ate better!

Driving through the night, we saw little but the occasional village with a cafe or two and shops with their wares spread out to look more numerous and displayed on ancient cabinets with mirrors, presumably also helpful in exaggerating the amount on offer. We arrived at Krasnada to find a pleasant Mediterranean town with long streets, quiet and dark at that time of night, with few lights and deserted. The main street of Krasnada is wide and would be imposing with a bit of work and a coat of paint on the buildings and the cast iron railings that divide the pavement from the road.

Vladislav asked if we minded him stopping to see his grandmother in Krasnada as there would be time, with which we agreed, of course. He guided our driver up a cobbled side street and tram lines, to add to the unevenness. Pollarded trees lined the pavement, and the cobbles were wet. We stopped before some sheet iron gates, and Vladislav got out and beat on them with his fist. In due course, a voice called out and he announced himself using his surname. The gates opened a little to allow a check of the visitor and then wider to admit us. We left the taxi driver in his car to sleep and went in to meet Vladislav's granny. She was quite elderly and apologetic for not being better dressed to receive guests. The yard we walked through to the house was small, with a vine of some sort and a few pot plants. The front door was open, revealing the inside of a small bungalow decorated in turn of the century style with romantic prints of wispy maidens sharing the walls with hanging carpets. It was warm and I wondered whether it was always like that or whether the heat had been turned up for us.

Through Vladislav we said our hellos and left Granny making tea and went through to the sitting room to sit down and stretch our legs out after the cramped car ride. Vladislav, apologising, asked if we would mind if he left us to talk to his grandmother. We told him to act as though we were not there, and I watched the evident affection between the two of them. Knowing something of the tragedies of his family, it was quite affecting. I cannot get the relatives in the correct order, but so far as I could make out, the bungalow was built by his grandfather, who died some four years since. He went to prison twice, each time for two months for "investigation" through the jealousy of his neighbour, who informed the authorities that he was obtaining building materials illicitly. As a result, every last brick and load of sand had to be accounted for. Quite recently, the neighbour had been imprisoned for running a bordello and Vlad joked that maybe his Granny had informed on him. The family was now split over the fact that Vlad's mother had divorced and remarried. Vladislav's great grandmother had lived in Siberia, and as a teenager was forced to work in a factory sixty kilometres from home. One day, she had not gone to work and had gone to see her parents. She was arrested and sent to prison for five years. Happily, the prosecuting judge fell in love with her, arranged for an early release after two years and married her. The authorities discovered this irregularity, and he was in turn imprisoned. I think he was the Cossack who was later murdered by Stalin's forces, along with others, for being a Cossack. Vlad's other great grandfather was a churchman and spent forty years in prison for his beliefs. And finally, his granny's sister married a Greek who was executed by Stalin — for being a Greek. Were it not for the fact that such things seem to have been commonplace, one would wonder at the veracity of it. Unhappily for those affected, it would appear that they also see them as commonplace and put little emphasis on their stories.

Vladislav remarked that his grandmother was without any pension and had, from time to time, to sell her crystal from the sideboard to eke out a living. We were invited into the small dining room for tea and homemade grape juice from the vine outside. It was touching to see them together, a tall thin young man and his obviously very dear little relative. I felt guilty for having so much and wished somehow to assuage the inequity. As we left, I told Vladislav to translate directly to his granny and told her she had a grandson to be proud of. He translated, embarrassed, with his eyes on the floor.

We left Krasnada, Vladislav with a jar of pickled cucumbers and us with our thoughts. We got a bit lost finding the airport but eventually I saw runway lights off to our left and pointed them out to the driver, who dropped us and set off back to Novorossiysk. The flight was enlivened by the presence of more passengers than seats. George found the additional pair standing, strap hanging, at the back when he went to use the facilities. They say it's wise to organise your victualling such that visits to Aeroflot toilets can be avoided, and so far I have achieved this. We got back to Moscow in one piece and found our driver, who took us to the office to collect the tickets for the next stage and thence to Vladislav's stepfather's flat. There we were to waste an hour or so before going to another airport, myself to the international and the others to the one serving the Ukraine; Moscow has seven airports of one sort and another. I was terribly glad that I had found sufficient reason not to be travelling with them. The flat was what might be called a studio in the West. It would probably fit into our living room and kitchen and still leave some over. The rent, however, is apparently a dollar or a so a month, so maybe there are compensations. Quite incongruously with the snow outside, there were impala skins from South Africa on the walls and some bits and pieces from other countries his stepfather had visited. We got to talking international politics, not very cogently at three o'clock in the morning, and George remarked on the close relationship of Greece with Russia, pointing out that there are one thousand two hundred Russian trolley buses in Athens. Vladislav remarked, with a smile, that maybe the good relations were because Russia had never "liberated" Greece. He told us about the war with Finland and how initially the Finns had lost a few thousand to the Russian's tens or hundreds of thousands of dead and wounded. The Russian command had then put a huge army on the border and the Finns had capitulated rather than face such odds. It was then portrayed as a major Russian victory. He was despairing of his country's abilities, and I wondered what his compatriots managed to find pride in of today's efforts rather than yesterday's.

Another airport and the comfort of a Lufthansa flight to Frankfurt with a cabin crew ready to do everything they could for your comfort. The fact that it was late, I missed my connection and arrived home after twenty hours of more or less continuous travel was immaterial. I had been travelling hopefully for long enough and to get home was sufficient of itself. The others got to Odessa that evening after twelve hours on the train. There is now a direct flight from Vienna, so I have probably missed my chance of the train journey.

31st March '98 — Skopje

Another communist block dump, but not as depressing as Russia. They talk a lot about the war and the blockade by Greece, but apparently the Greeks are getting over their worries bit by bit. The Greek railways are here in a few days to celebrate a hundred and twenty-five years of railways to Macedonia, but the name Macedonia is expunged from all their correspondence by way of thank you letters to their hosts. The Macedonians invited them to a performance by the Macedonian Symphony Orchestra and the reply thanked them for the opportunity to listen to the Skopje Symphony Orchestra. All this was vouchsafed by Betty of the red straw hair, fetchingly attired in what appeared to be a spare set of loose covers.

Betty, another central European with an incredibly convoluted life story. She used to live in Czechoslovakia so speaks Czech fluently, but learnt English at school. She has worked for the railways for twenty-four years and now finds herself to be the English translator. She flies to Prague once or twice a year to see friends but can't use her free rail pass — "I am a railway woman" — because her passport is no use for getting into countries. She would like to go to America but can't, not that she is unable to afford it, but because it is so difficult to get a visa unless you travel with a tour company.

At lunch, Will, the tour leader, said, "OK, let's all come clean! How much did we each pay for the ride from the airport?" Stan — thirty, Will — forty, me — fifty US$. The trip was about thirty minutes in a wreck of a car. Tomorrow we drive to Sofia for a hundred and fifty US$ — three hours in a modern Mercedes and the average worker gets a hundred and fifty US$ a month to live on! Well, at least I was not alone.

Stan is our sewers man — or environmental consultant. What harm will a container terminal do to the environment in a place like this — none. Why did Stan come all the way from the US to attest to this — any lending bank will have to have an environmentalist report to let them lend the money.

"Arm loosin' mar pee-ergs"? Well, according to Stan, a farmer he knew in North Carolina was losing a hundred and fifty lbs of pig some nights and reckoned an alligator was thieving them. Stan and the farmer sat up one night to check out the veracity of the farmer's theory. To keep themselves going, they had a bottle of Eastern North Carolina Beverage with them, sometimes known as moonshine. In due course, the alligator came cruising up the creek after the pee-ergs and farmer vows to shoot the beast.

Stan protests that the alligator is protected, to which the farmer says, "Well, you ain't goin' to talk about the moonshine, so why the alligator?" The reptile apparently filled the back of his pickup — with a twelve-foot bay-erd — and had all of its tail to lay along the ground behind.

Now in spectacular hotel in unspectacular Sofia. What a dump.

Sofia Cathedral

From memory: the stone bridge — Skopje was the scene of a devastating earthquake in the sixties. The stone bridge across the river and the castle were just about the only surviving monuments. The result is that Skopje is a mishmash of hideous Soviet-era architecture, exemplified in full by the central post office, which can only be rivalled by the disastrous Chinese-built port off in Cochin. Well, I forget entirely what these other tow aides' memoires were about — the restaurant up the hill, cows in the road, eight-hundred-year-old Macedonian Orthodox church.

1st April '98 — Czech Airlines — Coach Class April

There is a quite a small gorilla in the seat in front, which restricts my leg room a bit. Beside him is the man with the Sony camcorder and beside me the man with the flash camera. I think they must all be contract workers building things in Macedonia. They are all designed for lifting heavy things around. They feel the need to record the pleasures of flying Czech, so they are all jumping up to take photos of anything remotely different. The meal has arrived, so all the smokers, including those in non-smoking, have put out their cigarettes. What you are unaware of until now is that I have just been to Prague — that's Czechoslovakia? Were you in on this little surprise, or was it thought up by CSA all on their own? I think the latter. Searching my conscience, I cannot think of anything that I have done that deserves five hours with CSA coach class. By the way, missing letters, etc. are because there is only room to use one hand to type.

Well, it was interesting to see Prague from the air. Some new housing being put up with their own swimming pools, a brand-new airport with modern equipment and tidy. Much better than Russia. Dinner was fairly desperate, but maybe I will eat in the hotel — if the room is not let go. The pleasures of travel. Hope I can get to an internet type phone — talk to you tomorrow, P. Oh! And by the way, can you make sure the next airport you send me to doesn't have helicopters and cars with UN all over them in big letters. Got safely to Sofia — Bulgaria is awful!

1st April '98 — Skopje & Sofia

My Eastern European geography was never that good but "Skopje via Prague" — you must be joking. Anyhow, the flight is late, which means I am on it, as the incoming from Amsterdam was late too. Swiss Air did a terrific job of establishing confidence that all was being done to help. A selection of stewardesses asked what flight I was on, expressed concern, advised hope, smiled, said they had been in contact, they knew the flight, called me by name and said there would be someone come over to pick me up. We arrive, not on the stand with the walkway, but out on the tarmac with a bus. No one to meet me and wait while the bus fills, go to the transfer desk they said, so dash for the transfer desk.

"You can't check in here for Skopje — terminal B on the right." Walk miles to terminal B and find the transfer desk queued with extra problematic people. Cast about and find lady behind desk reading a paper.

"I need to get on the Skopje flight leaving now, can I get help somewhere."

"Certainly, just give me your ticket." There was no way of knowing she was even at work, let alone helping passengers...

I am in the departure lounge looking out at a most beautiful Swiss day. As we came into land, you could see all the Swiss out on their bikes, walking, picnicking and watching the aircraft come into land and take off. I had returned to Holland to pick up my thick coat for eastern European climates — not sure it is going to be necessary.

So why Bulgaria? Railheads! I have no papers on the visit at all except a complicated dissertation on the exact duty of the American taxpayer to fund this little jaunt. I have a vague instruction to get myself to the Grand Hotel and await results. Someone will find me there — hopefully not carrying an umbrella with a poison tipped ferule. Never trusted a Bulgar after those awful tomatoes we used to get at prep-school — a sort of vegetable balloon containing warm red water which soaked into your fried bread, converting it to pink mush. Somewhere in the middle of the week, we transfer to Sofia. The agent will take us to the border where we walk across to the other side and are picked up by the agent for Macedonia. I wish I could get used to the idea of a shipping agent rather than keep drifting around the idea of Special... or Secret... I can see an alp — a very big alp — I wonder which one.

Hopefully the seat will be on the correct side for alp viewing. I have been relegated to coach class... I hate coach class. I think, after the number of hours I spent last year in the air, I have a right to hate coach class. The worst part is trying to find a place for your carry-on luggage, followed by the inevitable back ache twenty-seven and a half minutes after sitting down. Just going to check out the aircraft, which seems to have arrived.

Prague Airport — I've discovered that I am going first to Macedonia where Skopje is — not Bulgaria — that's Sofia. This piece of news arrived via my diary atlas… And then I got to wondering, since Prague was closer to Amsterdam than Zurich, whether there was another Skopje somewhere — sort of Siberia direction. It seems not.

The flight is filling with farmer types and looks as though it could be uncomfortably full. I wonder what all these people travel for! Was our secretary in on this little surprise, or was it thought up by CSA all on their own? I think the latter. Searching my conscience, I cannot think of anything that I have done to our secretary that deserves five hours with CSA coach class. By the way, missing letters, etc. are because there is only room to use one hand to type.

Well, it was interesting to see Prague from the air. Some new housing being put up with their own swimming pools, a brand-new airport with modern equipment and tidy. Much better than Russia. Dinner was fairly desperate, but maybe I will eat in the hotel — if the room is not let go. The pleasures of travel.

The Hotel — no one to meet me at the airport. Never use helpful people in airports that offer you a taxi, even if there is no other transport to be seen anywhere. Got ripped off, didn't I? He stopped the car and pointed to lights some distance away, and using the English he was ignorant of before, told me that was my hotel, pay up and walk the rest. Anyhow, I am not willing to take issue over the company's money in a dark street in Macedonia, so he went away happy after an hour's work. I hope it chokes him.

I don't like to see UN cars and helicopters when I arrive in an airport —leaves me feeling uneasy. I must find out what the local time is and go to bed.

6th April '98 — Answer phones

I thought to find at least one of you back in UK, but maybe you are all in Beijing (I liked the name Peking much better — redolent of Gilbert and Sullivan, Puccini and the Opium Wars). I am just back from a little diversion to the Balkans — Skopje/Macedonia and Sofia/Bulgaria. I thought I recognised Skopje from somewhere and assumed it was to do with the last lot of Balkan bother, but it turned out it was the earthquake which I thought was not so long ago. It was 1963, while I was still at university. Nothing shook while we were there, but by the look of the architecture not much had been left up after the quake.

Not a pretty place. The only remaining attraction seemed to be the castle walls and one tower, for the rest communist block neo-blockick! The post office had been designed by someone suffering from blockick rejection and probably a stupendous hangover. It looks like a sick octopus. However, the cover on his reinforcing bar being a little scant, the whole lot will probably fall in a heap even before the next earthquake comes along. I picked up a fearsome cold somewhere; people moved away from me in the aircraft — a bit pointed, I thought. I am improving, I think, so will have to toddle off to the office this afternoon for a bit, else the backlog will confound me. Back to Blighty for Easter and the dentist — must not forget the dentist, he seems to punctuate all trips home — and thence together to Oman for a few weeks. Hope all is well with you all, Procter.

5th June '98 — Oman

I am in the flat in Salalah just at present, waiting for a large Dutchman to return from a fishing trip. He, being a member of the Holiday Inn club, can get me in for free. The company would pay, but seems silly if there is another way. Holiday Inn sounds infinitely bourgeois, but hereabouts things are different. They have succeeded in shedding all semblance of American customer focus and established a thoroughly Middle Eastern regime of "if you want it, why not get it yourself or wait until we feel moved". They do smile a lot. The manager has only once been seen to frequent "'front of house"... on his way to the heads.

We finished in the office yesterday about four and then went down to sit on the beach and swim a bit. The monsoon is not far away, and the swells are beginning to build up from the SW. The beach is not a particularly safe one, so it makes for interesting swimming. This morning it is quite cloudy, and the temperature has dropped several degrees over the last week, so relief is at hand. It has been forty-nine in Muscat and set to go higher, I would guess.

Work has been exciting. The tribes are really upset, or their sheiks are. We opened a recruiting centre and one thousand six hundred people — all unemployed — came through the door. Of these, three hundred and five got onto the training scheme which, if they complete it, guarantees a job at the end. Since then, the pressure has come on to hire a whole lot more of friends and relatives who didn't make it. The hill tribes got the most jobs because they are prepared to do the jobs we need done most, like drivers and mechanics. The townies all wanted to be Public Relations clerks = visa fixers. This is the best sinecure going — you get a car, a mobile phone and job which entails going to see your friends in the government offices and drinking tea. We have one such position and a hundred and seventy-one applicants!

I spent a whole day on demographics, as our Omani board members are out of their various trees as their tribal mates are bending their ears about what we've done to them. It is not about whether it was a fair choice of individuals on their merits, but whether or not we had favoured the ones we should have favoured according to the lights of the various interest groups. The government did tell us to make a special effort for the Yemen returnees. This lot fought the rest with Kalashnikovs from the Russian-influenced Yemen when life down here was real fun and now are unemployed freedom fighters. The lads that had sat it out in Salalah with the rockets going overhead feel a little miffed about that too.

We will never understand the difference between our loathing of nepotism and the Arab belief that you must help your family first. Our bold leader is today doing battle with the board members — rather him than me.

The physical side goes reasonably well, but time is running and there is a lot to do before the first vessel in November. I will attach a couple of aerial views to this if I can. Our staff has thickened up a bit, which means petty disputes are culturing nicely in the warmth. Gary hates Joost, Joost hates his boss, John, John hates everybody when he is in one of his blacker moods, etc. etc.

Time for tea, I think! Your work sounds fascinating and I'm so relieved you got it to work. You know your grandfather's satirical motto — never repeat a successful experiment. As for cloning another Bill — we could all profit from that. You would perhaps have to modify the software a bit to ensure greater amenability — you wouldn't want the clone making up its own mind whether it preferred going to the pub to cleaning the car or doing the washing up. The date for demolitions is scheduled to be the 25th and 26th so to arrive/depart any time either side of there would be fine. I would like to grub out the old concrete in front of the garage as well, preparatory to putting paviours down, so we might get to that as well while we have a skip.

Patricia is kitchening wildly and it will all be paid for by the Dutch government/taxpayer. How, you might ask — well, I made my return in 1996 to the accountants with a comment that I had been out of country a hundred and twenty days — would that help? They said and did nothing and I forgot about it, then last year I told my boss that paying for a flat in the Hague and living a double expat existence was receiving precious little recognition from my employers. He got on to personnel, which came up with a wizard wheeze whereby they could get the govt. to contribute having my status changed to non-resident taxpayer — and it worked like a charm. The accountants feel that they are due five thousand Guilders for their efforts = Ca. one thousand five hundred St. Pds, if you please. I have yet to take issue with them. The tax rebate was a joy to behold.

As to the break in, we have yet to find out anything at all as the police will not allow anyone in until we get back. I fear one of the casualties will be the five hundred mm lens. I hope they took all of the stereo, as a new one from the insurers would be nice, but I am afraid they will have got some gold bits and pieces from beside Patricia's bed. Thurber's aunt had a phobia of burglars gassing their victims, so she used to put all her valuables in a pile outside the bedroom door with a notice on it saying "This is all I have. Please take it and don't use your gas" — or so Thurber said.

7th June '98 — Internecine strife

I am in Salalah again, having been up to Muscat for two days to attend presentations on accounting software. We flew down this afternoon on the Airbus commuter flight which keeps Salalah and Muscat in contact. There is a bus which must take twelve or fourteen hours, but it crashed a few weeks back, killing two or three passengers, so possibly air travel is safer after all. We flew through some porridgey air on the way down, the plane shuddering but not that desperate falling sensation of a Dakota or a Viking. Did I tell you I landed at Lyon just after Christmas — I think so.

I came down with Jack and we sorted ourselves out in the flat, and I took myself off for a walk while he phoned the family in Texas. There is a path behind the sand dunes along the beach and outside the fenced off archaeological site that is the prehistoric town of HmHm, as the Dutch say, when we might say whatsit. I have a book on it somewhere, which I have not yet read. It is being excavated by a German university and they are making an excellent job of displaying it for the public. I crept through the fence a few weeks back and walked round it. There is a large tell which shows evidence of massive fortification and a lot of fallen walling in the shape of scattered dressed stone blocks — quite accurate too.

I saw a bee-eater and a few bulbuls but that was about it for bird life (there are some long tailed sea birds flying around the cliffs here — any ideas? White but have not had the binoculars on them (frigate birds!)).

Where was I — walking down the track behind the dunes and then cutting through to the sea and walked back along the beach, watching the monsoon rollers crashing on the sand, occasionally, when the combination of out and in coming was right, throwing up spray off the beach where reflected wave met new wave and then building up the depth and throwing a stream of water up the beach and over the lip of the sand and onto where I was walking. Like watching a fire burn.

I've been thinking about sand crabs. They dig themselves holes in the sand and throw the spoil up into mounds beside their homes. I thought this was like a dog might throw the sand in one direction until it built a pile until I saw one little chap carry a claw full of sand up to the top of his tip and drop it so that the mound was quite pointed. I have concluded that sand crabs are thoroughly middle class and wish to brag about the size of their houses. Since no one can see them, as they are underground, they have to build the biggest highest possible spoil tip to show how big their invisible home is. Must go to sleep. The tribes are gathering.

23rd June '98 — England

It is wet today! Yesterday in Stafford, talking to people about health and safety. Despite all their assurances, I didn't get the feeling they were on my wavelength. I need someone to lead the charge when the balloon goes up and the tanker terminal catches fire, but every time I got the conversation round in that direction, another set of forms seemed to emerge from a folder. Currently I am getting better from the Omanis than some of the round eyes. It is a bit depressing when you think you have recruited someone who is going to reduce the workload and you find that rather the opposite is occurring — came well recommended too!

8th July '98 — Oman

I am at thirty-seven thousand feet over, I guess, Turkey or somewhere, quite honestly glad to be on the move again. Great flight, including the Sunday Times dissertation on how to crash a Boeing 737. The co-pilotess went down in history as having started a scream which ended in the sound of the impact. If I happen to end my days that way, I am looking for a laconic "Oh Damn!" (BA) or "Yee Haaa!" (American) for an epitaph, not taped panic on the black box. Perhaps I should write to the Times.

Great flight! The people who record the in-flight music got the idea we were all ready for classical education in the more esoteric and arcane branches of music. No! What we want is all the good old thumpin' stuff from Elgar, Bach, Tchaikovsky, Verdi etc., none of your abstruse stuff, please. Anyhow, today we have a sympathetic ear and lots of the above together with a very passable meal of salmon and baked cod.

Been here a couple of days now and listened to all the grievances that I can handle. I hope it has done some good. The round eyes have got really out of sorts with each other, mainly through the lack of someone to knock their heads together. Add to that the decision to employ their wives as their secretaries on a sort of 'anything you can do, I can do a lot worse' policy and it was about reaching critical mass. We still have to extract ourselves from the wives issue, but the rest is a bit more peaceful now — I just feel a bit drained! It would be interesting to relate my experiences here to those of Mother and Dad in their day. Salalah is much more like what Shambat, Sudan, must have been in '48 — the services are much the same and the shop could be Souza Fig's at a stretch. There are no donkeys going to market with the cooks flapping their slippers from their big toes, but there are the fields with chaps tilling by hand and flood irrigation. I must build a saqya (the Sudanese irrigation device) one day.

The monsoon has started, and the days are warm, wet, and dull. It has drizzled most of the time I have been here, but the cranes arrive on the weekend so I shall not lack for something to do. There is quite a swell running outside the harbour and the limestone cliffs get the most terrific battering. The cranes received some of the same in the Southern Indian Ocean and sustained limited damage. The big ship handling cranes arrive 10th September, but the worst will be over by then. To see the pictures of those things on a vessel is just too improbable — one thousand three hundred tons each, three of them, and eighty metres high, if I recall correctly. It is close to bedtime, so will make myself a cup of tea and retire.

8th July '98 — London museums

What to do? The two weeks have vanished in a flurry of sledgehammers, falling masonry, plumbing, wiring, brick laying, plastering, and painting, all in aid of the new kitchen. I have kept out of email, fearing missives from work and wisely so. I have still not hit the company one, which must be knee deep by now. Maybe I will look at it tomorrow.

We did manage a trip to London to see the Science Museum. We had promised ourselves we would do it since Andrew was capable of appreciating it. It was a good day out for the three of us. Patricia stayed home to receive the new tumble drier. I just regretted not having more time to see the Natural History Museum and the V&A as well. The cost of the venture was quite ridiculous, what with train fares and a meal. However, I was, as usual, fascinated with how our forefathers, or rather fathers, managed with equipment so beautifully made, but to our lights antique, to discover all that we culturally walk around on. We saw Babidge's differencing computer, which was built in replica for the Museum's anniversary — something I had long wanted to see — and a four-megabyte disc memory nearly a yard across. The steam engines are magnificent, but for the more esoteric mathematical and research stuff you have to go to the top floor and progress downwards. Probably worth doing in future.

I had not realised that there was a polio epidemic in the fifties. I have wondered why it was such a preoccupation while I was at prep school. The iron lungs they used are quite frightening. Enough of that — I leave for Oman again on Sunday morning and will be there until the first week of August, then back to NL for a few days sailing and some work in the office, back here for a week round about the 20th and then to Oman until November when we open! Will try the phone — see if you are in!

8th July and back in Salalah — I am fortunate in having a friend working here who I worked with on the last project in Holland. When it gets too ridiculous, we can agree we have seen it all before — and this week it has been ridiculous. It surprises me that they haven't yet come to blows — it has been all but. I have spent two days of ear bending on everyone's personal gripes about their colleagues, their wives, other people's wives, their terms, other people's terms, the Omanis in general and in particular, budgets, expenses, who sneaked on who, you name it! Hopefully the present calm is not the one before the real storm and something has been achieved.

Our target of sixty percent Omanisation is looking increasingly suicidal, but we have got some reality into the thought processes of those that advocated it. We have retained a training company to set up a training programme, but the expectations that they will open the doors in three months' time and release into the community three hundred fully qualified all-singing, all-dancing Omanis has had to be adjusted downwards somewhat. Well, if it was easy, they wouldn't pay me this film star's salary.

Must go to bed — the monsoon has broken and it's like Holland, only warm and wet, not cold and wet. Not much to do by way of amusement, but we have the first delivery of heavy equipment on Friday so that is the weekend taken care of.

8th July '98 — Mugsayl blow holes

I'm sitting in the Mugsayl café, waiting for lunch to appear. Opposite me are two Omani gentlemen playing chess on a lovely inlaid chessboard with its own box. They seem to be old friends and the keys of the Range Rover seem to indicate a comfortable lifestyle. They encourage each other's moves with "Wallah hi" and the "Yala, yala". The older man sings from time to time and is the more vociferous. To my left, the monsoon waves hiss on the white sand beach; the water is green today. A pole stuck in the ground about six feet high shows no shadow from the sun at all, so my proposed check on the wave direction comes to nought. The café has an area for families with shelter with barty (Swahili for corrugated iron!) roofs covered with aesthetically pleasing coconut palms fronds. Nobody is using it, but they will no doubt emerge at sundown, as is their habit.

A friend has pulled up a chair to watch the game. In Sofia, in the park's entrepreneurs would sit on the low walls with chess pieces set out and a dual clock to time the moves. A good game attracted quite an audience, though I wonder who pays the owner of the equipment, the loser or the winner.

In front of me at about four hundred yards are the world-famous Mugsayl blowholes. You haven't heard of them? Amazing! I thought everyone knew of the Mugsayl blowholes. Do you remember, Helga, on our Zanzibar trip, the blowholes on the shelf of rocks over the sea. I think they were Kenyan rather than Zanzibar, but I'm not sure. The connection with Oman and Zanzibar and the East African coast is historically very significant. The Omanis ruled Zanzibar and the East African coast for years. They were into slaving ivory and cloves among other things. I was told by an Omani lady who was brought up and worked in Zanzibar that it is not the same at all now, and blamed it squarely on the ethnic east Africans; quite racialist, she was. I remember the horse-drawn carriages, the dusty roads and the coconut palms and the doors with brass spikes on them, which we were told were to keep the elephants out but not a lot else. Oh! Swimming on a beach, collecting shells which had Emperor purple insides and getting stung by a jellyfish and the flights in the Dakota dipping and diving among the cumulus clouds.

The Indian waiter has brought curry to another table of Omanis; it smells good enough to start again.

But back to the blowholes. There were crowds of people, but they have moved off in their cars now; the Indians like to take their families there, but the Omanis don't seem to bother with them much. I suppose it's the Salalah equivalent of Disneyland, really. Along the coastal cliffs, the mountains have turned green, yet the kharif or monsoon is only a week old. They told me in Bombay the monsoon always breaks on 16th of June — except for the years when it is a week or so late, and others when it can be a week or so early. Certainty is a malleable commodity in this part of the world. My lunch of Arab mezze — tabbouleh hummus and flatbread — was a good choice for a day like this, but the curry would have been good. The chai has arrived.

Musgayl

The two gentlemen got up from their game to wash and say their midday prayers together on a prayer mat thoughtfully provided by the management.

Before that, the younger of the two came over and remarked on how peaceful a place it was for writing anything you wanted. I agreed and asked him who the winner was. He indicated the older man and laughingly dismissed it as luck — in all previous games, he was the loser. Nice people.

I left with some reluctance and drove over to the parking area for the blowholes to leave the car and look out over the breakers crashing against the rocks. I didn't walk down to the holes that snore and spout foam and spray, as I had been several times before, but just watched for a bit, lent my binoculars to three of the local lads, and came away to drive on south a bit. I found our finance supervisor stopped for refreshment beside the road, so pulled over and chatted for a while to him and his friends. He is an Indian and very pleasant and enthusiastic. I have concluded that my colleagues overall are incredibly intolerant. They seem to find fault with everything and everyone; not the plan if you take an expatriate contract. I'm getting tired of being the buffer. I am supposed to be out for dinner tonight, but the chief engineer, true to form, has not told me his plans yet, so I will get myself down to the hotel bar and see if they are there.

On the way here, I took a track up a wadi going into the hills away from the coast. It was quite well worn and followed mostly the riverbed to a couple of huts out of sight of the coast. One day I will follow it a bit further when I have told someone where I'm going, but I thought it wise to limit my exposure to a puncture and a long walk, or rather two punctures. The valley was quite steep-sided and some of the flanks seemed to have been picked up a good shower of rain and turned green before the rest. The cliffs of limestone have underlying strata of white chalky rocks which might be the gypsum very common in Dhofar. I have an enquiry in the office for loading gypsum in the port.

On the way back, I was flagged for a lift by a tribesman looking very Thesiger-like, wild with a be-tasseled scarf around his head. He climbed in and we recited the greetings to each other, which exhaust ninety-five percent of my Arabic. However, not to be deterred, he essayed a few questions of the where are you from variety, so I gave him some answers, probably unrelated. As I dropped him off, he shyly said thank you in English, "Afwan" I said in Arabic, score fifteen all.

Despite my mobile phone being still in range, I have escaped the exigency that is the project work for a few hours. The vessel bringing the stack cranes has a bow ramp of forty tonnes like a cross channel ferry, or rather had one. The bow ramp was swept away in a storm off the south Indian coast on the ship's way from Singapore. The Chinese engineers who are here to commission the cranes now have another problem: to build a new ramp. Through the good offices of the civil contractor, we have got hold of the only available heavy steel sections in Oman and trucked them to Salalah. They came from another construction site, being the cranes rail beams for the cranes there. The Chinese had to get a design from Shanghai that could be built in Oman in short order. Mike, our plant manager, said he could do it, but I was worried and would have preferred a simpler design, but it was a problem for the Chinese. Luckily, our consulting engineers had a Chinese engineer, so our problems were not compounded by an insuperable language barrier.

A stack crane being loaded by crane in Shanghai

The Chinese needed the whole stock of welding rods available in Muscat, so we bought that and trucked it down to Salalah. The ramp would have to be lifted from the quay onto the ship and happily we had a one thousand ton crane of sufficient capacity (though not in a condition which meant it was insured). I had the Omani engineer of the port make a drawing of the lift, which resulted something you might get from the last class of the primary school. Once the ramp was installed, the ship was brought to the quay bow first and moored with warps ashore and to anchors laid out astern. The ramp was lowered, and the expectation was to start work of unloading the rubber tyred, hundred and twenty ton cranes under their own power; however, there was a problem. The ship began to surge to and fro under the influence of incoming waves, which you could hardly see and were of a very low frequency. The infragravity waves, we later learnt, were about a hundred and twenty seconds peak to peak and of no more than a foot amplitude. I watched the ramp moving a foot, two feet, three feet, six feet and then the heavy wire cable coming ashore to a bollard on the port side snapped, whipping back on the quay. Happily, there was no one standing by, as on those occasions it can kill a man. We could not discharge the ship in these conditions and discussed what to do. It appeared that the ship was resonating to a low frequency waveform from offshore that we could hardly see. We could possibly change the resonant frequency of the vessel by putting a tug, pulling a quarter ahead, on the stern of the vessel. I arranged for that, and the vessel fell quiet, and we discharged the cranes. The low frequency waves became a severe problem when we started working the big ships in the Khareef. The vessels would range up and down the quay until the mooring warps parted and yet you could not see the waves causing the disruption. This turned out to be an un-researched phenomenon which occupied two or three years of measurements and research work.

You find me in Salalah at the bottom end of Oman, not very far from Aden and just across the Indian Ocean from Colombo. I know American geography of this part of the world is similar to ours of the Americas, often rather scant. We have a consulting engineer here with us this week from Mobile, Alabama, and he asked whether we were North or South of the equator. We pulled out a small map and I remarked that we were on the same latitude as Khartoum — a complete blank. I asked where he did know in Africa, and he said well, nowhere really, as he had never been there! We are actually just South of the Tropic of Cancer.

Today is Thursday, the start of our weekend. Friday is a full day off, but we work half days on Thursdays, so this morning we had a four-hour staff meeting. It was supposed to last two, but we have a lot to cover! The project here is proceeding reasonably satisfactorily. I once read a guide to project management which advised the novice that if he thought all was going well, he was undoubtedly missing something. Today, an important part of the team decided to resign after only two months in the job, so that was unwelcome, however, he was obviously not happy in the position so has probably done us all a favour. Unfortunately, that means that I have to carry his work until we get a replacement — not something I know very much about either.

I took myself for a walk along the beach this evening. It is a straight stretch of two miles with dunes and an ancient site to the landward. The sand is white and devoid of any pollution at all, and I saw four people, two of whom I knew. The only other occupant was an Arab horse being given a sea water bath by its Indian groom. I was quite surprised that it was so relaxed with the surf thundering at its back and the water up to its belly. I am not a horse person — we don't trust each other and have no reason to anyway.

It is not a busy resort, but it is a resort at this time of year for the Arabs from the Gulf states who come here for the rain — yes, the rain! The monsoon or Khareef broke a week or so back, and it will be drizzly and overcast for the next several weeks. The sun breaks through sometimes for a couple of hours around midday, and then the heavy black clouds roll in again. Most of the rain falls on the thousand-foot high circle of mountains that enclose the coastal plain and the town, cutting them off from the desert to the west. To the south, all the way to South Yemen, the coast is composed of high cliffs and the mountains get up to over three thousand feet. The country is very similar to East Africa, but unfortunately the game was all hunted out years ago.

The coastal plain, where it is not inhabited or desert, is used extensively for agriculture. The overall impression is of coconut plantations, but in among them they grow papaya, bananas, sweet potato, citrus, sugar cane (for pressing for juice in the many shops and stalls selling fresh juice) and other tropical varieties. One quarter of the population is Indian, as someone has to do the hard work, but the wind of change is blowing a bit chilly and the Omanis are having to get themselves jobs. The oil price is down to twelve US$ a barrel and the exchequer is suffering along with the private economy.

There is little or no social insurance, so the family will support its unemployed dependants as much as it can, but we are seeing anyone able applying for jobs with us, and this includes the girls from the families who have been to high school and now are prepared to use their skills. This has some strange repercussions. Down here in the South, they are much more conservative, and all the women go veiled, so we have two in the office of whom I have only ever seen their eyes. It is quite strange to get a wave goodnight from a black body and a pair of eyes. The new recruits who are in training have asked for special consideration, as they wish to remain veiled outside when they visit the port. They will think about un-veiling in the office (so that the manager can see what they are thinking and hear them a little more clearly), however, no one goes on the terminal without a construction hard hat. I am sure you can imagine what it will look like when they are fully robed and veiled in black, topped off with a white hard hat walking around under the cranes. Our operations manager cannot wait.

8 July '98 — Grave mounds

Khor Ruri: I'm sitting on a rock in the middle of an eroded outlet to the sea carrying the flood water from Wadi Dharbat. Apparently, Thesiger mentions Wadi Dharbat, but I cannot find a reference. The sea is pounding the beach two kilometres in front of me; to my left, the water of the khor reaches to a slight cliff below a bluff coming down from the high ground. On the beach, I can see camels and cows in the monsoon mist. To my left, in the foreground, some ruins of a canal or something, and beyond that the dunes between two outcrops of the high ground still left from the erosion. Distant camels standing among what looks like grave mounds — damn big ants if they are ant hills this time. As I arrived at this spot, I passed some graves, probably aligned east-west so, if Muslims point to Makkah, not Muslims. Behind me, another outcrop surmounted by the remains of some fortifications; it is fenced off as a significant site.

Driven in by the rain

All around me are cairns about four feet high by six across the base, built of rocks collected from the limestone pavement I'm sitting on. About two dozen of them are out on a spit of rock running down to the water's edge in the khor. Who built them and when?

A she camel is watching me write from twenty yards away and over in the shallow water are five flamingos, not very pink in this part of the world; they must need more crustaceans. My camel is getting closer, and the flamingos are bickering over a crust. All the other camels have couched themselves — are camels couchant a heraldic device, I wonder. The monsoon waves are throwing themselves fifty feet up the cliffs. Another camel has arrived to join her friend and is groaning, as they do. Above me, a desert lark is marking his territory and the sun has come out. I could do with a hat. The camel has gone for a paddle. All the camels are brought down from the mountains during the Khareef; I think it may be because they get sick from the rain and the unaccustomed glut of green grass. I can see the fortified hill now; the walls must be seventy-five yards on a side. The camel is up to the tummy now.

I moved on from Khor Ruri down towards Mirbat, and looking to my left inland for a road up into the mountains that reach one thousand five hundred metres above Mirbat, with the scarp to make access difficult. I found a road, but it stopped regrettably but attractively in a carpark. Well! There was a forty-gallon oil drum among the rocks for rubbish, so it must be a carpark. I could hear the young voices of children herding goats by the sound of it — Oh no! He was singing! Before me was a dump of boulders with the knarled trunks of trees growing out between them. Their tops were bright green with the monsoon rain and hopping among them a beautiful (I think) blue robin. I saw south of Salalah another robin-like bird without much colour except a dramatically striped brown, black, and white head. I saw three herons today, grey, white and another one which I must look up but could have been purple. Also, glossy ibis, something like a lily trotter, extremely well camouflaged, a large seabird-like a gull but all over black when at rest, white underparts in-flight and a white collar.

Above the top of the trees, the ground dropped away a thousand feet to the plain where the greenery stopped. I could hear the surf, a background to the small boy's singing. In the valley, the Jebalis have pitched their tents, which regrettably are either of bright orange or blue plastic tarpaulins, not a pretty sight.

1st Aug '98 — Khor Rouri or Sum Haram

A successful day! I decided I would go back to Khor Rouri again and poke about some more, and thought I might get our tug man to join me with his wife — Brian and Tina. They both speak with a pleasant West Country burr and are possessed of a sense of humour, so make good companions for poking about.

The Khareef is in earnest in the mornings, so we left town in the rain along the Taqah road. I wanted to look at Sum Haram this time, since I had been told it was the Queen of Sheba's city. I think she moved about a bit because South Yemen also claim her as a past resident, if I remember right. There are the ruins of a prehistoric dam at Marib in South Yemen which she was thought to have had something to do with — must look it up.

You have to turn off the made road to a graded track running over hills towards the sea, which shortly droops down to the levels approaching the khor or water, and you can see the hill which is Sum Haram with ancient walling and debris obviously not natural. Behind, the khor continues on towards the sea, lined with reed beds and providing a home for the bird life, chiefly moorhens, coots and flamingos.

We stopped by the fence which encloses Sum Haram and got through the rather large hole to wander round the ruins. They are pretty rustic except for two items, a beautifully constructed well about a hundred feet deep and some inscriptions on a wall. The well is square, about a yard on a side, and built of carefully dressed stone without mortar. The walls looking downwards are stepped in every three or four feet by an inch or so, forming a ledge which might be used for access by placing planks across, but the ledge does not seem quite wide enough for comfort! The average cross section remains about the same all the way down. We dropped a rock down which took 2.5 seconds to hit. My Physics tells me it was therefore ninety-two ft deep — or thereabouts, which concurs with my visual estimate above.

The walls surrounding the well were all built of inferior material and craftsmanship, the stones roughly shaped and built dry — hardly more than boulders. Frankly, the Queen of Sheba deserved better by reputation, but if the palaces were built like the well, it would be more likely that she had some connection. Later, I had a look on the internet for Sheba and it seems she is claimed by Israel, Ethiopia, Yemen, and Oman — must have had a bike. Apart from the well, there were just two stones in a wall that had been inscribed and some evidence of the builders of the later structures having used some of the stones from the better times.

I looked hard for artefacts in the rubble, but found only a few pieces of pottery and one granite pebble — imported, as it is all limestone — showing evidence of having been used as a hammer. The inscriptions were not in a script I had seen before and included matchstick men. Tina thought Lowry might have been round earlier. We speculated on the ancient inhabitants and what it might have been like, looking out from their walls over the khor and the surrounding desert hills. I imagine their chief interest was trade rather than agriculture, except in so far as collecting frankincense could be called agriculture.

The khor might at one time have been usable as a harbour, but it is difficult to see how, especially with the monsoon waves beating the beach back on itself. I suppose if there had been more water flowing from the mountains, it would have cut a channel to the sea with a bar like Orford Ness. At some time, it must have done, to erode the landscape the way it is. I was with some archaeologists looking at the old site of Salalah and the tell I think I told you about. They were of the opinion that there had been a built harbour with quays, and they even pointed out the remains of a bridge to me. I went to take a closer look at the bridge, which consisted of a gently sloping ramp of dry stone construction, but without anything on the other side sloping the other way. The dry stone construction was, to say the least, of indifferent structural integrity. If it was to be an arch, it would need a lot of divine intervention to keep it up. If it was the buttress for a planked bridge, it would have been very narrow waterway, because all their buildings span no more than six feet before the short lengths of timber they had available called for another column. And in a land like this, why a bridge when you could walk round the end — except that the experts also postulated a moat. Now I think we were really getting to the flights of fancy.

Which reminds me of a story from a friend of ours, who as a child was taken to the local a castle for the afternoon out. He and his little friend found a long chain running down into the water, so they pulled it up and found a thing like a large bath plug on the end. The moat was dry when they left in disgrace.

But back to Khor Rouri — we left Sheba's place and set off for the grave mounds — or whatever — that I told you about in my last letter. The camels had moved elsewhere, so we were able to wander around at will. Apparently, the other graves are dug into the limestone to stop the floods washing the contents away, but the mounds have not been excavated so no one knows what lies beneath. I would love to be there when they dig the first one.

Brian and Tina had been to Khor Rouri before but had just gone to the beach, and Brian remarked how much more there was about the place than just the beach. We were watching the flamingos a few hundred yards away when they decided it was time for a move and all took flight. They are wonderful, even in the limited quantities Oman provides. Their legs behind and their necks stretched out in front an equal distance. Tina thought they resembled the Push-me-pull-you from Dr Doolittle.

I had robbed a bottle of white wine from the fridge in the flat and so we set off for the fortified hill overlooking the sea, parking the car at the bottom of a sandy slope and climbing up through a gap in the dry stone wall to the flat top of the hill. You walk about a hundred yards towards the khor until the hill comes to an end in cliffs above the beach. We sat down and drank the wine, ate nuts and watched the endless succession of waves crashing against the cliffs on the far side, throwing spray forty feet into the air. Apart from the camels, it could have been Wales or Western Ireland.

The new tugs we had ordered had to have names, so a competition was organised by Ahmed, our harbour master. I put up two names, Khor Ruri and Khor Taka. Since I had bought the tugs, I thought I should at least get some consideration, but I heard nothing, and they were called after a couple of fishing harbours to the south. One evening, in the bar of the Holiday Inn, I was with a mixed crew of Omanis and Indians and the subject of Khor Rouri came up. An interesting place to talk about, I thought, but the Omanis put a damper on the subject. Khor Ruri is inhabited by djinns that ride around on hyenas, so people don't go there much. And nor they do! I was a bit surprised, as I thought Islam frowned on that sort of superstition.

The tugs would come out from Holland on their own bottoms and with them came Mack. It is said that, at one time, you could open any engine room hatch in the world, shout Mack and a head would appear of some Scotsman or other. With the new tugs alongside, I asked Brian if I could take a look. Sure, he said, go and ask for Mack. Sure enough, he appeared and gave me a conducted tour, a slight Scotsman with a tousled head of red hair. Damen, the builders, had, as usual, produced super yacht quality of finish. Months later, after Mack had re-patriated, I went to see Brian in his office. On a chair beside Brian's desk was a blow-up plastic clown figure with orange hair dressed in full protective gear — helmet, hi-vis, safety shoes. What's that, I say. Oh, that's Mack, says Brian and when I have a problem, I do what I always did: I ask Mack. I warned him to watch out for when "Mack" begins answering back; it might be time to leave.

As we sat watching the world, the gulls on the beach suddenly took flight. I had noticed another arrival, which through the binoculars turned out to be a very large eagle indeed.

2nd September '98 — Georgia

As to power boats, our tugs for pushing one hundred thousand-ton ships around are four thousand five hundred SHP, so what do you fix three times four thousand five hundred SHP to in a fifty footer? — I suppose you don't. You just fix the boat to the engine instead. The tugs are building in Holland as of September (Uh! That's today!) so when I get back, I will toddle down to the yard and allow them to show me round and eat lunch. They are for delivery in February and March, and it would be great to go on the delivery voyage, but in a sea way I am reliably informed that a tug is like a pig on a trampoline or something. I shall not be there.

I think my Georgian trip went unreported! Lucky you. Well, it is a lot better than the North of the FSU, and a lot more prosperous, I would say. They do seem to have some vestige of initiative. This means that, industry being moribund, everyone has returned to the soil and bought a cow or three plus some pigs and sent them out to forage. Driving in Poti at night is risky, as the cows are un-lit, as are the pigs. The port that I went to see is the usual Soviet mistake. More cranes than you could shake a stick at and nowhere to put anything down once you've picked it up. See that sow's ear, Procter, with a little ingenuity and some hard work there has absolutely got to be a silk purse in it somewhere — and some profit for our Wall Street management.

Hotelling! No longer is one supposed to have an office; you have to book a desk when you happen to be in town. Well, it is not quite as bad as that yet, but I do have to share my office with someone else instead of having one to myself, the rationale being that we are both so often away it makes sense not to waste the space. Since the last trip to Rotterdam of fourteen days doubled my residence for the year, the argument carries some weight. I go back to Rotterdam for just a day at the beginning of August and scurried around, trying to assemble scattered thoughts and get off to Georgia the next day.

As I was scurrying, a strange personage asked me in broken English a series of broken questions and I despatched him rather rudely in search of my office sharer. The following day, waiting for the flight in Schipol, I saw the visitor also waiting and approached to restore the damage. He turned out to be Costa, director of our Turkish agents, and my hello unleashed another torrent of stuff about Istanbul and wanting to develop a new berth and... and... and. I gave him my card, which he stopped long enough to read and decided that any project manager was good enough for his purpose, and said that it was obvious that I should want to look at his pet project. I had been thinking that my schedule put me in Istanbul on Saturday morning and out again an hour or two later, when I could stay a night and see the place — most particularly the Blue Mosque — all I needed was an excuse and no one at home in the Hague to go back to. I told Costa I would look at his berths if he would arrange for me to see the Blue Mosque.

"Of course! Of course! I will send my driver to get you from the airport we will see the berths and then have lunch. After that, my driver will take you to the Blue Mosque." Brilliant. Luckily, Costa was travelling elsewhere in the plane, otherwise I would have had three hours of shipping.

At Istanbul, I had to wait for another Turkish Air flight to Tbilisi but found the KLM lounge there, leaving the Dutch lady who had sat next to me on the flight to fend for herself. She was a sociologist from Amsterdam University on her way to Cyprus to have a bit of holiday and to write up something on the tourist trade there. She admitted to living in a house on the Princes Gracht in Amsterdam — a bit like having a villa on Hyde Park — and having the family farm on an island in the Ijselmere. She was a scion of the KNSM shipping line, but no airs and graces to go with it. She was quite interesting on the subject of immigrants to the Netherlands — liked the Turks, but in common with all the Dutch I have met, loathed the Moroccans.

I got to Tbilisi at close on midnight, having travelled with a Dutchman who was a sort of one-man trade mission for the Netherlands. He went off to get his visa from the gaggle of supplicants around the visa window. I was in the process of joining him when my name was called, and I was shuttled off to the VIP lounge to have everything processed for me while I sat at the bar with the Sea-Land rep who had arrived to meet me and see me on the next stage of the journey to Poti.

"Do you know what is ahead of you?"

"Two-hour taxi drive?"

"Well, a bit more, actually, about twice that." He lied. It was pouring with rain, and we wondered whether we would make it through. Coupled with the rain, Dan had established through a Georgian with broken English that the car we were to travel in had a leetle probleem. What, like no engine, no roof, only three wheels. I was accorded the front passenger seat and before we could really get started, we had to pick up a couple who needed a lift to Poti. I got to Poti at 0730 after seven and a half hours in a Lada with a driver, a lady and her daughter and her husband who proudly told me from the back seat that he had learnt English "Don Teacher" This with his hands over his ears. It turned out that he had learnt entirely from tapes and a book. This was his first opportunity to practice with a real English person. After the first forays into subjects with ready access to the relevant vocabulary, the questions became prefaced by extended silences as he massaged the words around to get the next sentence/question assembled and submitted. It became apparent that his wife had her own command of the language and was able to help out from time to time. If she had not been so shy, she would probably have been better than her husband; but he was far from shy. 0330 — "How… How you like…" 0400 — "What you…" Etc. The wife was a violinist in the orchestra of the Tbilisi opera, but she said the productions were terribly limited because they had no money. He listed their performances, supposedly recent, which included all the big names he could think of.

We found our way through the darkening streets of Tbilisi, now and again coming upon some clues of how interesting the town would be if you could see all of it. It took us half an hour to get out into the country, where the roads were at least straighter and the pothole negotiation could be planned somewhat in advance. Arriving at the hotel was diverting.

Here follow notes for a script which sadly I never completed. I must now fill a few gaps, at least:

Tbilisi — the old city walls with the houses built on top of them — neo-classical but with the addition of balconies strutted from the walls with filigree balusters

The drive from Poti to Tbilisi — the old and careful taxi driver in his ancient sixteen-year-old Russian car. Cows and other vehicles have no respect for life or limb.

The stalls beside the road — Georgia then was sadly poverty-stricken

Honey camps — up in the hills the bevies of beehives

Red pottery — up in the hills again, a village totally devoted to pottery. The roadsides lined with pots, for what purpose I cannot now remember

Petrol — Huh?

Hammocks — well, I suppose there must have been hammocks for sale

Baskets — and baskets?

Bottled water

The mountains to our left or the North — this was the drive back to Poti and now that it was light, we could see the country we were passing through clothed in beautiful deciduous forest. We gained height steadily, and at the watershed there was a village street entirely composed of restaurants or cafes. So it seemed. We had to cross over the pass, but stopped for lunch. We stopped in one of the cafes, where we ate of rough peasant bread and bowls of excellent stew. There were a multitude of bus stops beside "the home for the bewildered architects". All the buildings that I remember had been built of scrap wood by people without the benefit of a saw. They were, for the most part, of timber, but the lengths being random and recycled from some other purpose, they just used them as they were. Our colleague, a young Dutch accountant, had eaten unwisely and was in desperate need of the facilities. We asked the way and were directed to a hole in the ground with a pottery squat to stop you falling in. The shed and its door were of the same random construction as the rest of the buildings, but our man was past caring and disappeared into the ammonia cloud, reappearing later with a smile on his face, much relieved. Our experience of the same facility was simply to take a deep breath and sue whatever time was available before inhaling to get the business done

Throughout Georgia, pigs, sheep, and cows use the roads, foraging for whatever comes to hand or mouth. Yes, that's Cow-crash: they and the pigs wander all over the road at night and they don't carry lights, for some reason — like cyclists in Holland — too mean to buy the batteries — like cyclists in Holland. We were driving to the hotel, too fast, when a cow appeared about three metres from our bumper out of the glare of the oncoming headlights. I swore, which I think drew our driver's attention to the fact that we had a significant problem. We swerved and the cow swerved, fortunately in the opposite direction. We slowed down for a few metres before resuming the breakneck rush.

Enclosing the roads are avenues of plain trees, the trunks of which are painted white, hopefully to prevent too many car crashes in the inky nights.

Very little of the old Soviet industry survived. We saw the rusting bones of factories, warehouses, and machinery yards, too many to mention and none actually working. The loose animals were there to find a living for their owners before being slaughtered, and as we drove, we saw multitudes of little plots growing maize, vegetables, anything that would find a living for itself. Along the road and most upsetting of all, elderly people stopping the traffic and crying — I have nothing to eat — shouting at us in Georgian.

We took a short diversion to Stalin's birthplace, Gori — the little house and the man with no title or inscription on his statue. The house was of clay bats, braced with diagonal timbers, with the museum built over it. The grass unkempt and the marble paving uneven and unloved. The massive museum behind was closed. Magnificent castle up the hill with very Turkish battlements

Back to the derelict factories. Fertile land and everyone growing maize and cows. At that time, all of Georgia's Soviet-era industries were derelict. The people had had to revert to their peasant roots and subsistence agriculture to get by. They grew maize on any tiny piece of ground flat enough and everywhere cows and pigs scavenged for food and grazing of whatever type they could find.

The visit to Poti port was to see what could be done to improve matters. I was accompanied by Dan, who ran the operation for us. He had two messages for me; where driving is concerned, all you can do is work the probabilities as best you can to your advantage. And living in Georgia as an American, you are at the top of the food chain. Or put it another way, if you must, you get first pick of the girls!

I was travelling with a young accountant from Holland, and we stayed the night in an ex-Soviet holiday camp for young Comrades with babushkas guarding the head of the stairs and your room key. The food? Don't go there.

At some stage in this venture, I had met our Turkish agent on a flight. He wanted me to look at a couple of quays where they were working containers and see whether we could improve matters. I made a deal that I would look at his quays if he would book me a hotel and allow me a day to look round Istanbul. He was good company. I remember well an excellent meal in a fish restaurant in the sunshine beside the Bosporus.

Sultanahmet — The Blue Mosque

Impressions unexpanded sadly:

Lead roofs

Mellow grey stone

Domes

Wondrous geometry

Towering spires of minarets — regular section, not tapered, with lead points and gilt ferrules — spears

Six minarets

Smooth stones of a thousand footfalls under my bare feet

Cyprus and cedar trees

Gilded crescents mounted on gilded balusters

Candelabra of wrought iron ten metres across

Wrought iron ties to take the thrust of the arches

Carpet for each worshipper, with a prayer mat pattern woven into it

Bosporus through the grills in the windows no glass

The stained glass in the galleries

My guide, a sad-faced man with a moustache, been there twenty years and once was young — the foreigners must go, but sit down there and you can pray if you would like to.

Because you are English, I show you the plaque from Queen Victoria — a hundred and sixty windows, forty domes. Six hundred mosques in Istanbul

Sat in the court outside

The small trough with the brass taps and a cube of marble with a wooden top to sit on while you wash your feet before prayer

Shoes off

Fountains carved of white marble with the tree of life, three black stones from the Kaba in Mecca

Lane of flowers between the walls of the mosque and the old city walls with houses built on the walls and flowers — a steep hill with granite cobbles and the man to clean my shoes

The Lebanese charmer with the hotel and the carpet shop and the apple tea: I was looking around for the Blue Mosque when I was approached by a gentleman who, from his dress, was apparently on his way to play tennis. He asked if he could help, as I was obviously looking for something. He told me the Blue Mosque was closed but would be open shortly. He had a café round the corner and if I cared to join him, I could wait there, so off we went. It was a carpet shop and he introduced me to his nephew and ordered tea and to please take a seat. The nephew, on cue, started dragging out carpets. Would I like this one or that one or a larger one or a smaller one. I tried to remain polite, but eventually I had had enough. I picked the most expensive I could see, even I can pick out a large silk carpet, and asked the price. The pocket calculator evinced a sum in excess of two thousand sterling. I thought so, I said, and that is not money I have for carpets. They put the tea things away immediately and I left for the Blue Mosque. I really hate being hustled and it is always on the pretext of helping the stranger. Had the same in Spain once.

The full moon over the Bosporus and the covered bazaar

Must catch a flight... CSX (our parent company) shares are down to thirty-six or something from sixty — it grieves me something rotten to think of our bold leader worrying over his next bottle of champagne and where it is coming from. I think Sea-Land will need to invoke another war to put their fortunes back on track with CSX. They prefer to deal in railway engines than in unstable things like ships. Got to Muscat this morning and must now go to the office and see whether I am needed or not. There comes a time in projects when the permanent team moves in, and one becomes surplus to requirements. Best to leave before that is too painfully apparent, but it is a bit galling to have to share and finally hand over your toys to the new lot. Beirut is on so expect to be there end of Sept. I gather it's quite a place now so should be a good diversion.

4th October '98 — Beirut

Had to think of you — flicking through a Lebanese paper before throwing it away and came across the photo of a tourist in a museum looking at what turned out to be a "skinned human on display at the Beijing Museum of Natural History"... along with a lot of other bits and pieces of people, "brains, spines, ...body..." Well! I'm sure you've not missed this opportunity to broaden your knowledge of human physiology and keep the dinner party conversation alight.

I got here via Beirut, where I had three days of putting up a bid to run their new container terminal. What a crazy place! They live as though the war might start again tomorrow, though the investment in the city and suburbs is huge. The whole place is a building site, with flats and villas going up all over the surrounding hills, and in the city itself, reconstruction of the centre and old part and the hotels that were on the Green Line. Our hotel was one side of the Green Line and the office the other, so we had plenty of opportunity to look over the effects of twenty years of war.

The old Holiday Inn is much as the press corps left it after they were shelled inside it — big holes. One of the high rises had all the windows of the stairs up a blank wall over ten stories or so. The top small window had had a sniper in it, as it appeared. It was like a dart board surround. They must have been pretty lousy shots. The port, as you might expect, is chaotic, but it does work. They could get twice as much through it if they had one organisation, but it's not like that. If you have a ship to work, you find yourself a gang of lads with their mobile crane, strike a deal and set them at it. We have a new definition for "intangibles". They are what end up in numbered Swiss bank accounts, so the intangibles budget was getting on for a million dollars a year and more for twenty years — nice work if you can get it. I think we will tell them to get out their kite and go fly it. Great place to visit!

Much later: on arrival, I met my colleagues, got cleaned up and then asked about dinner. Yes, just round the corner. They took me to the Hard Rock Café, would you believe. It was karaoke night to boot and some of the performers were unbelievable; however, the Brit compere was a good lad and kept the irony going for the rest of us. The glorious old part of Beirut has been rebuilt where, for some of the buildings they are working on, you would think one more round from an AK 47 would bring the whole lot down. There were families living in flats with no walls, just the concrete skeleton, their property piled along the edges of the floors to stop the children falling off. Years after this, I had a presentation from a Bouygue engineer for a project in North Africa; he talked about other work and mentioned Beirut, where they had rebuilt the waterfront breakwater and promenade. During the war, the residents had been unable to leave the city, so they threw all their rubbish in the sea, creating a new waterfront. In constructing the breakwater, the engineer said they found a new geological stratum — used AK47s.

New Beirut container terminal

We got the first cranes ashore in Salalah in the last couple of days — one thousand three hundred tons of machinery, sixty-eight metres high, rolling along a beam between the barge that brought it and the quay. It's not as if no one ever dropped one! The monsoon is over and the weather perfect, though today it is a bit cloudy. Patricia is in UK and should be here in the next couple of weeks or so to spend three weeks with me. We should be back in Europe mid-November hopefully, to look at a project in Gdansk and pursue the Beirut one a bit further. Gdansk you can keep but I would like to get into Beirut.

5th November '98 — Oman

I have no idea whether you got this or not! See below! I am still trying to escape my old PC! It does not want me to leave and the new one is not very helpful. I now get my mailbox to work part of the time and I even have my old message files installed, plus the addresses, but getting through to the heavenly host is a very hit and miss affair. I even got involved with techno forums. That was a mistake. It left me feeling more inadequate than was entirely necessary. Some Japanese was explaining in broken English how he managed to connect through the whatsit gateway in Tokyo. Talk about knitting patterns.

We are both here in Salalah at the moment. Patricia got in a week or so ago and I have been out of Europe for a month, I notice. The stopover in Beirut was fun and the resulting political intrigue incredible. A week after the bid was in a column appeared in the press saying that Dubai Ports had won the contract. The CEO flew to Beirut to sign up, but our lads got to the prime minister or president — Hariri, who owns Saudi Oge — and pointed out that there was a very strong smell of rotten in the state of Lebanon. The port director was told that the PM was not signing anything, and furthermore, the port director is scheduled to become the past, or emeritus port director. We have to wait for the end of November when new elections are held to see whether we still have a chance. I very much hope so.

It turned out that their lawyer had copies of incriminating documents. Being a public-spirited chap, he could make these available to our team for a consideration running into some millions of US dollars.

They are firing people again in Rotterdam and centralising in Cork! A hundred and fifty jobs to go around Europe and Cork will employ two hundred and fifty. No one knows who will end up where. The official story is that the new software demands that everyone is in the same office. Horse manure! If they wanted to, they would tell us that the new software would allow everyone to work from home.

Salalah — the weather is perfect at the moment and will no doubt remain so for the next few months. We had the "soft opening" last week when two very large vessels came into the port, loaded some token boxes and went away again. As usual, the horny-handed engineers were notable by their absence at the tables of the great, however, Brian the Tug and I marshalled the ladies and took them aboard one of the charter tugs (our own have not yet arrived) and took a trip round the bay. Patricia drove! Made it all worthwhile.

The new ones are building in Rotterdam, and I will go to see them when I get back. How much longer in Beijing? I will be pretty much disengaged from this by the end of the year unless things change dramatically. I shall be sorry to leave the country and a couple of friends, but it is getting a bit too political — too many ego trips.

29th November, 1998 — The Casino Hotel

India was a great trip. I had to go to Bombay — now called Mumbai — for a day and stayed in a very good hotel close to the airport and our office. The flight to Cochin in the south is now run by a private airline which measures up to international standards. We are thinking of bidding for the management of the container port there, so I was there to have a look before getting too involved. I was last there in 1988 on a visit, but had very little time to look around and things have improved since then. We used to stay in the Casino Hotel because it was better than the Malabar. One night sitting in the bar, I watched the mice under the table, like rugby players, picking up and making off with the spilt peanuts from underneath the low table we were sat at. Times have changed. We were booked into the Malabar, now run by the Taj group. It is an old colonial building with a new extension and is bounded by water on two sides. The whole of Cochin and environs is islands and back waters which are used by the locals for transport and fishing and the hotel looks out across the access channels to the port.

Much later — that would be Willingdon Island, which used to house the airport. The runway was very, very short and if the pilot overshot, he had two choices: the main road through the town or the airport fuel tanks.

My room in the old part of the hotel was floored with teak boards and all the furniture of the same material. Through the window, you could see the garden, a riot of greenery and bright tropical flowers. Fortunately, we had time for a boat tour, complete with snacks, drinks and a waiter to ourselves. Cochin is known for the "Chinese fishing nets" which are erected in suitable spots along the coastline where the fish congregate. They consist of a wooden gantry constructed from small trees, from which hangs a four-cornered net of thirty feet on a side. The whole contraption is hinged and counterbalanced so that the operator, by shifting his weight, can dip and recover the net at will. As the sun went down, we sat on the roof of our boat out in the centre of the stream, the lines of nets lit from behind by the reflections on the water — and we get paid for doing it.

Holland

I was to be in the UK today, but the weather had disturbed the flying, so my aircraft was already hours late when I went to check in. I came away and all day have watched the squalls of rain, sleet, hail and snow whip their way across the port. I'm glad I was not flying today, however, I have to go to Denmark tomorrow so very much hope the weather is back to something like normal.

Next month, the third, I go back to Oman again and thence to India. I shall be away three weeks and then to South Africa for holiday with Patricia and Andrew. In April, I will be in India again, it seems. I keep expecting the travel routine to come to an end and it may yet, as there are rumours of the company being for sale. We shall have to wait and see, as there is no information until they drop it on you. Fortunately, the Dutch law is very much on the side of the employee.

30th November '98 — Oman

Yesterday, our chief engineer gave his notice in after a couple of months on the job. It is not unusual out here. I don't know whether it is bad selection or bad luck, but it creates great difficulties either way and we now have to do a lot of what the Navy calls "Damage Control". He has a guaranteed job back home so will be all right.

To leave work behind for a bit, I drove north today and investigated tracks and ruins I had seen before but not had opportunity to tarry. I find that if you are out with others, it is difficult to divert the convoy on what might be a wild goose chase, so I leave exploring for very understanding and like-minded companions or for solo trips like today. I spent a good hour or so in a place called Khor Rouri. Khor means an inlet from the sea in Arabic and historically were often the centres of trade and civilisation, so anywhere of that type you tend to find fortifications, graves etc. which in this part of the world are, for the most part, unexplained.

Salalah has a pre-historic city tell which lies just behind the beach I told you of earlier. Tells occur all over the gulf and are the accumulated rubbish and building materials of aeons of civilisation. (By the rubbish they leave around they are still building them today) This one is square, about fifty yards on a side and about forty feet high with exposed masonry of the old walls built from roughly dressed stone.

Khor Rouri below Wadi Dharbat looking out to sea

But back to Khor Rouri, where the khor widens to about a mile of swamp, reeds and open brackish water contained at one end by the sea and on all sides by hills and cliffs about a hundred feet high. The open water has flamingos and other waterfowl, and the beach today had camels and cows. Apart from two other cars, I had it all to myself. At the furthest end close to the sea, there is an isolated hill with cliffs going down to the sea on three sides. The steep approaches to landward some previous owners had converted to fortifications with the addition of a wall along the top, six feet wide and a hundred yards long, built of readily available rocks. What amused me was that, where they had finished the walling at the seaward end, where the cliffs started and walls were not needed, there remained an area the size of a tennis court with spare rocks that some poor workers had had to bring there for the builders. I lifted one of them to see what might be underneath by way of evidence of the age of the wall and found only a desiccated leaf. Whether it was a hundred years old or ten, I have no idea. My father, when he was a don at Cambridge, had something to do with the re-building of one of the sixteenth century courts and was presented with a mummified rat they had found in the walls, preserved by the lime in the mortar. Despite a rather desultory search for stone implements, lithics as I learnt I should call them the other day, no such evidence of antiquity was forthcoming at Rouri.

12th December '98 — Finland

It is a long time since I have done this and partly it is the fault of my old PC and its battery; partly my own fault for not doing it. However, here with a letter, albeit by email, but my Montblanc seven thousand dollar diamond-encrusted pen has run out of fuel. Our finance director in Oman uses the cheaper solid gold variety — he remarked that his salary was somewhat less than the revenue from the family property in Bombay or Delhi, so I guess the pen was the result of rental rather than earned income! Today they are having the official opening in Salalah with the great and the good in attendance. I had begun to get the impression that my presence in Oman was becoming inconvenient, so arranged to be away when the opening happened.

I will be back in January to finish off some details but that should be about that. I am on my way to Finland at the moment, to a place called Hamina, very close to the Russian border. We have a brief to manage the container operations there, as the local stevedoring company are more Russian than Finish in their attitudes, it seems. Apart from that, there is hope that we can get the Beirut management contract and we have a bid to put in for Gdansk, and I hope, Cochin. I would love to get the Beirut and Cochin jobs, but Gdansk and Hamina require antifreeze in the veins — I don't have any.

I packed for this trip, trying to remember what was a "good idea" for these latitudes. I think I have what is needed, but the shorts, cotton slacks, short-armed shirts (as William used to have it) are stowed for the time being. Once I get all my clothes in one place, I will have to sort what is really necessary. The knickers population is getting out of hand, engendered by a middle-class nervousness that there may not be sufficient at the other end — but I already left some there…

I suppose I had the best part of two years in Oman, which compares with the two years I had in Cape Town, but CT seems like a lifetime while Oman was just a few trips. Strange! Patricia was out three times this year, which made a lot of difference, and she greatly enjoyed most of it. The last trip, it was all getting a bit too political and the atmosphere among the expatriates strained, to say the least. I think now that they are underway, it should be a lot better.

We had an unofficial opening on the 1st of November, which was really enjoyable for everyone. The VIPs did their kowtowing and we got on with taking photographs of the ships and the tugs, and when all the programmed stuff was over, took all the wives on one of the tugs for a trip round the bay. We have a picture of Patricia driving! A week ago, we were sitting on the beach at the Al Bustan Palace Hotel with a view over the ocean from under the coconut palms. Now the temperature is down to below freezing, and the Dutch will be talking about running the Elfstedentoch, the two hundred kilometre skating race they manage to hold every six or seven years when the canals freeze deeply enough to bear the weight of two thousand competitors and the spectators.

Finland — the port of Hamina.

"Is there no night life in Hamina?"

"Yes! But tonight, she's in Kotka." Hamina is ten thousand souls and was founded by a Swedish count in 1600 and something. The centre of the town is still laid out in an expanding series of octagonal roads within the old city walls and the buildings are timber, dating back to the foundation — and that is about it. The port is well away from the town and is everything for the town. The Port Party is the consensus party covering all the political spectrum, and the council has thirty-five members, thirty-four of which are known to be members of the port party and one is suspected to be — so says the port director. The latter is an old Finnish sea captain, and you could imagine him driving his sailing ship loaded with timber to windward in a force ten gale across the North Sea. His English is probably better after a few beers. Last night, he entertained me and the chairwoman of the town council to dinner in one of the three presentable restaurants and told tales of runs ashore around the world. In Iskenderun, they were all arrested and carted off in an iron tumbrel drawn by two horses. They had mistaken a wedding for pub and in Jeddah their skipper had been thrown in gaol for winking at the Arab women. We are talking fifties and sixties now. Today he and the consultant working on the port development are off to see the management consultant employed by the town to look at the council employees. Good luck to the management consultant!

Much later — as we were touring the port, we fell to talking about facilities for the road truckers and how much space to set aside. I was confused by the size of park the managing director thought appropriate. Maybe you don't understand, he said. The truckers come here from Russia to wait for orders and meantime they maintain their trucks (which need a lot of maintenance). This can mean taking the head off or the gear box apart. In winter, they will still work in minus temperatures by working until they cannot feel their hands, when they will put them in a can of hot diesel to warm them up again. He said that the German invasion failed largely because they were unable to maintain their equipment, unlike the Russians.

I will shortly leave for Holland and a weekend in the flat before going to Spain for two days. The Spanish trip is to see the architect we will use for the recreation centre in Salalah. I am instructed that we will be touring Moorish architectural sites to talk aesthetics etc. I am deeply grateful for having been exposed to the architects of Queens College so that I am not completely out of my depth when it comes to architectural speak. Wasn't Corbusier Spanish? This individual designed Sun City in Bophutswana, or is it Botswana? I am hoping for something a little more restrained!

The opening went off in Salalah in my absence. Our head man made the trip all the way to Oman from the US but forbore to spend fifteen minutes to see his employees. Apparently, the Sultan failed to show up too, which is a bit strange — probably had to see to some affairs of state.

Must get to fighting with Autocad again. This is incredible drawing software that allows one to produce drawings on a PC instead of a board and it does everything — if only you know how to tell it what to do.

22nd January '99 — Wimps

Eid feast and a few days off to wander around Dhofar. My colleagues are not often allowed out to play — wimps — so two days I had to go by myself. I did manage to drag them out for a foray into the mountains, but I missed the Riyadh spirit of adventure in some of the crew — mainly the wives, who wanted to be by the pool polishing their nails or something. Fabulous views up and down the coast from a height of some one thousand metres dropping away below you to the desert and the sea.

Today I went for a swim at a beach you reach via a track and a steep walk. It is ringed by cliffs, which come down to the sea at each end so it is completely isolated and is overlooked by Ras Hamar, or donkey's head. The next challenge was to get my leased Landcruiser within range of the top of said head. As you know rentals can reach the parts other cars can't, so up we went. The edge when I got there was so precipitous that I couldn't enjoy the view for very long — too nervous.

Fine sight of falcons from above, a turtle which must have been six feet across the flippers and two dolphins fishing for their lunch. I have just about done all the things I would like to do down here, in case I don't get back again. Absolutely wonderful scenery, but wish you were here to come along too.

Had dinner with Donaldson in Dubai and on the way to the café, we phoned Catriona and she showed up later with Charles. Not really fair on Charles, as we talked of another life, I guess. He is a decent stick — he's a banker, after all — and must wonder at his good fortune to end up with the devastating Catriona. She has cut her hair short and looks a million dollars. The kicker is that Jessica is 5'11" and fourteen years going on twenty-five; C is battling to keep the parental reins on the lass. I asked what she was going to do after school or something and Catriona replied with the caveat "…if she lives that long." The inference being that her mother might throttle her first.

Much later — Jessica to Catriona, "You don't know jack shit"
Catriona to Jessica, "No. Who is Jack Shit?"

We had a great evening. Peter is as full of beans as ever, captain of Abu Dhabi golf club, fit as a fiddle and waiting for Heather to finish her university course and hopefully join him in Dubai (he is going to move from Abu Dhabi). I was supposed to be in Dar es Salaam next week, but the US got weak-kneed over a project in Africa. You can just hear it in Charlotte: "…isn't that close to Somalia?" We were going to apply for pre-qualification for managing the container terminal there. As it turned out, I was very disappointed not to make the trip, but it meant I got the chance to spend some time here over Eid. I shall still be going to Bombay and Cochin — as I write this, anyway — which will be interesting. I was last in Cochin ten years ago or more, but I doubt it has changed much. The mice will still be catching the peanuts as they drop off the tables in the lounge bar.

31st January '99 — Anti-gravity

I am on my way to Muscat from Salalah and will continue to Mumbai at 0100 tomorrow morning. I am booked for dinner with our chief financial officer and his wife; always a pleasure, as they are good company and the cook they brought from India, while living up to cooks' reputation for Woodhouse-type moods, has a rare touch with the curry. He is a very slight little chap and Nandita asked him to walk their too-boisterous Labrador puppies. This had to be stopped, as he retired to bed for two days, exhausted, and the kitchen suffered, so now Nandita does her own dog walking. They have a beautiful two-year-old daughter with honey coloured hair and eyes to match. Both parents have jet black hair and dark brown eyes. I suggested that, since they are from Kashmir, Alexander's troops may have been instrumental in her make up.

I have been having a wonderful time in Salalah. The weather has been perfect; we had two days of holidays and I've had a Toyota Landcruiser hire car. I have always resented Toyota's shameless plagiarism of Land Rover, but had to put that aside and enjoy the ride. It has been relatively easy to inveigle others into my ventures, but I did have to do a couple of solo trips as the ladies took exception to the road conditions. The first joint trip was instigated by a conversation about the anti-gravity field which occurs (sic) to the north of Salalah. We were sat round a table in one of our Dutch family's houses when our Omani accountant said they had been to the antigravity place and how amazed and impressed they all were by this freak of nature. You can imagine my jumping into that one, and when one of the Brits attested that he also was convinced, the challenge was issued to prove it. The following holiday we set off in two cars for the place with eight witnesses, and after establishing to the satisfaction of the analytically minded that it was all an optical illusion (Kotaiba was very disappointed because what he remembered happening failed to recur. I gave him Father's advice: "Never repeat a successful experiment") continued on up the dirt road into the hills.

Some of the heavier ladies felt that sports underwear was necessary for restraint; in fact, Jenny thinks she might be able to market a line of "Off Road Lingerie" to be sold along with the vehicle. Perhaps you include the vehicle name like the Porsche merchandising… Eventually, we got to the top and found a track going north into the higher ground, which we followed until we arrived at a large house, almost completed construction, apparently well-sited for the view. How well-sited we discovered on pulling up and getting out to investigate. The garden had been walled and by hanging on, you could get round the end and walk along the outside until the wall finished to let the residents see out.

The garden finished in a slab of rock the size of a squash court above a steep drop, followed by the land falling away a thousand feet to the desert and the beaches below. The view was from Marbat to Raysut, a distance of maybe a hundred kilometres, with Khor Rouri centre stage the mouth of the Wadi Darbat where it exits to the sea, with two outcrops of the hills guarding either side. I sat, legs dangling over the edge, and soaked it up. I have not my camera with me this trip but it's perhaps as well; it's so difficult to get shots of those vistas that mean anything.

We continued on to the top and Brian and Tina in my car said they thought this was where the sink hole was, so we turned off and found it very shortly along a track leading to a farm of sorts. It is a little difficult to get too excited about, but it is the largest sink hole ever discovered in… well, Dhofar anyway. It's main claim to fame must be that Ranulph Fiennes went down it on the end of a mobile crane hook, looking for the lost city of Ubar. Why he went down it is beyond me, as people don't often build cities where the only access is via Coles Crane. After all, there were not so many Coles Cranes around when they were moving frankincense up to the Roman Empire.

Tearing ourselves away — a stone took six seconds to hit bottom so it could be five hundred feet deep — we picked up the dirt road across the tops to Madinat al Huq, a well-known centre of not very much in these parts. The road winds among farms, well huts with bomas of dry stone walls (do I mean bomas? That is an African word) and drops into wadis where they have concreted the steeper grades against the monsoon rains. Where the farms had thinned out, we found a patch of savannah leading to the head of a wadi, so I pulled over to stop and look. Everybody piled out, except the two ladies in the other car, who were beginning to wear thin and sat smoking, hoping to leave soon. An Omani drove down in his truck to throw spare corrugated iron over the cliff and then came over to offer us — the men — milk, tea, meat, anything… This would mean leaving the ladies, who don't count, and wandering off to a kraal with the inevitable slaughter of a goat. We could have been there all night while the stones got hot enough to cook on. Kotaiba declined on our behalf, and we got the impression that, duty done, he was quite happy not to have to carry out the threat.

We hit the tarmac again and it was quite clear that if we decided to cross it and take the dirt again, we would not be popular. The following day — holiday again — I couldn't get any one to join me; obviously gated.

I took myself off to look at the bay below Ras Hamar or Donkey's Head. It is only fifteen minutes' drive across tracks from the port. The hills come down to the sea and end in cliffs, one of which, Ras Hamar, stands above the rest and is sheer to the water below. It's a landmark from almost anywhere around Salalah. The beach at its base is very difficult to access except by foot, since the road was washed out in the last rains, so I walked down and put my bits and pieces on a rock with the intention of swimming. The surf was quite lively and the absence of anybody at all and the presence of a dolphin or two left me wondering whether getting out of my depth was such a good idea. I walked along the beach, enjoying the view, and then set off back again, all the time debating with myself as whether it would be foolish to go in or not. I noticed that the foolish side was getting the better of the argument, so gave up and took the plunge, watching carefully to see whether the cross bearings were changing too much in the wrong direction. I had a wonderful swim and survived to listen to the stories of people lost on that beach through the tricky currents etc. etc. later the next day. Nobody, we agreed, ever relates whether the victims could swim in the first place.

Thoroughly refreshed and encouraged, I decided to see whether I could get the truck within range of the tops of Ras Hamar. Being a rental, it has, of course, greater climbing power than ordinary four-wheel drives and after some low ratio stuff, I found the right line and got to within a hundred feet or so of the top. The view was breath taking, and definitely heeby and jeeby by turns. You wonder if it's time for the next earth tremor — they had one forty years ago, so it could easily be. I was walking along one cliff and noticed a fissure, followed by another, followed by a line… of fissures… the San Andreas fault, and me on the sea side of it. I hopped quickly to the landward part.

All along the nether edge grow plants with grey stumpy stems, some nearly a foot across and as high, with no leaves but the loveliest pink flowers on the ends of their swollen fingers. They must live on the dew. Below me, I could see two dolphins catching their lunch and a turtle come up for air and a sight of the beach where they lay their eggs in the season.

The day before yesterday, I went back with Rob to the same place, but in view of marital obligations, he suggested maybe 0600 in the morning. I got up wondering if he would remember and he did, so we set out in the dark to get there before sunrise. I had thought about whether I could find my way and we did, after a couple of false trails. Rob had not been there before, so he was suitably impressed. We watched the sun rise and then I suggested we go up to the head, so we did. We sat above the sea and watched the sun light up the mountains and the desert until it was no longer possible to ignore the fact that we were supposed to be at work.

Another day, I took our architect and his wife, newly arrived from retirement in Spain, south to about twenty miles from the Yemen border to a place I found overlooking the deserted beaches between Rakyut and Dhalkyut, two little fishing villages at the end of wadis draining into the sea. The cliffs are at least a thousand feet high, but I think I've told you about them before. Previously I have been ill-equipped, but that day we had a chicken, bread, beers, salad etc. and a mat and chairs. We sat for a couple of hours, had our lunch and watched the ravens playing in the up draft. They remind me of lads in the street, cruising on their motorbikes, looking to left and right to see who is watching their swoops and dives, shouting to each other across the air stream with sly remarks about the talent. One time, two of them swept across the face of the cliff, escorting a hawk off the patch, and came back together, congratulating each other on their bravado. Did I tell you about the black eagle? I last saw them on the Taif escarpment above Jeddah, noticeable for their white flash above the tail. This one was circling, a black dot, above the waves and I watched him climb on the air currents to a tree halfway up the cliff. He perched there for so long I was about to give up watching through the glasses when he took off back towards the sea carrying a lizard. He dropped it, or it wriggled free,, and folding his wings, he dived down, caught it and climbed back to his original altitude. This happened twice until he lost it completely and sloped off, disgruntled, to look for another less obstreperous prey.

This morning, I was on the road again with our bankers who wanted to see the sink hole and the plan was an early start again. The result is that I am thoroughly tired and just wish I could climb into bed rather than climb into an aeroplane. I very nearly didn't, as my seat was cancelled through the re-confirmation procedure the airlines have out here; however, there was a seat.

India

Bombay — and what a change from the open vastness of the desert — people and more. The poverty is still as bad as ever, but I was spared the run into Bombay South, as they had booked me in the oddly-named

Kempinski hotel. This is right beside the international terminal, and last time I stayed there was a bit of a dump, so was not expecting too much at 0500 in the morning. Luxury! I was on the Privilege Floor, where there are flunkies available day and night and solicitous ladies in saris to check you in, book a car, confirm reservations and generally look decorative.

I got three hours sleep and then went to the office, which has moved north from its old location in a rundown merchants' house beside the railway to the environs of a soap factory. Not as bad as it sounds; the soap people are the rich of the rich, and own a huge plot of real estate almost in the country. The gates give on to gardens and warehouses converted to offices and large tracts of grassland. I found my host and toured the old friends from the Gulf who have all been shipped back to Bombay — not very willingly.

We lunched back at the hotel, and I slept until four when I took a walk in the garden and then to the bar for a drink before dinner. No shortage of curry. I had meant to get to bed early, but the email intervened so it was not until eleven for an early start to fly to Cochin.

Cochin — I was here in 1988, I think. We are billeted in the Taj Malabar hotel; it used to be a dump, but the Taj group took it over and it is delightfully colonial — my room is teak floored, doored, wardrobed and bedded — clean and well-served, with public rooms similarly attired with teak and a lovely view over the harbour.

We used to stay in the Casino, as it was superior, which was why I was able to observe the mice making off, like rugby players, with the spilt peanuts under the bar room table. The Malabar is situated on a corner site, corner to the water that is so you have views across the waterways on both sides. The whole area is islands and backwaters, very low lying, with multitudes of coconut palms fringing and backdropping everything. However, if we get the contract, we'll build a container terminal and fix all that soppy stuff.

The evening before last, we took a boat, and on the excuse of researching the access to the berths etc., chugged round the islands, attended by our waiter with a supply of Kingfisher beer and other refreshments. The Chinese fishing nets are the local tourist speciality. Towards the end of the trip, we left the backwaters and went closer to the sea, just at the point where the backwaters widen into open ocean. This is obviously a very productive site, as the nets are lined up ten abreast. So far, as my hosts were able to tell me, Chinese fishing nets only exist in Cochin, so I am hoping you will seek out their ancestors in China. As I was saying — a black kite flies by — this is Cochin, and I am sitting in the lounge of the hotel with the water on two sides. The one has old Cochin, where the go-downs and staithes crowd the water's edge, yellowing walls roofed with handmade clay tiles and slips for the coastal craft with artisan's houses surrounding them; above the roofs, coconut palms. I can see one of the go-downs now, a wooden staithe in front, yellow painted walls with doors for cargo on the ground floor and above, the windows of offices or perhaps where the owner lived, with a balcony where he could walk out and survey the vessels working. Above all, the mottled tile roof, brown and terracotta. The traders have painted their names on their buildings, names like Hookken Dewassy Ouseph & Sons.

Cochin Synagogue

The area is very Catholic, but there is also a synagogue looked after by the one remaining resident of that persuasion. The boats are mostly called by saint's names, and the taxis have supplications in the back window to whomever the driver thought most likely to save him from his own earthly aberrations. The foreground is the hotel garden, with a riot of tropical plants and trees and between the water, where earlier three rice boats had diverted me at my breakfast. They came close in to avoid the tidal stream, propelled by a small sprit rigged sail, two men with oars and two more poling with bamboo stems, walking up, dropping them in and walking back with their shoulders to the top end. They were making for the other bank and cut diagonally across, the steersman sometimes helping by paddling with his steer board. The rice boats can be as much as fifty feet long, the planks sewn together with coir; they used to be used to bring the rice down from the hinterland with a barrel shaped cover of rattan, bamboo and plaited palm fronds for a thatch. The hotel has one as a restaurant, cut in half; you sit round with your back against the gunwale with the table in the middle.

While I ate breakfast, the crows kept up a continuous cacophony of caws, squabbling with each other while maintaining a beady eye on any chance of a bite. The cheekiest of the lot hopped down from his branch, bounced onto the table and made off with two envelopes of sugar in his beak.

The other waterway gives access to the new container berths and a ship is making her way there just now — she is Japanese, on the Far East run. The other side, the port want to build the new container terminal in a few years' time, which is why I am here. I guess it will spoil the view. The Environmental Impact Assessment says nothing about the view from the old Malabar Hotel. The new port offices are such an eye-sore that perhaps it doesn't matter anyway. The old ones are lovely, wide eaves over verandas, one room deep with the French windows open both sides to let the sea breeze right through. The omnipresent collections of files of cheap paper tied together in dusty bundles is so typically Indian. I looked at some in one of the offices, expecting them to be thirty years old, and they were only from '94 or so.

We went to see Mr Koshy in the old port office, a garrulous civil servant and civil engineer, to talk about their project. The accents are pretty thick on the Malabar coast, so I only caught three words in four and when they are fired at you… How he got the job, I have no idea. We also saw the port director in his office, quite a different case. His last position was with the police, fighting dacoits on the borders somewhere, so dealing with the Malabar unions was chicken feed to him and he has done a lot of good for the port. The new office was not his idea. The port directors are political appointees, so can know next to nothing about ports — cf. Tuticorin, which is another story.

I have sketch of a go-down on the back of the hotel booking in card. It shows a building with a pitched roof above a subsidiary pitch showing inset gables at the level of the collars — such a simple and pretty design.

Last night, after seeing the port and all (as they say here), we returned to the hotel at four o'clock to join our vessel for a port tour. We boarded at the hotel staithe along with our waiter and sufficient refreshment to keep us going through the arduous task of surveying the waterways and the new site. I don't think I can do justice to the evening. The coconut palms fringe every view, from the wharves, to the open marshes, to the houses set among the plantations, to the fishing fleet, moored for the night alongside the villages where they sell their catch. We left the hotel, chugging gently up the channel to the old port, built on land reclaimed by Sir Somebody (Willingdon), to port the ferry berths for the vessel that plies to the Lacadives, and to starboard, the old town. A few dugout canoes fished with nets and the ferries carrying people to and from work passed us from time to time.

My companions, Ravi, Kumar and Aspi, told me what they knew of the history of the place and also tales of bygone Sea-land nutcases who worked in the Middle East and India. We came back past the hotel and set off for the opposite bank to circle Vallarpadam, where the new berths are to be. The whole coast is a labyrinth of waterways used by everyone as a transport route for goods, chattels and people, as well as being a source of fish, not only to humans but also to the dolphins that we saw just briefly from time to time. The fishing fleet were in or coming in and from time to time we were passed by a boat laden with sardines and some smaller fish. They were selling their catch in the villages along the bank, where the cafes and shops, garish with home painted advertisements, lined the water's edge.

The opposite bank was part of the island where the new terminal will be. At that point, there will be no development, but the farms and plantations will persist, for some time at least. The whole island is ringed with a dry stone sea wall, well-built but not maintained and breached in places, which serves to control the water in the inland lakes with sluices placed in the wall. There must have been reason for the effort, as it does not occur elsewhere, and might have had to do with fish ponds or just flooding.

Cochin market

If we get the contract, we can find out and perhaps put it right. The work that has gone into this country over the years is incredible when you consider how much of it was done with bullocks and bare hands.

Talking of which, I was asking about sacred cows — with some diffidence, as I was not sure of my interlocutor's (?) sensibilities — and I gather the government has tried to outlaw the slaughter of cattle for meat. Apparently only the cow is sacred, and you can do what you like with the male of the species. Beast me! Actually, that was supposed to be beats me, but the other will do as well.

Bullock power still trundles through the streets and occasionally you will find a couple of pure white ones dressed for a carnival or something, waiting patiently by the road for the fun to start with their float ready behind them. Passing the Catholic church that the fishermen regard as particularly faithful in bringing them home safely, we continued to follow round the island into more deserted areas. The bird life is wonderful, and I had my binoculars with me. I have a book of Indian birds in Holland which I will pore over when I get back; I bought it and never had a chance to go bird watching here before.

The Chinese fishing nets

My hosts debated whether we had time to see the sunset and decided this was possible, so we rounded the island and headed out to sea. The boats are built with high topsides and even higher prows, so when you get into a chop, they roll like pigs, and so we did in the slight swell running in from the Indian Ocean.

Cochin is famous for its Chinese fishing nets, and all during our trip we passed these gantries, projecting out from the bank into the stream in favoured places. Closer to the sea, just at the point where the backwater widens into open ocean, is obviously a very productive site, as the nets are lined up ten abreast. They consist of four curved poles about fifteen feet long arranged in a horizontal cruciform, suspended from a wooden gantry some thirty feet high. This operates on a hinged horizontal axle just above the water, running in slots in the top of two piles driven into the seabed. In the stowed position, the net hangs above the water, four cornered with the centre pulled up by a pulley system. To catch fish, the operator walks out along a bridge of single poles anything up to fifty feet long (good balance is required) to the inner end of the gantry, which carries counter-balance weights on which he stands. He then releases the lashing and walks further out along the gantry's lower arm, allowing the hinge to operate and the upper arm to descend, dropping the net into the water. When he thinks it's full, he walks back along the now sloping lower arm until his weight brings the whole lot back to the rest position. I guess he then hauls in on the centre pulley and the fish get rolled to the outside of the net, where he can rake them towards him.

As the net descends, the lever arm of the counterbalance weights decreases and the mechanical advantage of the pay load increases. To overcome this disparity, they have a knotted rope threaded through additional counterweights which are picked up progressively with the advancing deployment — clever!

As we motored out, the sun was dropping behind a dozen of these gangling structures over a burnished bronze sea — no camera.

Others were taking the air and the sunset in their boats too, among them Sir Clive somebody. I wonder if he was related to the original knight that built the place. I met at breakfast one of a pair of American ladies who later introduced me to her companion. The latter had lived in Riyadh for five years while we were there, while her husband (now deceased) project managed the new airport — pleasant people whose friends could not comprehend why they would holiday in India when they could be in Hawaii

The new container berths from the south

playing golf. They had been in Kenya and Tanzania last year and found Africa much harder going.

Back now in Bombay — what a city, filthy, decrepit, crowded, bustling, polluted and still better than New York. I am leaving for London tonight. To say I cannot wait to be out would be an untruth, but it will be good to sleep in my own bed for once, quite apart from being with my family again. I just realised the other day that it is now February and I've not seen my office yet this year.

This morning, I was driven into town — I am staying out by the airport — for a meeting with our co-conspirators, P&O. Their offices are in the old port building, and unlike us latecomers, are thoroughly established and clubby, with etchings of steamers and earlier on the walls. We only go back to the first containers — not a lot of romance there. Cochin is delightfully Conrad in everything, even some of the vessels still working would not unduly surprise him with their modernity.

So, London tomorrow, the Hague on Wednesday for a meeting with the Finns, and then a week before going to Denmark for a day. It looks as though I shall have to be back hereabouts in March for a week, and then we go to South Africa for a holiday; after that, who knows.

5th February '99 — Cochin

Sitting in the first-class waiting room in Bombay, waiting for the flight to London — and waiting. The systems were down for an hour, so we, that's a good three hundred people, stood and waited and got hotter — but what's new!

I got back from a quite delightful trip to Cochin yesterday and had a meeting in Bombay city this a.m. I have been staying in the Leela hotel right by the airport; only three hundred and fifteen US a night, except we get a special deal at two hundred and sixty — cheap at twice the price.

Cochin is worth a visit, as is the rest of India, but I cannot think that P. would enjoy the filth and the squalor, so I shall not be bringing her along next trip. Driving to the hotel from the airport is enough to make you feel ill with just the anticipation of what it would be like if you were. One of our lot was taken ill with the kidney stones in Cochin — put the frighteners on him — and was admitted to the Cochin Port Trust clinic, I think it was.

They dosed him and shipped him out, but only on the condition that he had no truck with the witch doctors in Dubai. The Cochin quack thought they were not to be trusted!

I got here via a few weeks in Oman, mostly in Salalah. Conveniently, I was there for Eid Al Fitah (Al Fita, Al Fitter, Alf Eater, who knows?) so got an afternoon or two and a day to wander round the lesser-known parts of Dhofar.

The 4WD I had hired learnt some new tricks in the process, I think. As a result of a late-night debate on the antigravity spot which is said to occur a few miles from Salalah, we set off one day to find it and prove one way or the other whether there was a quirk in the firmament just for Dhofar. The Indian population love it and make a big thing of taking visitors out to see cars run uphill. We did all that was required of us and concluded that, as optical illusions go, it wasn't even a very good one. Apparently, they have them in Scotland and are known as Electric Braes. From there, we visited the greatest sink hole in all the... well, Dhofar, anyway, and then took the dirt road across the tops. I see I said something of this jaunt in my last missive.

I have been having trouble getting into my email, and after a phone call to Dubai, find the only way from abroad is to dial a number in Dubai and change all the settings in my software/protocols. Now, you might think that that displays superior knowledge of PCs. It doesn't — I followed instructions like a cake mix packet and when I pressed the button, it worked. Amazing!

The port is beginning to look pretty industrious, with six cranes and twelve stack cranes rising above the desert, we just don't have much by way of cargo at the moment. This should change by April, when the lines reorganise their schedules. We got cheated out of the Beirut job, and so I will be in Aarhus, Gdansk, Finland, and Southampton when I get back. I guess I will be back here again in a month to make progress on the Cochin job and to check out the drawings for the new recreation centre. I've seen the sketches and they look good.

I forgot to mention that I met the widow of the Bechtel project manager for the new airport in Riyadh on holiday in Cochin. Did you know them? He left Riyadh to get on with his life of leisure and "dropped dead at fifty," to quote the lady. She and her companion take a major trip every year to the surprise of their friends, who wonder why they knock around the third world when they could be playing golf in Hawaii.

This place is beginning to look like a refugee camp — comatose bodies spread around in chairs, leaning on tables etc. Thank goodness for frequent flier programmes. Hope all goes well with you lot. Over… somewhere and keep expecting to get there, forgetting I've come from India not Muscat.

21st February '99 — GM Foods

I hope you have been following the GM foods issue from your Chinese ivory tower. The papers and news programmes here have been full of it, allowing some nice headlines of the "Killer Cornflakes" and "Prime-monster" variety. The latter referring to Tony Blair's support for the industry. Apparently, it all really got started when some unfortunate scientist fed his rats on an exclusive diet of GM potatoes and stunted their growth as a result. He got fired for his efforts — it was said — and then it seemed he was still employed. Monsanto scored an own goal by ignoring safety rules in an experimental plot designed to prevent cross pollination and got fined seventeen thousand quid. Someone suggested that that was cheap at twice the price for an American company to conduct an unstructured test of escape into the environment possibilities in a foreign country. I have not yet seen an informed dissertation on all the bits and pieces of the argument. If you find one, I would be grateful for a faxed copy! Apparently, the only GM foods on British shelves is a variety of tomato puree, plus maybe some other things that no one has noticed… um… and…

Off to Southampton tomorrow — Suckling Airways, I guess the pilot wears a leather hat and goggles — thence to Aarhus. Not sure why the latter, but will find out on arrival.

7th March '99 — Moodies

Typed this once but there's a key somewhere — or more than one — which, when hit, deletes everything without so much as a by-your-leave. Bill Gates has put all these are-you-sure windows in the software and did-you-know-what-you've-just-done windows; I would have thought he could have eliminated that particular glitch. I have found one of the keys — Esc — which one generally uses to cancel the last command, not the last five hundred. There's another somewhere — lurking for the next slip of the finger.

Yes! We will be there for the Navy Lark. Give us a call on the mobile phone telling us which pub you're moored to. Did you see a climber was rescued the other day off a vertiginous mountain face. Hanging on by his fingertips and one eyebrow, he was able to press the recall button of his mobile phone with his nose and ask the last person he spoke to for assistance. One wonders who it was — his just-dumped girlfriend, his manager who thought he was off sick, endless possibilities. But anyhow, so long as you are sailing in conditions of sea-slight, we will be there. Sea-state moderate, choppy, severe or gruesome and we will listen to your stories afterwards. Sorry to be so wet, as it were, but I thought I had it cracked in Dubai and then the evil green monster — not the envious variety — took hold one time we were supposed to be racing. End of race and of yachting for a few weeks until I got my breath back.

I was sitting on the veranda of the club in Dubai last Thursday for a few beers and lunch, weather perfect and nothing too desperate to get done. I was interested to see your thoughts on GM foods etc. I found an interview with the potato chap, but he didn't allude to any toxins, though my sister pointed out that un-cooked potatoes are mildly toxic of themselves. Apparently, the genetic mod increases their toxicity in some way. I was listening to the Today programme on Radio 4 some time back, and as they do, they had a piece of quasi-scientific news which went to the tune of "Liverpool scientists have discovered that, where sex is concerned, big is beautiful the sssssssssxxxxxxxxxxggggggg..." I had just gone into the Benelux Tunnel. I was particularly upset, because my nephew had just published his thesis from Liverpool University on the attractive attributes of having larger pincers than the other chap if you happen to be an earwig. It seems they were talking of this, or a close parallel — nephew regrets his life's work so far should be reduced to a cheap shot at scientists by the Today Programme.

So Dubai — after lunch, I was dropped off at Charles and Catriona's sumptuous villa in Jumeira to spend the rest of the afternoon drinking tea in the garden overlooking the pool — with paddling area — and mini one hole golf course for sharpening up your tee shots (or green shots or whatever). Charles' predecessor nearly lost his job over his wife's extravagance with the bank's money spent on properly landscaping her abode. A lot of oak panelling and bells in every room to summon the staff — including a foot-operated one under the dining room table. Now there's style! Where are you in this race to keep up?

Now in Salalah, and will be here for another few days before going back to Muscat and thence to Bombay and Cochin again. Once back from there, I have three days in Holland before going to Cape Town for hollies. After that, I fear the gravy train grinds into the station, though another trip to Bombay threatens. Will have to get one of these bids soon or they will stop allowing me to wander and demand that I sit behind the desk and do some real work.

The company is not as much for sale as it was it seems. The CEO wrote, saying we were all bad lads for listening to rumour, and then went on to confirm that fifty percent of them were correct. It is a fair guess they will sell off the terminals if they can get a good price, just to jack up the flagging share price. It used to be sixty-three $ and is now just breaking forty, but the Dow has put on a lot of weight in the interim, so applying the correction makes forty look more like thirty. Beijing should be almost bearable just now — hope so.

17th March '99 — Mumbai

This is Bumbay — no wrong — Mumbai. The error was, I have to say, a genuine one. Madras is now Chennai and VT, else Victoria Terminus, the central railway station, has a new name even the Indians can't remember.

Just spent a pleasant evening in the Indian restaurant in the hotel with entertainment provided by the new Ravi Shankas and a dancer. The music was actually played on a type of Indian squeeze-box, not a sitar and the dance was to tinkling bells without the sounding cymbal, plus a drummer who tuned his drum with a little silver hammer banging the wedges down to tighten the raw hide, stretching the skin of the drum. The dancer was a smiling lady of considerable panache, dressed in full Indian rig with tassels and bells on her ankles, bare feet and a sort of modified sari. Alan, my companion, when I asked him what he thought the first dance meant, suggested it was to do with waiting for her nails to dry. As you probably know, there's a lot of gesturing with hands and fingers fully extended. Nice one, Alan — ten marks. She went on to another dance which started with lots of eye movement and neck exercises. I don't transmit much idea of grace, but she was very graceful and attractive to watch, particularly if you knew what was going on. She passed our table as she left for her break, so I asked her and she stopped and explained very animatedly what the dances were. The first was a tribute to Lord Krishna and involved some bowing and supplication. The second was "merely foot work". I asked about the eye bit, and she said "Oh! That is only to get the attention of the audience." Well, it did, too, because they were just slightly licentious! She came back for another dance later and stopped unasked to tell me about that one too, which was rather charming. Apparently, Lord Krishna's girl asks her friends to go and find him and the gestures describe what he looks like, but the friends tease her by purposely misunderstanding. The food was excellent too.

Later — it is Saturday the 20th, and I would be very happy if I was home, but that is not for a bit yet. Tomorrow, another day off and Monday, our office here, followed by Tuesday in Dubai. Wednesday in the office in Rotterdam and Saturday to Cape Town, where Patricia is already installed with friends. I expect to be back in Oman at the end of April and over here by the 26th for a meeting in Cochin. Fortunately, while the company makes no monetary concession for all this, the Dutch government does, and I get effectively twice as much salary for a day spent out of Holland. Even working at home in England is in the same category, so long as I don't spend too much time there — crazy. I am a non-resident taxpayer! This involves our secretary in a huge amount of work producing photocopies of all my air tickets and expense forms, which has the pleasant corollary of P and I taking her and her husband for a slap-up meal where we toast the generosity of the Dutch Inland Revenue. The other aspect is that when planning a trip, one has to give serious thought to its longevity.

The lounge has really livened up — six people now. The almost life-size statue of a four-armed god is still playing the flute with two of its arms. Sexy beasts, the Indians. It must make religion a lot more fun — pulls the crowds, I guess. Most corners of the hotel have bronze figurines that would shock the living daylights out of the bible belt. However, I've not heard anyone complaining at the front desk. The hotel is certainly well done. The decor is heavily Indian, but a pleasant mixture of temple architecture and colonial club. The staff are as engaging as Indians almost always are, and there's a retired Ghurkha to press the lift button for you in case the effort might be too much for the honoured guest. There is, however, a price to pay of around two hundred pounds a night — fortunately, I don't have to do that. I doubt I could run my own business and have to think of that sort of money coming out of my pocket. One advantage of working for an American company is that you get to stay in the best hotels while abroad, as they regard it as some insurance against an attack of the Delhi Belly, Montezuma's Revenge, Gypo Tummy or whatever is the local epithet. Our head of finance admitted to spending a miserable night in a similar hotel as he was afraid to sleep, except on his back where he could be sure his mouth would not touch the sheets.

I have been meeting our competitors, P&O, to discuss bidding for the management of the container terminal in Cochin. They are managed out of Australia, so might end up there at some time for a trip. They are building a new terminal in Bombay, using Australian consulting engineers, and we met their site manager, a young man with a good grasp of his subject — what a pleasure after geriatric Americans in Salalah who knew nothing of our business and couldn't be told. We were to have gone down to Cochin this weekend, but my colleague had to get back to Washington, where he is obtaining American taxpayers' money for studies in the Balkans. Seeing all those observers crossing the border into Macedonia was a little close to home after a trip to Skopje.

20th March '99 — Italy

Well, I'm sorry your Vien, no sorry Venezia, trip was so blighted. Last time I was in Italy, it was a petrol drivers' strike and you couldn't get fuel at the pumps. Wishing to re-route, as I could not make Genoa, the only way to get the flight changed was to phone the travel agent in Rotterdam. It could not be done in Firenze (ah! Those continental names again), after all, it was Saturday morning. Yes, parlez-ing the local names is a minefield, particularly if you are abroad. At home, you know very well that your audience will be either totally ignorant of where it is you are talking of, impressed and wish they had thought to use Torino when they told you about the vehicle break down in Turin, or more generally struck by your pomposity. Abroad, they think of all sort of stupid names, which floor you completely, all for the same place — particularly on road signs. Best stay home.

Well, no one will be at home when you're in London, but I expect your friends want to see the bright lights. As for the chances of getting to Prague, except by mistake again, they are fairly slim, I have to be honest. Whenever people get to talking about holidays in exotic places — we have a standing invitation to Beijing (or was that Peking, and do you have Beijing duck in restaurants now — not that I've seen). My mind drifts off to my cellar in Hampshire and a walk up the hill as the sun sets. I guess if the job brought me back to a desk in UK, it would not be long before the wanderlust struck again.

The lounge has really livened up — six people now. The almost life-size statue of four-armed god is still playing the flute with two of its arms. Sexy beasts, the Indians. It must make religion a lot more fun — pulls the crowds, I guess. Most corners of the hotel have bronze figurines that would shock the living daylights out of the bible belt. However, I've not heard anyone complaining at the front desk.

23rd March '99 — India

You owe this to an enforced hour or two in Bombay airport waiting for the Emirates flight to Dubai. It would be nice to be on my way home, but this will do for the time being. I've been in India a week, just short of, and time to go after a bout of the Prawn's Revenge (prawn curry is an Indian Russian Roulette, there is one of the little pink blighters waiting for you, but which?) that could have won an Oscar. Fortunately, I was not wandering airports at the time. Tomorrow to Holland and Saturday to Cape Town — well it's all go. Patricia is already installed there with friends and hopefully Andrew got in yesterday, so the three of us will be there for a fortnight. I hope someone else is going to do all the organising, as I am through for a bit.

To Dubai and the worst excesses of consumerism. I would hate to live there now, mostly because the small puddle has become a very large lake with not a few large predatory fish in it and I don't fancy being one of the small fish. I shall be there only for tonight and have decided I am not going to stay in the dreaded Ramada, our hotel of choice for the company's cash flow, again if I don't have to, so am bound for the Meridian, which I am advised is half decent. My phone bill in Bombay was the best end of one thousand US$, so am thinking of a mobile with a selection of SIM cards for different parts of the world.

We have friends in Beijing who were in Riyadh with us, and the following are some thoughts on India which I wrote to them. Tully says in the introduction to his book, 'My visitors ask how do I put up with the poverty in India and I reply "I don't. The poor do that"'. Glib? I think so, even if purposely so. You find yourself wondering where, if one were in power, would you start — like the Victorians, with the sewers, perhaps? They have enough education, of an indifferent sort in some areas, but basic health is obviously desperate and could do with attention, but I don't think that answers the problem. Possibly the problem is ours, in that we can't understand that this is how the majority want it to be or are prepared for it to be, lacking the Western urge to make things better and tire yourself in the process. However…!

I have been plodding along with Marc Tully and his book *No Full Stops in India* — don't know if you've read it — and wondering why I don't see it quite as he does. He is a vehement critic of the Raj and all that follows from the West believing, it would appear, that India could be much better if it was not for the influence of the West and the implied inferiority of the Indian way of life. He contrasts Chinese communism's success at relieving poverty with the failure of the Indian adopted capitalist system to do so in India. Driving back from the office last night through the streets of Northern Bombay — all right, Mumbai, if you must — I was struck, from the insulation of my air-conditioned vehicle, that the only people who actually seemed to be working were the very poorest, worst dressed and worst accommodated.

They are putting in a sewer or water main in one area and flyovers in another. The workers have their accommodation on site, which consists of whatever they can make out of plastic sacks sewn together and stretched over a pyramidal frame of poles on a footprint of no more than one and a half square metres. This is home for the family and all that goes with it. The odd sacred cow is in attendance to lend a rural air and the traffic meanders past hooting, encouraged by the injunction painted on the rear of most vehicles "Horn Please — OK". Their tools consist of their hands, maybe a pick and shovel, and tin basins. Excavating the trench is done by ladling the soil into the tin basin, passing it up to a woman in a sari with a grass ring on her head where she places the basin and carries it to the tip. The men work in the trench and when rocks need to be heaved out, they have to break them into sufficiently small pieces that it can be done by hand. I asked my Indian consulting engineer: why the basin, what about a wheelbarrow? Procter, it's the maintenance, he said.

The flyovers are rather more mechanised, as the precast sections have to be craned into place, but there is no contractor's yard other than the road, so all the sections are piled precariously in the middle of the road or placed temporarily in position on the bridge support columns. The men seem to do most of the work, which frees the women to hassle the traffic for alms, carrying their children with them with the odd pinch of a leg to extract the required crying.

And what of the rest? The streets are lined at every possible place with businesses providing services to the individual. Some areas specialise; there are the marble and granite sellers, the light engineers, the non-ferrous foundries, and the motor re-winders. Printing is big business. The polished stone lot are in an old quarry area, beside the road, long since closed for quarrying but with the remains of the equipment and the loading chutes still there. The shops and services along the way inevitably tend towards food and drink, but with side-lines like a row of barbers in a sacking lean-to along a wall, with two concrete blocks for the barber and another two opposite for his customer.

The three-wheel taxis provide occupation for as many people keeping them going as are required to drive them. The occupants of the businesses are better dressed, seem to live somewhere else and if at any one time, five percent of them could be shown to be actually contributing to the GDP, it would surprise me. Everyone chats, wanders, sits, eats, drinks, thinks, but no one clears up the mess until it reaches their feet when they kick it somewhere else. Beats me! But having said all of that, why is it different here from maybe China or Korea or Taiwan, the latter of which have surely adopted the West's culture, or at least capitalism? I think it has to do with the overall Indian attitude of "near enough is good enough". Their only lasting and great architecture that I know of was imposed upon them by the Moguls. I must find out what there was before that.

Outside our office in the Godrej Soap compound, there are some fairly reasonable office buildings, by Indian standards sumptuous, one of which was being extended somewhat. The shuttering had been erected for some in situ concrete work on the first floor, and now it needed filling with concrete. The ready-mix truck had arrived and was parked on the verge adjacent to a scaffold which had been prepared earlier. The scaffold advanced upwards in about eight steps of bamboo poles, each a yard higher and a yard further forward than the last. On each pole of about six feet long sat two men one at each end. To get the concrete from the ready-mix truck to the top, it was placed in the omnipresent tin basins and passed from hand to hand up the bamboo stair and tipped into the shuttering. You can't blame the Raj for that, can you?

However, progress is in the offing. They now provide the women workers on the same site with blue plastic hard hats with… wait for it… a moulded ring on top that serves for the grass ring to put the basin on.

I asked our Indian consulting engineer, "Why not wheelbarrows?"

"It's the maintenance, Procter!"

I think we must have got past Iran and the Black Sea and be up to Rumania by now. The Iranian landscape is more forbidding than anything in Oman, I think. It's bigger and more desolate. Without a track in many parts closer to the Gulf, as you go north, water increases, marginally, and the mountains acquire a scattering of snow, which fails to translate into any sort of greenery until much closer to the Black Sea.

We passed over Shiras, a town in among the desert mountains, with a little water for the fields from somewhere. Perhaps when it opens its doors again to the West, I might get a chance to take a look one day.

23rd March '99 — Above Iran

Many thanks for Island Girls — quite cheered me up — and for the email which I also enjoyed. I'm glad to hear I am not alone in the search for physical perfection. As I said, I've been to the gym in Petersfield twice now, so that should keep me going for a bit. My real regret is that I've not been more, as CT is better enjoyed without the pain of those first trips up a hill. I thought I should start gently with a stiff walk up a hillside every evening for half an hour. Glad you enjoyed the coastal path — I have had so little contact with the natural world over the last few weeks, I begin to wonder whether it still exists. I will attach some thoughts I wrote to friends in China which might give you an idea of what Bombay is like, but after your own sub-continent experiences, no real surprise, I think.

The last trip to Oman was fairly quiet. I have a couple of things to get done and then I'm through, unless they call me in again. The chief engineer that I had a hand in hiring is, I think, useless, but the top man couldn't bring himself to fire him, or rather accept the proffered resignation, when he had the chance. The man is now jogging along until his years' tax immunity has been established and then he says he's off back to Australia and good riddance. This policy is not public knowledge but admitted to another probably after his usual number of beers. His wife had to be taken home, heels dragging, between two friends from a party in Salalah. This in a Muslim country! How did we get into this predicament? He came hugely well-recommended from inside the company and by the consulting engineers they use in the US. I happened to remark at the time that my one concern was that he was recommended by them!

I am over Iran somewhere and what a landscape — desert mountains with snow on their crests and the rock formations all running parallel to our route. It is a wonder that man found it necessary to penetrate through these wastes and establish himself on the most outlandish bit of earth with a meagre water supply. You would have thought he could have pushed up a bit closer, where life was easier. I saw what I think was one of the ancient falaj systems where they tunnelled underground for miles to create a catchment for the ground water. From the air, I could see the track of shafts with the circular heaps of spoil around them, each no more than fifty yards from the next. Amazing. I thought Mt. Ararat was around here somewhere but haven't seen Noah's Ark yet.

Dubai! The road that led out of Dubai to Abu Dhabi past the Hilton apartments and the building with the doctor's surgery in it is now a New York canyon, only wider and glitzier. The World Trade Centre, the big white honey-comb tower, is dwarfed beside the other buildings, which are all sculptural shapes with mirrored glass, and mirrored glass, and mirrored glass. What used to be roundabouts and traffic lights are now four lane overpasses and underpasses and the new airport will put anything you care to name in Europe in the shade. They say the glare from the shiny roof is confusing the pilots coming into land. The new building is a wing shape about a kilometre long, I would guess, with all the passenger loading arms coming off both sides.

I stayed at the Meridian on the beach and felt completely out of place. It is built on land just beyond the Jebel Ali Sailing Club, if you remember it, and they demolished half of the one hundred villas to put it and other hotels up. Not sorry to leave.

Well, as you say, a laptop and a long flight gives lots of opportunity for letter writing — not sure how successful email from SA will be. I got into mine via Beirut the other day — I was very proud of myself. I asked our guru about access via other service providers. He said that worldwide connectivity meant USA, and if you were lucky, Mexico, or words to that effect.

2nd April '99 — Things general…

What a nice surprise to get a message from you down here, south of the equator. I managed to get hooked into Compuserve after giving up on the semi-automatic and punching in the number. I had taken the precaution of researching the number in CT before leaving Holland. The Microsoft routines are ridiculous and designed for Americans who never leave America — wish there were more of them.

Got here in good shape after an all-night flight in tourist and Patricia and Andrew picked me up from the airport — renamed to CT international instead of the old politically incorrect D.F.Malan! The place is busy beyond belief, but you have to assume that they are living on legacy systems to listen to the locals lament the economy, the government, jobs, education etc. etc. It is obviously difficult to come to terms with real life. Patricia was talking to a shop assistant who earns two thousand five hundred Rand a month, or two hundred and fifty quid. Patricia said flying to Europe on hols must be unapproachable, to which she agreed. However, how many UK shop assistants can afford a trip to Cape Town? Expectations!

We are now in Knysna in the holiday log cabin Patricia booked — excellent — with views over the estuary or lagoon and all the other cottages and country mansions spread around the hills. The lagoon was formed behind a ridge of hills and then the river broke through to the sea, leaving what are known as The Heads guarding the entrance. Very scenic.

Yesterday we took the railway to George, about three hours, the line runs along the coast, finding its way as best it can up and down valleys and across the estuaries and lakes. The last section is along a rocky coastline, right above the waves breaking on the rocks below. Very much worth the trip, but we were quite pleased not to over-egg the pudding and did the return journey in an air-conditioned coach over a period of forty minutes. Lots of birds on the way and in the estuary where we walked for an hour this morning across the sand banks.

Tomorrow, we are off to McGregor to spend the night in the hotel we used last time — great food and in the middle of nowhere. Glad you enjoyed the lakes so much — you don't need to climb on aeroplanes necessarily, nice though it is. I also note that there are places in UK that can compete food-wise with SA on the home-baked versions. We have eaten very well here of scones and cakes and apple pies and things. The average cafe fare in the UK would not be well-received, I think.

29th April '99 — Poland

Hail from Poland — I have been trying to induce some rationality to the Polish port's strategy, but it seems less than a doddle. The politics of post commie-crash privatisation, shareholder rights and turf issues will, I am sure, defeat sanity with the same consummate efficiency of the lads behind the cannons to right and left of them when the Light Brigade came by. Apparently, the port authorities of Gdynia and Gdansk, names to conjure with, are to be privatised, but only partly, so as they will still be owned forty-nine percent by the province and fifty-one percent by the Ministry of the Treasury (are you following me so far?). However, the six thousand five hundred employees, past and present, have an entrenched right to fifteen percent of each company, so they will get thirty percent of another company, because no one wants a share in the port authority since, by law, it will be non-profit-making. Easy really.

We are trying to bid on a port management and construction project for Gdansk, but Gdynia has all the cargo and is not about to give it all away to their rivals seventeen kilometres away. So, once I have had enough of that, off to Cochin for a repeat performance — but at least it's warm and coconut palm infested there.

Left Holland in some dismay. Jill Dando murdered outside her home and the Dutch police using live rounds on their football supporters. It seems they were a trifle justified, as the riots had been very cynically choreographed to ensure the police were divided into three parts trying to control different elements. I think the run-of-the-mill Dutch attitude was that their police should have aimed higher and better — a lot of leg wounds apparently.

Patricia and I went to view the shipwreck last weekend but found the boat in pretty good order. Motored out to charge the battery, but not having any sails aboard, did not venture too far. Cold but beautiful spring day. Brought the tiller back for varnishing and spent a happy hour or two fixing it. P asked how it was that all the other boats in the marina looked so pristine compared to ours. Well, says I, their owners knock off at five thirty, home for a bit of tea and then down to the staithe for an hour or two's boat worship before home for supper. Then I wondered what I thought I was doing with my life…

The BBC World Service ran an excellent programme on Slobadan Milosovich and his lovely wife Mila. What a pair. I wonder if you saw it. According to his close friends and colleagues, Slobadan is entirely directed by Mila through tens of phone calls a day, during which he says yes, no and OK. The newspaper editor who was the most outspoken and who was, at one time, very close to them was assassinated last year after writing an open letter to them pointing out the error of their ways. Mila runs a political party called Jul which has all the trappings of fascism: the ranks of men in suits, the massed choirs and her statement that communism and capitalism had failed and now was the time for the new beginning.

I am in our Warsaw office, filling time before going off to catch the flight to Schipol. A three-day weekend, so I may get a bit more boat done. I have her scheduled to come out at the yard and get painted on the 31st of May. I am hoping not to find anything wrong with the hull after so much time in the water. There will be no point in cleaning decks and such until then, so will stick with a bit more varnishing. The tiller is out on our veranda waiting for another few coats and I must get the hatch boards back and do them too.

Poland has turned out a lot better than I expected, lumping it together with most of Russia. The people are friendly and apparently conscientious, and the mood is one of getting on with life and making a living — not something you could say of Northern Russia. Georgia I found more dynamic, in that their industry was dead as the dodo but the lads seem to have gone out and got on with their old skills of farming the land. Every last possible square metre seemed to have been planted with something; even a patch in the forest on a forty-five-degree slope had been cleared and planted with maize.

LOT — the sun is out and below, what I guess is Germany, flat, a patchwork of fields with the ever present yellow of rapeseed in bloom. I managed, by some device, to end up in business class, which means there is enough room to extract the laptop from the case and use it. Funny how flat everything looks from the air. Only by analysing shadows, tree and river patterns can you get any idea of the topography. This has been an interesting trip, though I'm quite confused over what to do about what I have learnt. Poland is very obviously not Russia or the FSU, and the people I met are enthusiastic about the future of their country and the immense strides they have made over the last ten years. They look down on Russians as a bunch of cowboys or much, much worse. However, they believe that the West needs Poland to act as intermediaries with the East, because we don't know how to handle them. True enough!

They are talking about landing, so had better put this away before it upsets the auto-pilot.

Safely back in the Hague and we have had a three-day weekend in honour of the Queen's birthday. Been to the boat to pick up some things to varnish, been out on our bikes to see the spring and been to the shops, coffeed around town and been generally pretty idle, but much of what was needed.

I have to write letters to the folks in Poland next week and try to get the Ministry interested constructively in their port's policy. I wish governments and such would talk to users about their ports instead of daft consultants generally from finance and economics rather than operations and engineering. I think half of the problem is that these people have a vested interest in something being built as a result of their involvement. How many reports start off with "Don't be ridiculous".

The port of Gdynia is getting a report on their intermodal future. We offered to take the money, three hundred thousand US$, but were declined (because it was a really lousy submittal) and I asked who had got it and what were they doing. The port president told me he could have written the report himself in a month and I suggested he could have done that and bought himself a reach stacker with the money instead and done more good, with which he concurred. The money came from the American taxpayer.

2nd May '99 — Poland

We have had a three-day weekend in honour of the Queen's birthday. She should have more of them. The weather has been cool, sunny spring days and we have been on our bikes and down to the boat to collect the hatch covers for varnishing and whatnot. On the way back, we came across Lex on the way to his new boat with the rudder in a trailer — big boat! She was out of the water, but we climbed aboard for a look — now Patricia is talking seriously of bigger, better boats!

Poland was interesting. Totally unlike other former communist states I have been to, being obviously on the make. The place is quite Western in aspect, and you could be in any rather rundown city in the North of England — parts of Cardiff, even. The people I met were very friendly and welcoming and there are seemingly a lot of Poles who emigrated and then returned to their homeland to make a living and a life for themselves. I flew LOT, which was very presentable, and stayed in half-decent hotels. Even the cars are OK, not the dreaded Ladas you get in other parts — and radio taxis which actually charge according to a tariff on the meter. India on Wednesday and thence to Oman. Had an email today telling me they had decided to move the radar to another location, which has been agreed three times already. Every time I go away, they come to a new conclusion without considering why the original decision was made, then I come back and we go through the same discussion again and we get back to the original decision. Now it has happened again, and nobody has the courtesy to tell me even why they changed it

19th May '99 — The Malabar Coast

What follows is part of a letter home, so why not inflict it on you too! Hope it helps to pass the time on the China station. Seen any good demonstrations? Does not that ring of Conrad and Kipling? The ghosts are all about here, in a manner of speaking. The Raj put this lot together and they've not fixed very much of it since Mr Bristow — MICE, M.Mech.E etc. finished building the harbour masters office in 1940. A plaque remembers him and his stalwart efforts. Perhaps I'll get a photo of it later if the rain holds off. And the Raj is back in one or another guise to help out again. I and my colleague wandered round after dinner last night, surveying the scene and wondering what it is that encourages the Indian lassitude about their surroundings. Why do they never ever clear anything up? If someone takes charge, they can do as good work as anyone else, but no one wants to see anything through, it seems.

Just now they are facing another election and Sonia Ghandi is leading the Congress party against the BJP. The former seem to be the rational choice, having achieved the liberalisation of the economy and the current increases in GDP — six percent p.a. The BJP are the ones behind the new xenophobia and communalism, even to the extent of being accused of involvement or at best disinterest in the hassling and murder of Christians. They are attacking the Congress party on the basis of Sonia not being Indian and seeking votes, currying favour with the Hindus, by conniving in religious intolerance of the others. Not very pretty!

We are in Cochin again — now called Kochi — and it's Sunday so I am in my hotel room with the window open and a view over the water with some chaps in a dugout canoe fishing for lunch just across the lawn. Hope it's not my lunch, as the water looks a little soupy. I ate fish in Bombay the other night and felt a lot worse for the experience. I suppose if I had recognised the fish, I would not have eaten it, but its rather stale flavour was probably due to just that, rather than its species. Got to the plane yesterday feeling less than perfect but felt improved later.

Last night we attacked the Hyderabadi buffet festival — not my idea at all — and survived all manner of copper pots with nameless spiced gunge inside. This morning we had breakfast on the terrace — porridge, toast coffee, bacon and fried tomatoes. All right, so I'm a dyed-in-the-wool Brit, but I enjoyed breakfast. I do enjoy Indian food, but I think the guts are beginning to draw the line at the more exotic

We looked to see what there was by way of tours, and decided to take the easy route with the town tour rather than the eight-hour marathon to the south. I rather regret not doing the full day but on balance, a bit of rest might not be a bad thing. Alan, my co-driver on this trip, was in India with me a couple of years back and had twenty-four hours in which to see Agra and the Taj Mahal, so flew to Delhi and took a five-hour taxi drive in the monsoon with a half blind driver to Agra, two hours there and then drove back again. Mad, but he says it was worth it.

It's just rained, and the air is heavy with tropical wet earth smells — must assemble the gear and go to see the Jewish synagogue et al. Back from the synagogue and the church and the fort, more of that later, and just dealt with the afternoon with a swim in the pool and a sit on the swing seat in the garden, overlooking the site of our proposed container terminal. Across the water from here, it looks like an English meadow with green grass and stands of trees behind the sea wall, which could be a ha-ha. It is difficult to imagine it with container cranes and stacks of containers, but if India needs container terminals, which it does, they have to go somewhere.

This morning at breakfast we watched the fishing boats coming and going and took some photos of an old man in a Chinese hat and a dugout canoe fishing with a bamboo pole. The dolphins put in a brief appearance.

We booked a car for 9.45 to tour the old town for ostensibly two hours. Peter, our driver, turned out he had worked in Bagdad, spoke reasonable English and was an engaging character, so we chatted to him along the way. The hotel is on Willingdon Island and is named after its creator, I think, who dredged the harbour and put the fill where I am sitting. It's a big island for something dredged up sixty or seventy years ago. To get to the old town you cross a causeway and a lifting bridge which no longer lifts. Immediately, on the other side, you are in among the tiny shops and houses of old Cochin, which was severally occupied by the Portuguese, turfed out by the Dutch who were in turn turfed out by the British. The houses and go-downs are all roofed with baked red tiles, and the baked bricks they still make are Dutch size, not English — quite small.

"]]]\ — A crow has just dumped in my laptop in the area of the square bracket key.

Well, I can tell you about the hat now. I have been trying to find a hat of suitably classy design so that I don't look a complete wally wearing it. I found a pretty novel leather job in SA which, though not quite imparting the full "Raiders of the Lost Ark" image, comes very close. This is to replace the floppy Australian cricketing variety which leaves one with the impression of being approached in the mirror by a manufacturer of tents turned milliner. Anyhow, the leather job was bought and I brought it out this trip to get its first airing. And a crow dumped on it! Patricia looks askance at it as well, but I think she's just afraid it might turn heads.

Dutch tiles in Cochin

Back to old Cochin — our first stop was the Jewish synagogue. Apparently, there was quite a large population here up to twenty or thirty years ago, but they left for Israel when opportunity presented. A few remain and look after the synagogue; we saw one old gentleman of distinctly Middle Eastern aspect, rather than a Keralite, talking to some tourists. The building is in an area of various other religious shrines and temples and is surrounded by the old Jewish area and spice market, narrow streets with all the shops now converted to selling antiques. The synagogue, not a large building, is noted for its history, of course, and one thousand one hundred Blue Chinese tiles laid on the floor. I hope the photos come out. They had some murals telling the history of Judaism in Cochin and they seem to have been very well treated and respected by the Rajahs of Cochin. The first Jews arrived on the Malabar coast sometime between the destruction of the second temple (OK I'm reading from the book) and 600 AD, when Mohammed got going. It seems 400 AD is the closest. A Dutch Jew visiting Cochin in 1686 records that eighty thousand Jews arrived on the Malabar coast in 370 AD. But I wonder where they got the boats. They worked in the government, presumably as accountants and scribes. Outside, we looked into the antique shops and found a wonderful array of carvings, teak furniture and brass work.

Candy pan?

I fell for some beautiful cast brass bowls used for making sweets, about two feet in diameter and quite shallow but with lovely handles on either side and turned ribs on the circumference; those and brass temple oil lamps hanging from chains.

Next stop, the Dutch — actually Portuguese — palace. After driving quite some way, we found ourselves just over the wall from the synagogue. Peter parked outside and we followed his directions to the steps up to the first floor, each step a piece of granite about two metres long with a design carved into the riser at each end. Inside, a marvellous collection of rooms with a few objets d'art scattered about, plus a picture gallery of the Rajahs. Objets were pretty much confined to palanquins of varying degrees of privacy and weight; one all of lacquered timber with shutters and small windows, another of ivory open on all sides and with a silver wire embroidered cover now placed in a display case alongside.

Merchant's house in Old Cochin

Less prosaic were the wall paintings of the Indian pantheon working out their differences over mortals and pieces of geography. The one I have some idea about is the bit about Sri Lanka and the monkeys building the bridge over to help out their particular god, however, downstairs in the harem were some rather different murals which the Victorians would have scrubbed off the walls given half a chance. They have this blue god called Rama, is it, who seems to get his pick of the best "Gopis".

The ceilings of all the rooms are intricately carved wood panels made from a wood, maybe teak or jacka, a timber like teak, the same as the doors and floors of my room in this hotel, and almost black.

I think I have mentioned the Chinese fishing nets before. We drove further out towards the sea and stopped at a place obviously popular with

Deities mural

the locals, where they were selling refreshments and all sorts. Along the beach, the Chinese fishing nets are set up and today they were working, so Peter took us to talk to his friend, who was in charge of a gang of six or so who were raising and lowering the net into the tide as it streamed by — but only three very small fish for their trouble. The net was down, and they pulled it up again to see what was there — not a good day.

The boss spoke passable English of the "Where you from — England" variety — pleasant man. I have had to revise my net mechanics. The story about walking the plank was rubbish — much cleverer than that. As the net descends, the leverage of the gantry decreases and the net would crash into the water if there was just one counterweight, so there are several, each on a length of rope and being a granite boulder of a good two hundredweight. As the net goes down, an increasing number of weights are hoisted off the platform, nicely keeping the balance. When the net is down, you can see from a distance all the weights hanging from the gantry, one below the other. Dash clever, these Chinese.

After shooting off a lot of film, we set off for home via Peter's house. He had said it was close and invited us to stop. I think Alan would have declined, but we had also stopped at a Catholic Church and he had been rather unfair to a lad selling bits and pieces, stringing him along instead of telling from the start he wasn't buying. Anyway, I thought we would do our social duty, but was a bit concerned that we would get at the very least tea with the bugs that might arrive with it. Mother, two sons and daughter were there and we sat and drank tea, ate mango, declined jack fruit and declined lunch. The son, reading politics and economics, told me he would like to see the BJP win the next election. I asked him why that was, as, not being Hindu, he might suffer as a result. He said yes that could be, but the BJP were better in terms of development and also were not as corrupt as the Congress party. We made our excuses and Peter drove us back to the hotel.

The crow has just had another shot at me — been eating raspberries by the look of it — but hit the aluminium table with a noise like the copper spittoons are supposed to make in Wild West bars. I will take the hint and put this away.

After dinner in the Chinese restaurant and after typing another paragraph or two which got eaten by the software I know not how — I mentioned the Catholic Church but did not mention the gravestones and memorial plaques. The Dutch stuck to the bare facts — Johanna, wife of such and such commander of the garrison, died 1600 and... — the Brits, on the other hand, were more forthcoming. BA, Caius College, Cambridge, MICE etc. lay member of the church... good of the people... education... health... etc., etc. but dated in the 1900s. One wonders what drove them to leave their home shores and come to India, with all the uncertainties of health and future, and then set about creating so much that has served for so long after they left — most of Cochin, in fact.

Well, must to bed and will put this in the outbox — if I don't lose it down the email worm-hole — I hope not too many yawns and Dad off on his diatribe again — lots of love to all of you from Cochin.

Last evening, we did the boat trip rather as last time, with a similar crew of passengers, but this time it rained, so we had to retreat inside for a time while it chucked it down tropical fashion. The hat is now spotted all over, but the patch where the crow scored has merged a bit into the rest — it does keep the rain off your glasses. Drinks were served and refreshments and we did the rounds of the old container terminal, the navy berths, the ship-building yard and a huge new tanker just fitting out beside the yard that built it, and then into the country areas a bit and passed where the new terminal will be. There is a story going round that the site is alive with snakes — we are to interview the snakes tomorrow.

We never got to see the snakes, but we spent all day with the Port Trust. The chairman is a most engaging and professional individual, and it is touching to see his wish to see things done right for the port. Apparently he is an ex-policeman more used to fighting dacoits on the Northern Frontier (as it used to be called). He said that for preference he would like to negotiate a contract with a chosen company rather than go through the rigmarole of an open tender, but that would not be possible politically... The fact that he is honest and many of the others not forces them into this.

On our wander round on Sunday, we came across a very presentable looking hotel which we were advised later is owned by German and had been restored with state assistance. We invited our co-conspirators out to dinner and told them we were going to this place which we understood to be decent but no guarantees. Our driver set off into the night along steadily narrower and darker roads, which we sort of remembered, at an ever-increasing pace. Now and then we would remark that yes, we knew where we were, and the hotel would shortly appear, only to dive down another road full of potholes and unlit bicycles. We did get there and were astonished at what we found. The building had some architectural attributes but a lot of Critall steel windows. However, the internals were delightful and decorated with local furniture, carvings and wall hangings. The floors were all of granite flags and the veranda roofs tiled so that you could see the underside of the tiles. Each tile has a design on it so that, looking up, you see a pattern of tiles, timbers and the design on each tile from the mould. Outside, they look like an ordinary fired tile roof.

The food was good and the rooms, which we looked at afterwards, very simply furnished but with great taste — the sort of place to sit, contemplate, write a bit and consider.

20th August '99 — Holland

I am here on the boat on Vestingdagen in Hellevoetsluis, watching the displays of aerobatics when I feel inclined, drinking tea and generally not doing too much. I picked up a germ and feel a bit fragile as a result, and having no crew, another great sailing day gone to waste. Vestingdagen or Fortressdays (I think) is when the town gets to party with a fayre, steam engines, rural japes like jousting a ring on a string while riding one of the Friesian draft horses, aerobatics, and later tonight, fireworks. We have attended three years now, anchoring out opposite the town along with a flotilla of other yachts and watching the fun from inside sleeping bags. This year it will not be much joy, I regret. The boat has remained in good condition and clean despite the neglect. We had her out earlier and she was cleaned up and antifouled by the yard, so she moves a little slicker through the water than when she had the garden underneath!

This little bundle of joy has just announced that it is hungry, running out of juice, needs mains power... I wonder if it can swim... You know those Japanese toys that children have to look after, or they turn up their little toes and peg out — the toys that is. Well, I think the Japs gave us the adult version without telling us — laptops.

The first trip to Bombay was to work with P&O on a bid for Cochin port management. Having seen us perform before, they had asked for forty-five days' notice if we decided we hadn't the stomach for it and would pull out. By this time, we had cut that back to thirty days, as we would not have all the data necessary to get a board decision in time. With that in mind, we set to work with the P&O team to get the financial model trued up and consider all the angles. For make weight, we had with us our VP of business development, a dapper little chap, rather out of place in India, and like all Americans, desperately nervous of the place.

The P&O people are a good bunch and they have set themselves up to aggressively go after the port management and development market in India and the Middle East. Their head man was born in India, emigrated and then returned as an expatriate, which is why he can drive a Mercedes in India, where the import tax is a hundred percent or so. He is a bit liberal with the facts, which he puts down to strategy. He accused me of misleading him over some political issue and I told him I was only the dumb engineer around there and I didn't get into those issues. His look said well, it was worth a try anyway! He took me to lunch with Nik, his sidekick, at the Oberoi, where they have a very fine Mughal restaurant and chivvied the staff around because the roti had failed to appear at the same time as the starters, etc. etc. Jimmy, I said, never mind, the food is excellent. I know, he replied, looking glum, that's the trouble.

Steve, on the other hand, was so worried about his health that whatever was put before him, he would consult the third member of our party, Alan, as to its bacterial merits. Alan is paranoid about lettuce and ice on the basis that the water for washing lettuce and making ice probably come from the same convenient ditch. The rest of the culinary world seems, in his mind, to escape this contagion, I don't know how. Anyhow, except for the above, Alan was able to give favourable advice, rarely taken. P&O had sent out to the coffee shop of one of the three five-star hotels in Bombay for sandwiches, but Steve declined an invitation to eat one, saying that he wasn't hungry, as he was a bit off-colour but "...I have my vitamins with me..." While the rest of us ate, from the rustling, it became apparent that Steve had iron rations in the form of crunchy bars and organic dried peas secreted in his brief case. These he was endeavouring to eat covertly and wash down with his very own imported bottled water. The Indians were entranced.

On the next trip, Alan and I ate in the convenient cafe next door to the P&O office — I confess I ordered a Coke in the bottle and did not use the straw. They are said to wash straws out for re-use by the next customer. The cafe was a lot dirtier than you can imagine, but we survived, and the food tasted good as well. Alan ate until his meal got close to the plate and then stopped. Must have been that washing up water again. Steve is in the process of marrying a Chinese Singaporean — not sure the family back in the States will see it the same way he does. One gets the impression they are fairly orthodox. He is totally incapable of managing himself, let alone anyone else, so how he comes to be a VP is a bit beyond me. Doesn't even play golf. He collects maps apparently and bought a stack of them in the hotel bookshop of places he had never been to. Hopefully he has one of Kutch, as I think he needs to go there — see below!

I finished in Bombay on the Friday and flew early morning to Muscat to start the Muslim week with a catch-up session in the office. As usual, everybody had a dismal tale to tell. They do not have management meetings on a regular basis, so they all get the wrong impression of what each other is trying or succeeding in doing. Typically, and I have heard it said, "I don't need a meeting. I have nothing to discuss" — so what about the other manager, who has? Should he discuss it with himself? So, I try to act as post box… "But don't you think that…" without getting involved — I'm not supposed to get involved.

Had couple of days in Muscat and then down to Salalah for most of the rest of the time. I did not have more than a few days' work there, but I could as easily work in Oman as Rotterdam on some other projects, and by waiting, I could be ready to go back to Bombay when we had agreed on the 8th August, I think it was.

Well, I heard nothing from Steve until I was back in England, despite a missive asking for instructions. In Salalah, all was deepest gloom. Equipment failures. The Khareef, the Dhofari monsoon, was on, and either the resulting damp had found its way into a wide selection of the electric motors or the motors were suspect in the first place or both. Everyone including, to my annoyance, our head man had jumped on the Khareef bandwagon as the explanation for all the problems. I pointed out that there were five cranes still working in Salalah that had not had so much as a lick of paint from the Omanis in fifteen years, but to no avail. Our brave consultant, who doesn't talk to me if he can help it, came up with some spurious explanation. I suggested that the consulting engineers be forced to write a report on the failures — they didn't like that either, so I am beginning to wonder whether they are feeling the heat a bit. I hope so.

Enter stage left Dave Shotton from Stamford, what a breath of fresh, seen it all before and knew what to do with his part of the problem, at least, and had just finished doing the same in Lagos. Stamford supply generator sets are a virtual standard to the ports industry all over the world. The problem was bad design by the Chinese, making the forced draft engine cooling air drag all the water running down the outside of the generator cabin all over the generator before getting to the engine radiator. Easy! However, the American GE motors, the manufacturer specified by American consultants, turned out to have all sorts of rubbish, loose nuts and bolts and bits of welding rod, inside them together with heavy corrosion of the steel shafts, making it look as though they were wet before we even got them. They had twenty-eight motors burn out in total! They have all been re-wound by now and properly treated for the conditions, so that will probably be the end of the problem once they have modified all the enclosures.

Social diversions were provided by an old sailing pal from Dubai who happened by on a delivery voyage Suez — Suakin — Aden — Salalah — Muscat — Dubai. I had been warned to look out for him and his skipper, but did not expect to find them propped up at the bar of our social club. Hugely impressed by the port and by Omani welcoming bureaucracy versus the Egyptian, Yemeni, Sudani variety (graft everywhere). We sent them away to carry the message to Dubai. As delivery voyages go, this one seemed to be typical of what you read — rotten gear carrying away, rotten owners not paying the bills, rotten weather, no wind, and motored nearly all the way despite the SW monsoon. They are back in Dubai now and apparently did not have to hide the boat in Ajman or somewhere until paid.

The paid hand, the individual I used to sail with, had a boat in Dubai but was loathe to receive instruction from anyone on the finer points of sailing. We were coming onto the berth once, the motor having failed again, under sail and David brought the boat into wind with son on the foredeck, warp in hand, to make fast when we reached the quay under the vessel's momentum. Well, we didn't reach the quay. As we would drift down onto other expensive sailing hardware, I gave the order for the lad to go over the side for King and Country and all that.

"Whah?" it said.

"JUMP" And it did, with just enough line to reach the quay and bring us home. Being full of similar tricks, when David was coming back into harbour, members at the bar would put down their drinks and saunter outside for a better view of the action.

Our marketing manager had his daughter and her boyfriend out to stay. His father is butler to the Brocklebanks, by way of introduction, used to be Cunard-Brocklebank, yer kno! He had probably not been much further than Southend and she has travelled all of India, Switzerland, Holland etc. and affects a rather bored familiarity with it all; he, on the other hand, has boundless enthusiasm for everything, especially stuffed leather camels and the like.

Other bits of scuttlebutt: the chief engineer left the club late one night with wife, and instead of turning left at his roundabout, took a flying leap into the middle of it at something like thirty miles an hour. The lady was asleep, out cold in the passenger seat at the time, it seems, and well, blow me, if it wasn't that dratted Khareef again making the roads wet. Fortunately, no one else was involved and they didn't damage themselves too much. Last I heard, they were doing strengthening exercises under the tutorial of the physio in the Al Shatty hospital in Muscat — probably the first exercise either of them had had in a long time beyond right elbow raising — which they are both in Olympic shape for. The blood sample was sent to Muscat for analysis, but I think the results conveniently got lost somewhere on a camel in the Wahiba Sands.

So back to Muscat and turned left for Blighty just in time to turn round and go back East again. It was, though, very nice to have even two days at home with P. and we made the most of it. Mostly in the garden, which is looking very smart — must get the paving re-done. P. is keen on Hostas and they look good beside the pool — which is still a deep healthy green. The fish must enjoy swimming around in all that food. We bought freshwater mussels, who are regarded as the natural janitors of murky ponds. We have only three, so if they spend all their time eating, they will soon be elbowing aide the lesser fauna and cleaning up on the lilies as well. We are planning for them to have large families, but we are not exactly sure how. Boy/girl-type enquiries at the garden shop seemed too embarrassing for P. I think they are hermaphrodite, but O-level bilge might be misremembered.

So, to Heathrow again and check in at the Leela beside Bombay airport. The following morning, I found the hotel barber and got shorn. Not a bad job, but I could have done without the finger massage of the head and the quite gratuitous comment, while patting the intelligence, "Very small, Sah! But sides good." This was a reference to the relative thickness of the thatch.

I moved to the Taj in the centre of town so as to be close to the P&O office, which is in the old shipping offices street next to the dockyard wall. The old section of the Taj is a magnificent structure, even if the architect was Italian. It echoes Mughal architecture with European tones. The entrance hall that was to be, had they got the plans the right way round, is single storey and quite restrained, but it gives onto the staircase through two arches. The stairs ascend in a hall which must be fifty feet on a side, with balconies cantilevered out at each floor, the stairs rising in single flights to each. It is all in stone, apart from the intricate balusters, which are in either wrought or cast iron. I think the latter. From the stairwell, there are arches off to the rooms which are accessed by a double balcony on either hand, supported on carved timber pillars with open space from ground to the top storey between them. They have used the landings and walls to display some very collectable Indian antiques, chests, carpets, pictures and so forth.

We went to look at the Executive club facilities and were shown round by a charming Indian lady. Alan decided to move from his hoi poloi quarters and afterwards justified the expense with a report on how well he was looked after. I was leaving the next day and otherwise would surely have done the same. The facilities were really most attractive, with views over the Gateway of India and the port anchorage.

Do you remember that Mother was taken to see the Gateway when they first arrived in India, and she thought the betel nut spit on the walls was blood from some recent, if not on-going, revolution?

One of the girls in the office advised us to try the Indigo restaurant, so one evening we did. She had said it was a place for "…you people…" no offence intended, but we knew what she meant when we got there. Obviously the latest expatriate haunt, though Alan went again at the weekend and it was full of the rich young things of India seeing and being seen. We chanced across the Australian project manager for the new port in Bombay and his Thai wife. We had asked for a table, but there were none, so when Jo walked over and asked us to join them it wasn't difficult to persuade us. They had booked for a larger party, not all of whom had turned up. There were an American engineer, and Australian banker and the rest were Thai wives of the above or Thai friends. I think Jo was glad of the opportunity, as he put it, to get some different views and talk from new people. His little boy was there too and was passed from lap to lap until he fell asleep on the banker.

To the dismay of our P&O friends, the bid and its politics had reached low water in the US. I had to go to Kutch to see a project there and so was leaving Saturday morning early. We parted from P&O Friday night with expressions of hope that something would turn up. It did not seem likely. The drop-dead period for informing them that we were not going in was then down to four days, with a weekend in between. It was apparent that the USA had followed nothing of what was necessary to get the required approvals from the parent company, and on Friday morning, had holed the ship below the waterline with two pre-conditions, either one of which would have had the bid thrown out as not only non-conforming but also mischievous. We had a difficult meeting with Jimmy. Rightly so!

I had to leave and found out later that P&O had gone in alone and were the only bidder. Nik passed us the information in an email which closed with a very generous "Wish you were here".

So, to the airport again, this time with Indian Airways, not to be confused with Air India — "Your Palace in the Sky", for the flight to Bhuj via Jamnagar. Kutch is the littoral province of Gujarat, and the Rann of Kutch was where I was going. I can tell you a lot about the Rann of Kutch when you have very little else to do — it's a bit like the surface of the moon without the interest factor. For some reason, the company I was to see thought it would be a good place to build a port, so they did.

Apparently, the "Kutchis" are a race of entrepreneurs, par excellence, and made a lot of money beating up the rest of India and trading with the Gulf in the old days. They came home to their partial desert and built huge forts to keep themselves inside, along with the piles of gold and women — or gold and piles of women, not sure which. Khimji Ramdas, one of the big trading houses in Muscat, is a Kutchi family, now naturalised Omanis, so you see what I mean!

The port is built in a place that makes Holland look mountainous. When you've driven for miles across nothing, you come to nothing by the sea and a raft of oil tanks and some warehouses. They have built a kilometre and a half long causeway and bridge out to the deep water with a quay at the end of it — like Southend pier. Once out there, you can see all the nothing from another angle. To get to this wonderful place, Indian Airways will fly you to Bhuj in an ancient Boeing 727 that, when you get in, you wonder which bit will fall off next, your tray table or the port engine.

Bhuj is a military aerodrome in the front line in the fight against Pakistan, so mobile phones don't work in case the troops all have one to tell them what to do next. Mig fighters and other hardware, artillery and such, are there for a bit of fun. The ordinary individual on arrival is bussed five kilometres to the military boundary, where you can get a cab or park your car. We, however, were special, and the cars were close to the runway. The airport buildings amount to a loo, an office for two and a tree. The drive to the port is possibly best summed up in my official report:

"It would be unwise to allow readers of this report to go in ignorance of the general impression one has on arriving in Kutch. It is a province of the state of Gujarat, and in earlier years, was extremely prosperous through the efforts of its entrepreneurial citizens trading in the Gulf, Arabia and India. The evidence of this past is there in the form of derelict walled cities and forts. Still, some measure of remittance of wealth from overseas results in the construction of some extravagant villas surrounded by ultimately basic housing in the towns and villages. For the most part, the country between Bhuj and Mundra is arid, verging on desert in places, flat and featureless. Industry is virtually non-existent, and the economy poverty line rural. Bhuj airport and that at Jamnagar are heavily militarised, being close to the border with Pakistan. The real desert, the Great Rann of Kutch, is fifty kilometres to the north, straddling the Tropic of Cancer. There is also a Little Rann of Kutch to the east, which is skirted to the south by the railway line to Ahmedabad. The Pakistan border is a hundred and fifty kilometres to the north. Access roads in Kutch vary between the country or village standard through state to national. The national roads are generally seven metres wide in reasonable condition, state roads the same width but not as well maintained, and the village roads about three to four metres wide and vehicles leave the tarred surface to pass. In places, the village roads become dirt rather than macadam. Between Bhuj and Mundra, we passed over mainly village roads but commercial traffic from the north would use the state roads."

The staff at the port had been told, I gathered from Thiagarathan, my host, that the builder of Rotterdam and Salalah terminals was visiting and were suitably agog. Inaccurate, and I can think of a lot of folk who would be more than a trifle resentful, however, it is unlikely that the Bhuj Business News, if published, will reach the desks of the international shipping community with the news. Certainly, upon arrival, a reception committee turned out to greet me, before being ushered inside to their meeting room for a presentation of their business planning etc.

There followed a port tour in the prestigious Landcruiser FWD when I was shown the new berths they had built, the bleeding line for bagged soya, the conveyor belts, the storage tanks for mineral and food-grade oil, the warehouses and the site to be of the new container terminal they want us to help them to build. This latter looked a strange place to build a berth, being a creek only some fifty yards wide and a couple of metres deep, however, it's five metres of clay and then sand for far as you need to go, so dredging is cheap — comparatively. I suppose you would need to move about seven and a half million cubic metres at two pounds a cube or fifteen million quid — need to move a lot of boxes to pay that off.

We reconvened for lunch, but though the food was good, you keep wondering what might happen as a result later, particularly with a six-hour train journey ahead the next day.

Part Two will follow — I noticed a dysfunctionality in my software indicating incipient crash and burn so had to cut short before it did just that!

22nd August '99 — India part two

And so to complete what I started. I am in Copenhagen airport, passing a couple of hours before my flight back to Heathrow. I've done email — both company and personal — I've marched myself past the luxury apparel in the luxury airport shops, past the luxury watches and the luxury cameras, and books and food and wine and all that stuff there to entrap the unwary. The psychology of it must be awfully simple and therefore demeaning of the human mind. You are in an airport; you are bored stiff; you're a traveller who can afford to pay for an airline ticket so another few quid on a Cartier watch must be in your budget somewhere to help pass the time. I retreat to the business lounge for a free drink and a read of a free paper.

And so later — much, much later — I am now back in Holland in the office (not much going on). So, I missed the flight! With all that time to waste and my watch set on Dutch time, I dozed a bit, woke up to watch Brits getting up to go and catch their flight — my flight, did I but realise it — and sat and thought about nothing much until I realised I was there to get on an aeroplane. Too late! The flight had left thirty minutes earlier and there ensued two hours of traipsing up and down Copenhagen airport from the SAS booking desk to a gate, waitlisted, not on it, back to SAS, another gate until I eventually got on another flight. Then we aborted landing at Heathrow. As we climbed back into the sky above the Staines reservoirs, I thought about all those stories of people who had just missed ill-fated flights and the others who had just caught them. We landed in due course, the delay having been occasioned by another flight failing to clear the runway soon enough. So then we were at Terminal III with a very long walk to Terminal I where the car was parked. The ticket machine for the car park would not accept my ticket, and after yet more delay, I found the office — departures level, across the road, right hand end — and negotiated a new ticket, exit validated. Problem? Wrote the number of the parking bay on the ticket so the bar code reader got lost.

Back to India — while in the port, they took me to see the contractor's casting yard, where they had prepared the forty-metre-long pre-stressed piles. Generally in India, port construction is low-tech and they habitually sink a steel former pile, spoon out the earth, drop in a reinforcing bar cage and fill with concrete. The latter process can take days for one pile, as they do it with saucepans on women's heads, a kilo of concrete at a time, filling a pile that might be thirty inches across and fifteen metres deep.

This site used hollow piles cast in a forty-two-metre-long bed with strong-backs at either end to support the forces of jacking the reinforcing rods into tension before pouring the concrete. There are formers outside and inside, which are recovered before the pile is driven, and re-used. The engineer remarked that the piles were not centrifugally cast. I suggested that spinning the whole contraption might be a little bit difficult — Acha! (Which, being translated, is Yes! in Hindi. Acha-cha-cha-cha! is Yeah! Yeah! Yeah! in Hindi).

We left the port to see the rail construction site. They have started in the middle, being, I suppose, the most difficult terrain, as it requires an embankment and a cutting. We arrived at the site via some tortuous country road where the tarmac had run out to such an extent that the fields were the better going. On the way, we were shown the survey posts for the trace with some pride. I think, quite rightly, they saw it as an achievement that they had got through all the hurdles designed by the bureaucrats to prevent actual work starting. The country is not as flat as at the port, so we found ourselves on top of a small hill where a man was drilling a sample bore to see what manner of rock they had to cut through. The contraption he was drilling with was, well, basic, a frame, a small petrol engine, a belt drive and a drill bit lubricated by a pump providing water from a polythene sheet reservoir in a hole in the ground. Since they had to cut through the hillock anyway, all twenty feet of it, I couldn't see why they just did not get on with it. On either side of the hillock, they were preparing the railbed up to the level of the ballast a kilometre or so into the distance.

The only sign of other life was a small temple complex with a few red flags flying above it. Apparently, the faithful can stop over there for free to contemplate and whatnot before moving further on their life's journey. I have decided that if I was down and out in India, I would get into the temple or shrine business. Start small and build up. It is amazing how prosperous, relatively, the shrine minders seem to be. And you don't need to spend too much on the infrastructure and facilities. You could get started with a bag of cement, some sand and a few half-used cans of red, blue and yellow paint. Your average image is generally easily recognisable by the number of extra arms, elephant's trunks and monkey's tails. You can pretty much dispense with the more difficult facial features. Acha!

They pulled out chairs for us to sit on and had a board up with the project plan and parameters on it. The others kept wandering around, so I suggested that, since they had been kind enough to provide seats, we should use them, so we sat down and one of the site personnel took about a dozen pictures of me. I am now left with uncomfortable feeling that Sea-Land are going to leave them in the lurch, just like the others. I hate being involved in those deals.

We bid them farewell and set off for Kandla and the night's rest in the hotel they had selected. We did a quick tour of Kandla port, which was built to replace Karachi after partition and to provide a city for the Hindu refugees from Pakistan. It is a pretty dreadful place, flat, dirty and without any shred of interest apart from the professional one of port operations. All the freight in India that does not move by rail comes to the ports in ten-ton trucks and the port area of Kandla is swamped with them. The cabs are hand built of wood and garishly decorated. The bodies are similar, but the link between the two seems to be very tenuous. I saw two chaps with a hand cart moving a cab down the road — who knows why!

The port is outdated and dilapidated but works some cargo, and the rail connection to Delhi and the industrial areas thereabouts seems to work well enough for India. I was to know more the next morning.

We found our hotel and I found my room, which stank of sewage, but I did have my own shower and loo so it could have been worse. It's difficult to walk on carpets without touching them — but desirable. Ugh!

The meal was all right that night and the driver failed to show in the morning, so they drove us to the station. There we walked through the city of the dead, bodies in winding sheets scattered everywhere, through the booking hall, along the platform, on the steps of the foot bridge, on the foot bridge, down the other side and into the train. Our compartment was the air-conditioned sleeper. I had had some vague vision of ancient East African Railways and Harbours rolling stock, so I was not ready for the Soviet-style carriage with beds for sixty and one loo. The windows on one side were obscured glass and on the other more opaque still through the accumulated grime of ages. The beds were all plastic, covered in pea green and mercifully, it being Independence Day, we were the only occupants.

I got some sleep with my head on my laptop — incongruous? What happened to bedding rolls and the like? When I woke, we were still shuffling along through marginal agricultural land, ploughed with oxen and growing millet and what looked like sweet potatoes. From time to time, we would pass a village and a passing point, the line is single track, and as we neared Ahmedebad towns, one with a magnificent Raja's palace but too far away to see much detail. It was six hours and three hundred kilometres to Ahmedebad and fairly monotonous with it.

I was scheduled, for my better education, to take the night sleeper to Delhi. Had it been by day I would have done it, but in the circumstances, I dipped out.

We were met at the station in Ahmedebad and driven to the guest house where we dropped our bags and then set off for lunch via the apartment of one of the company's directors. He and his wife entertained me to drinks; Gujarat is a dry state, but the bold Captain Sethi told me that if you are old enough, you can get it on prescription. Charming couple who had lived in the UK and were very Anglophile (she apologised profusely for assuming I was American).

We went from there to a new restaurant that everyone was talking about — well everyone in Ahmedebad — and ate well of Thai food, I think it was. Ahmedebad is where Gandhi got started and founded his ashraf, or school. It has a substantial university and is one of the five large "metros" of India.

After lunch, we returned to the guest house, tea and a discussion with the chairman of the company and his technical adviser about the project. Later, we were driven to the chairman's house on the edge of the city, in its own twenty acres of grounds, complete with tennis courts, swimming pools, a stable of expensive cars and the house itself. If you had landed in Hollywood, it would not have been surprising. The house is perfectly set up and furnished with no thought for cost, and the grounds are manicured. We chatted at length about their business, India's economy, ports, etc. etc. and then got up to go out to eat at an ethnic restaurant where they served food to you sitting on the mud floor. He drove us in the Landcruiser down the half kilometre drive to the front gate.

Stopping at the gate, I am joined in the back seat by a man with an automatic weapon. The technical adviser explains that our host had a nasty experience with a kidnap and now travels everywhere with an armed guard.

Eventually on the journey back, tiring of the barrel of the gun wandering over the occupants of the car, not least me, I pushed it into the vertical position where it would do less harm if it went off.

"It's not loaded," he told me with that confidence bringing wave of the head prevalent in this part of the world. I think the big man is in greatest danger from his idiot guard if he ever gives him any bullets.

We drove to the restaurant at a good pace along a dual carriageway with no street lights and all the drivers with their head lights on full beam. The fact that the local sacred cow population finds the roads a pleasant place to sleep and chew the cud means that drivers must somehow pick out the unlit cows before hitting them — and they like the fast lane, that's the cows and the drivers. We got to the restaurant, which was entirely lit by hurricane lamps and housed in a series of village houses built of poles and palm leaves. The food is vegetarian and very good, though the method of serving is rather alarming. You are seated on the ground and a covey of rather grubby Indian servants comes round with steaming copper pots of who knows what, which they ladle onto your palm leaf.

Before eating, we were entertained by two lads with a puppet show. The children loved it. It was similar to Punch and Judy, but with no words, just a fizzy whistle made by the puppeteer and the drum of his assistant; one character specialised in losing his head and reattaching it to the wrong parts of his body, another had an extra-long neck, which meant his head could almost reach the audience and the children who shrieked, but the best was the snake, which leapt out at them from the curtains of the stage. On some nights they have dancers, but not that night. The next morning, I caught the flight to Delhi, on my way home at last.

12th September '99 — India part 3

I was booked into the Sheraton in Delhi — civilisation, at last. Delhi consists of the old and the new in close juxtaposition. New Delhi is the British Raj seat of government and old Delhi the Mughal one. I had most of the day to look around, so went and found the travel desk in the hotel and asked what they could do. Inevitably, they asked me what I wanted to see, to which I inevitably said I didn't know, why didn't they tell me. So, we got round that one and they gave me a driver with instructions to take me to the sights, being New Delhi and the Red Fort, plus some other bits and pieces.

He took me to his favourite curio shop and could not really understand that I was not buying and that he was therefore not getting commission for taking me there. Apart from that, he was a good lad and I think I tipped him round about the charge for the trip. Easily done, with the rupee at 43 to the dollar.

So, Lutyens! To read the books, he sounds a bit of a Philistine, but I expect taking remarks out of context was the media's stock in trade then as now. His New Delhi creation is worthy of any megalomaniac, masses of space for parades, with the centre piece of the twinned government buildings set on the hill at the end of the great approach, reaching out like a lion's paws to accept or to issue the magnificent. I could see myself ruling a continent from there.

The buildings are neo-classical with Mughal influences — which somewhat belies Lutyens' derogatory remarks about Indian indigenous architecture — and all of red sandstone. The "mall" that leads up to the building complex is confined at its nether end, a mile away it seemed, by the Indian Gate. It is a war memorial in the style of Roman triumphal arches. Beyond it and on either hand are gardens, the mall being a few hundred yards wide. When I stopped over here with Mother in 1969, we attended the national day celebrations, but I never noticed Lutyens' buildings being too far down towards the gate.

Independence Day in Delhi

My driver asked if I wanted to walk and stopped the car for me to wander round outside the government buildings. They form a stage for the Viceroy's residence, but it is gated so you cannot get to it, but I peered through the railings, wondering at the conceit of our forefathers in building such a vast place for two people to live in. The front door has as many columns as the colonnade embracing St. Peter's, and the dome would probably fit over St. Paul's.

Turning round, the red sandstone buildings frame the view down the "mall" to India Gate, and walking along the pavement, the ground drops beside you as the road declines. On each bluff above the road, there are two domed and columned red sandstone octagonal buildings providing shade and a breeze so you can stand and stare —, and if you've a mind, pat Lutyens on his metaphysical back.

Lutyens had competition. You can imagine the old bird looking at the Red Fort and thinking, "Well, one way or another I have to beat that — show these chappies what's what". The Red Fort is competition indeed. I was sitting in the back of the car, watching all the bric-a-brac of India going by, bikes, oxen carts, hand carts with enormous loads of old paraffin tins or sacks of rice and the press of people all going somewhere or, if not, tending tiny shops and stalls, when out of the melee the huge red sandstone walls of the fort stopped my reverie in its tracks.

They are huge and intricate, with towers and embrasures and battlements, and the stones are cut and laid with such precision even to the extent of having alternately deep and shallow courses to give life to the undecorated parts. The road runs round under the wall outside the moat until you come to the barbican, a later addition to protect the main gate itself from attack.

Views of the Red Fort in Delhi

Not the Peacock Throne, but close

Here, all the buses and taxis park up, and you can buy your ticket for a few rupees that gives you access to all of the site. I walked across the park into the barbican entrance and then left handed into the fort itself.

Rather to my surprise, you pass through the Lahore Gate and are immediately in the bazaar, which used to sell gold, silver, spices, dried and fresh fruits, perfume and so forth to the gentry, but now plies Indian handicrafts and Kodak films. The bazaar is arched but halfway down, it opens to the sky to let in light; you pass this and another side entrance that used to lead to the houses of the rich and famous, but the Brits knocked them down and built a barracks instead.

After sixty yards or so, you emerge into the sunlight to find yourself approaching another building with a central arch, balconies and whatnot that used to be the Drum House. According to the book, a band performed here to add resonance to the arrival of important visitors — resonance that kept the other visitors awake nights. Through the arch, you come into the presence, or used to when The Presence was there, sitting on his throne in the centre arch of the next building another fifty yards further on. What a throne too.

Pietra dura is the inlaying of precious or semi-precious stones in the base material of white marble, as employed in the Taj Mahal. The throne is a riot of pietra dura, flowers, birds, animals, a copy of a Raphael painting of a god charming the animals all enacted on intricately carved white marble columns, plinths, balustrades and arches. You stand and wonder how it is all possible. The throne is set back under the canopy provided by nine arches and a colonnade of red sandstone pillars which used to be decorated with hangings and carpets. It must have been fabulous in its hey day (or is that hay day?).

Behind the Diwan i Am, the building above, are the private areas of the fort, where the harems were and the palaces for the first wives among gardens laid out with canals in red sandstone for running water with little foot bridges, pools and waterfalls. I was fascinated by their designs of sculpted edges to the pools so that the water level just filled the interstices, showing the designs in relief against the reflective water surface. Regrettably, you must rely on your imagination for an idea of what it must have looked like, as the Indians don't do much maintenance and no restoration.

The river Yamuna used to flow at the back of the fort but unfortunately has moved itself further off, so when you look down from the private residences, you see only a grass sward with park land beyond. One of the buildings housed the Peacock Throne, which was snitched by someone. The plinth on which it used to stand is there, but the throne is gone. To judge by its setting, it must have been splendid. The building is open on all sides, with the roof supported by a myriad of square white marble pillars, each beautifully decorated with carving and pietra dura. Fortunately, there is enough of it not to notice the absence of a lot of the inlay prised out by vandals of all centuries and cultures.

Like the Al Hamra in Granada, it must have been a great place for lying around in on carpets and cushions. Peel me a grape! No camera, so I bought the book. A photograph can draw your attention to the details you passed over, and looking through the book, I would like to go again and this time with camera and of course more time.

I am completing this in Oman. Tomorrow is Friday and I might go and take a look up a wadi I have been wanting to see. Regrettably no companions available.

17ᵗʰ September '99 — Oman

Sitting here in the kitchen of the guest house in Muscat and going to Salalah tomorrow. Went on a wadi trip this morning to the Ghubra bowl. It is remote. Six kilometres of dirt road gets you to a cleft in the mountain, which turns out to be a wadi bed with the road running along it among boulders the size of a truck and steep walls ten feet on either side reaching up several hundred metres. The bed opens out to reveal a bowl in the mountains fifteen to twenty km across. The book says the mountains go up to two thousand five hundred metres.

Most of the road is pretty flat until you get to the other side, where the lads have built villages up the sides of the mountains where the springs emerge to water their gardens. The road up to these villages is graded shale which scoots from under the wheels of a Jeep Cherokee Larada. I think Cheep Jerrykey is a better description. An automatic with only three gears is no fun in bad going and if you drop to low ratio, it will take you all day to get over an anthill. It got me there and back so should not grouse, and I will hand it back to the office with a satisfactory layer of dust inside and out.

The villages are perhaps a thousand feet above the plane of the base of the bowl, so you get some fabulous views. The natives emerge in droves to practice their English, "How are you?". For some reason this is as far as children of school age get — in any village or town, "How are you?". Perhaps "The Early English Reader" for Omani schools has only three pages — Page 1: How, Page 2: Are, Page 3: You — roll credits. Beats me. The elder ones mutter Arabic greetings and ask for a French/English dictionary! On this occasion anyhow. I wonder what he thought to do with it if I had one, or maybe his "Later English Reader" had some useful phrases viz: Do you have a French…

The road up to one village has the required 4WD parked on its side two hundred yards down a glacis of rocks. Helga had a story of a notice in Uganda, which read something to the effect of "This is a private cemetery for careless drivers" just before a particularly hairy piece of road engineering. I was passed by one — I think German. His companion was wearing hot pants to walk through an Arab village.

22nd September '99 — William letter

The wadi-bashing trip sounded fun. How can they produce an off-road jeep with an automatic gearbox — I suppose the "shopping trip/school run" clientele now decides the latest designs in off-road vehicles. I recently saw one of the new Jaguars, which, despite now being designed by the Yanks, still retained most of the tasteful lines the old Jags had. However, upon closer inspection, I noticed two pop-out plastic Coke can holders protruding from the walnut veneer dashboard. I immediately cancelled my order!

The weekend in Cardiff was very nice, if a little wet. Andrew appears to be well settled in and has a suitably up-market student house — no signs of rat or cockroach infestations yet, but give it time.

Helen and I took a wander around the castle during a break in the rain. I can imagine that they felt pretty superior looking down on the local Welsh peasants from high on the battlements. We also inspected the Dragoons regimental museum, buried deep in the castle walls. The cavalry appeared to have a fairly macabre habit of chopping off Dobbin's hoof when he died and turning it into a snuff box. I guess you get three extra to give away to your friends or relatives. It reminded me of boxes I had seen in a market in Katmandu, comprised of human skulls inlaid with silver, inside which you put… tea, spices, paperclips, spare nuts and bolts, god-only-knows? Apparently, the Ganges is littered with skulls ready for the picking.

The frog-in-a-blender demo brought forth various squeaks and groans from the assorted lab people. I'm sure you could market it if you could replace the frog with various individuals — I certainly know of a few in computer support I'd like to blend.

The gels are calling, and I have a grant proposal to finish by Friday, so must go.

22 September 1999 — Dhofar

I am sitting a thousand feet above nothing — my feet over the edge of the cliff. To my right is a family of mountain people selling rugs — hand woven somewhere among these vast crags. They are ten metres from the cliff edge, and circling in the thermals just below them, four vultures and three eagles. The other side of the canyon, another mountain slightly higher than this one, with tiered cliffs below it with trees lodged in the fissures in the rock. The canyon opens out into the plain, stretching away north and west to the Wahiba sands.

Jebel Akhdar

I can see villages, just discernible in the heat haze, with date palm gardens around the white houses. There's a cool breeze, but the sun is hot on my back, the voices of the Omanis chatting among their rugs and the pitter patter of the hooves of a kid goat that has just come over to see what I am doing with pen and paper. It reached over the edge of the cliff to eat some piece of greenery. It should have fallen over, but then it's a goat!

The wind got stronger, and the paper kept blowing around, so I had to give up. What a place. It was so hard to leave. I bought one of the rugs from an old man, probably about my age, but they don't wear too well out here. We drove to the end of the road, where we found a family living with the most wonderful view at their doorsteps. I don't think the view could count for much with them in their hard life of goats and weaving carpets lived out in tiny stone-built huts.

A good day out in Oman

Date: 10/11/99 — Jebel Akhdar

This from Dubai airport, on my way back to Muscat, hopefully, as a prelude to a delayed return to Europe. I am just slightly concerned that by the time I am done here I will have to stop in Jordan on the way home. I have been two days in Dubai and last night had chance to catch up with old friends — here at dinner with one of them. Two I last saw in Salalah in the club, partway through a delivery voyage, and two others left for Australia where I think P. saw them a couple of years back. They are now back in Dubai, for the time being, at any rate, and if they can get the Sharjah government to pay their bills — which they are not prone to do.

I have been here to see the consulting engineers who are working on some new cargo sheds for Salalah. Ben, who runs their office here, asked me to stay with them for the night so I didn't suffer a hotel. He and his wife, Glynis, have been here for ten years, having originally only come for a year. Not unusual, I suppose. A very pleasant couple and very hospitable. Ben and I fell to discussing houses in UK. He had bought a place years ago in Clapham with subsiding walls. Being a civil engineer meant that he was able to fix it and they still have the house, but he remarked how everything was done on the least possible budget. He wondered once why on earth they had painted the spare room such an awful colour and then remembered that they had absolutely no money and this was a can of paint they happened to find in their cellar. The hall floor was a case in point at home — chip board was cheap!

Last Friday, I had decided that one way or another I would investigate Jebel Akhdar, but on the previous Wednesday I met a Dutchman who is building a tank farm for bunker oil in the port in Muscat. We were sitting in his Jeep, waiting for my port pass to come through, and got to talking about four-wheel drives and whether he liked his Jeep. One thing led to another, so on Friday morning we foregathered at the super-market out of town to buy food and set off. As usual with women, around the start time was already late and it got later as we debated the finer points of lukewarm pizzas and cooking bananas (Matoke?), but she is Turkish. The expedition consisted of Alex, two metres and big with it, girlfriend, Tilly — one and a half metres, Tilly's friend from Schipol duty free and Harry, master of the ex-oil minister's new yacht — big motor boat, actually.

I thought Harry and Duty free would travel with me, but Alex put his girlfriend and friend with me, and the two lads got in the other truck. OK, but did he have an ulterior motive? Possibly — Tilly, a charming lady but definitely to be avoided by donkeys; there could be a lot around short of a hind leg. The spring began to run down after an hour just short of Nizwa where we stopped for coffee in a local restaurant that didn't serve coffee, so we had to have tea.

Nakhl Fort

It would have been nice to look around Nizwa again, but as I said, getting away early was not in the plan. I visited Nizwa last year, I think it was. There is the most magnificent round castle just as you might build on the beach, and sand coloured, too. Apparently, they have a product now which looks like mud and straw and whatever they used to put in to hold it together (asses' milk? No, that was Cleopatra) but the new stuff performs like cement plaster, so it doesn't wash off in the rain.

Tilly works on the royal flight as cabin crew and looks after not only HM but also his guests, who tend to be knighted military and diplomatic (no doubt some are benighted, but I didn't say that). The story of how he came to power and all that went before and after must be written someday, but I doubt anyone will do it now. The old school know when to shut their mouths, perhaps, and it was all the old school who acted as king makers. There are stories that he killed his father, which he didn't, and that someone put a bullet in the father's leg so he had to go to UK to hospital and was not allowed back. He did, I believe, see out his days in a grand London hotel,

Date Gardens from Nakhl Fort

which, for someone who deprived his people of comfort, education and medical help for years in the name of religion, must be some sort of backwards punishment. I've no doubt he suffered in silence.

HM battles to control the avaricious lot he has as ministers. I think HM does not set the Good King Wenceslas example too much himself — no snow — but in comparison to his ministers and their like in the Gulf, he's a paragon. He has been down in Salalah for the last few days and will set off for his annual desert "meet the people" safari in a day or two. He travels with an entourage who have to put up with tent life for a few weeks and meet all the tribal sheiks and hear their woes. I don't think they enjoy it very much. Harry lived on the Isle of Wight for some years and skippered yachts for those too idle or too rich to do it themselves. The pay is better for motorboats than for sailing yachts, which is why he is out here. He was about to move the boat down to Salalah; though where he will berth it, I am not too sure. It is most unlikely that the ex-oil minister will want to get to and from in a rowboat and we are using all the quays for cargo — tough one!

After Nizwa, the road begins to climb into the mountains, following the wadi beds and eventually winding up the bluffs. It is dirt and well-graded at this time of year, as there have been no rains to wash it out.. They come in April if they come at all, as I recollect. I was driving an automatic Mitsubishi Pajero, not a bad truck, but the automatic is a pain off-road. You can manually select a gear, but there are only three of them, low is too low and medium is too high. It was its first trip out, so it went back to the driver thoroughly dusted up and exercised.

Deserted village

We passed a village in the wadi bottom, the hills on either side and set up on a cliff the old village built of roughly dressed stone, the colour of the cliff it sat atop of, looking like an organised extension of the rock.

At a place where the strata were dipping gently south, I took my eyes off the road following the rock pavement beside me and nearly went off the road. To our left, the great slab of black rock fell away to a view down two thousand feet to the desert below. It seemed you could see all the way to Salalah, nine hundred kilometres to the south.

Jebel Akhdar

The road wound on up steep turns until we reached about two thousand metres where the going was a bit less vertiginous and eventually arrived at a fence and military notices saying go away. We had reached the radar station and the unfortunates manning it all rushed to the fence to see what diversion had arrived. Having dealt with the necessary greetings, I declined coffee, knowing that that would mean long delays, followed most probably by having to fight off offers of goat to follow.

They directed us back down the road a kilometre to the turn which would take us south of a ravine, the final approach to the radar station being to the north of it and up another thousand metres. Following the directions, we found ourselves on a well graded road, travelling mostly on the tops with occasional valleys until we came out on a rock pavement, a shelf above the deep ravine we had not been able to see before. We were greeted by the local rug weaving family with their rugs, hoping to make a sale.

There was another four-wheel drive there from one of the tour companies with Dutch tourists negotiating with the Omanis. A detachment of carpet sellers came over to us to see what they could achieve, but we had been told they could get unpleasant if you showed a lot of interest and then failed to make a deal — fair enough, I would feel the same. It also seems to me that you owe them something as a fee for invading their patch, but still, honour must be satisfied, so after asking the price of a rug from the patriarch, I declined further interest on the basis of it being an unreasonable demand: about thirty-five pounds for a rug five feet by three foot six. The view over the heads of the rug seller and his extended family was superb.

Later, after looking around, the others wandered off while I said I would stay by the vehicles. Sitting a thousand feet above nothing — my feet over the edge of the cliff — to my right, the family of mountain people selling rugs — hand woven somewhere among these vast crags. They were ten metres from the cliff edge, and circling in the thermals just below them, four vultures and three eagles. The other side of the canyon, another mountain slightly higher than mine, with tiered cliffs below it with trees lodged in the fissures in the rock. Looking to the right, the canyon opened out into the plain, stretching away north and west to the Wahiba sands. I could see villages, just discernible in the heat haze, with date palm gardens around the white houses. There was a cool breeze, but the sun was hot on my back, the voices of the Omanis chatting among their rugs and the pitter patter of the hooves of a kid goat that came over to see what I was doing with pen and paper. It reached over the edge of the cliff to eat some piece of greenery. It should have fallen over, but then it was a goat! What a place. It was so hard to leave.

As we were going, I walked to the edge again, looking around me before getting into the car.

"Lost something?" from one of my passengers.

"No. Just can't leave!" I bought one of the rugs from the old man for a small discount, probably about my age but they don't wear too well out here.

We drove to the end of the road, where we found a family living with the most wonderful view at their doorsteps. I don't think the view could count for much with them in their hard life of goats and weaving carpets lived out in tiny stone-built huts. They came over with rugs and wool sandals, trying to make a sale. One old boy had a distaff with him and showed me how they spun the goats' hair, a handful of hair in his hand, the distaff spinning under its own inertia around knee height twisting the skein of hair as he tugged from the handful. Always wondered how that worked!

Jebel Akhdar Canyon and weaver's house

16th October '99 — Ghubrah Bowl II

You may recall a previous burble on the Ghubrah Bowl, in which I lamented the missing of a good walk as a result of reading the book and making the trip in the wrong order. Friday morning, I departed early to rectify the problem. I was tempted to go back to Jebel Akhdar instead, but decided not and in the event was most pleased with the decision.

The road from Muscat to Sohar and the UAE border follows the coast within a few miles. The land on either side is cultivated or devoted to the weekend villas and gardens of the wealthy, watered from wells bored into the aquifers fed from the mountains set back forty kilometres from the beach. The farms are largely devoted to date gardens, market gardening and deep green mango trees lining the driveways.

The Gubhra Bowl is beyond Nakhl, where the country road turns west and follows the feet of the mountains. After Nakhl, the land is deserted; to the right is broken ground and rock hillocks and to the left, the foothills and in the bright sunlight, exaggerated three-dimensional sawtooth mountains, bare of any vegetation beyond the odd thorn bush. In due course, a left turn leaves the macadam road for a well-graded dirt road heading for a slot in the mountain range through a plain of tamarisk thorn and bleached wadi bed cobbles.

I got there just before nine in the morning, with the sun well up and beginning a hot day. Immediately, the road dives in among boulders the size of a lorry following the wadi bed in deep gravel, the walls of the wadi at the narrowest being about thirty feet apart and rising at forty-five degrees to the mountains above. This is important data, as you will discover.

After a mile or so, the wadi opens out into a steadily broadening alluvial plain with spreading Ghaf trees, under which you can park to take a break from the hammering of the suspension. Further along, after another mile or so, you enter the bowl proper to find a few villages growing crops on the plain, surrounded on all sides by the limestone cliffs rising a thousand metres and more above the sedimented glacial rocks which form a sloping rampart to the foot of the cliffs. The base of the bowl is glacial conglomerate, originally sludge with larger lumps in it dropped from the melting ice floating above. I wonder who worked that out.

Gubhra Bowl and Wikan village

Apparently, the conglomerate is impervious so the water, percolating through the limestone, emerges in springs at the discontinuity which is five hundred to a thousand metres above the floor of the bowl. In the photo, you can see the change in gradient. It's fifteen kilometres across the bowl and at the southern end, the road begins to rise after crossing a deep wadi bed full of pebbles.

On a bluff above the wadi edge, I found a mound of stones which looked man-made, and it crossed my mind that it could be a grave mound, but then I thought I was being too inventive. Much later, back in the house, I found photographs of similar mounds described in the books as barrows.

The road climbs out of the plain and up the gentler slope to two villages. The first has a watch tower and is quite low compared to the second, which is well up above the plain. The altimeter in the truck read one thousand five hundred metres when I parked, and I think the base was

A falaj or water conduit

five hundred metres. There is very little space to park at the village — Wikan — but there were only three vehicles there, so I was all right leaving the truck parked on the edge of a cliff above the road I had just ascended.

I walked up into the village between close-set houses and was greeted by a little boy in Arabic. I replied as best I could, from which he assumed I could speak more and set about leading me up the hill among the gardens beside the falaj, his chatter competing with the chuckling of the stream of canalised water. The falaj is only some nine inches wide and six deep, but it runs steeply down the hillside so carries a good flow of water to the grapevines, date palms, pomegranate trees and plots of maize and vegetables.

The women in their bright dresses and shawls were tilling the soil, carrying water, washing clothes and children while the men were sat under a vine on a trestle, drinking coffee. I greeted them and plodded on up the steep path after my little friend, his bare feet and fuzzy head going before.

Schipol — the people loading arm has gone phut. We have been here for twenty or thirty minutes, but the walkway won't get itself to the aircraft door, so we are waiting for a mechanic to arrive to get it to move as it should. They thought they had the plane in the wrong place so were going to shift it back with one of those big tractor things they use — much gyrating below with towing poles and whatnot. We wait — perhaps we will get the chance to use the emergency chutes.

The village already has a magnificent view of the bowl, but as I climbed — puffed, the altitude, you know — and climbed again, it opened out more and more. There were a couple of stops for my tour guide to explain in fluent Arabic the significance of this or that stone-built hut. I believe one was a miniature mosque at some time.

Further up, small reservoirs had been provided in the stream, concrete tanks about the size of a small swimming bath with a drain plugged or unplugged by the branch of a tree with the right size end to it. As the ground grew steeper, the cultivation lessened to whatever could find a horizontal space to grow on, a grape vine here or a date palm with its own little diversion channel to carry the water to it. The grapes are grown on trestles or trellises made of poles and the spines from the palm leaves.

The path is formed of large stones set as steps so it is not too difficult to climb, and failing that, you can walk on the side of the falaj. Where

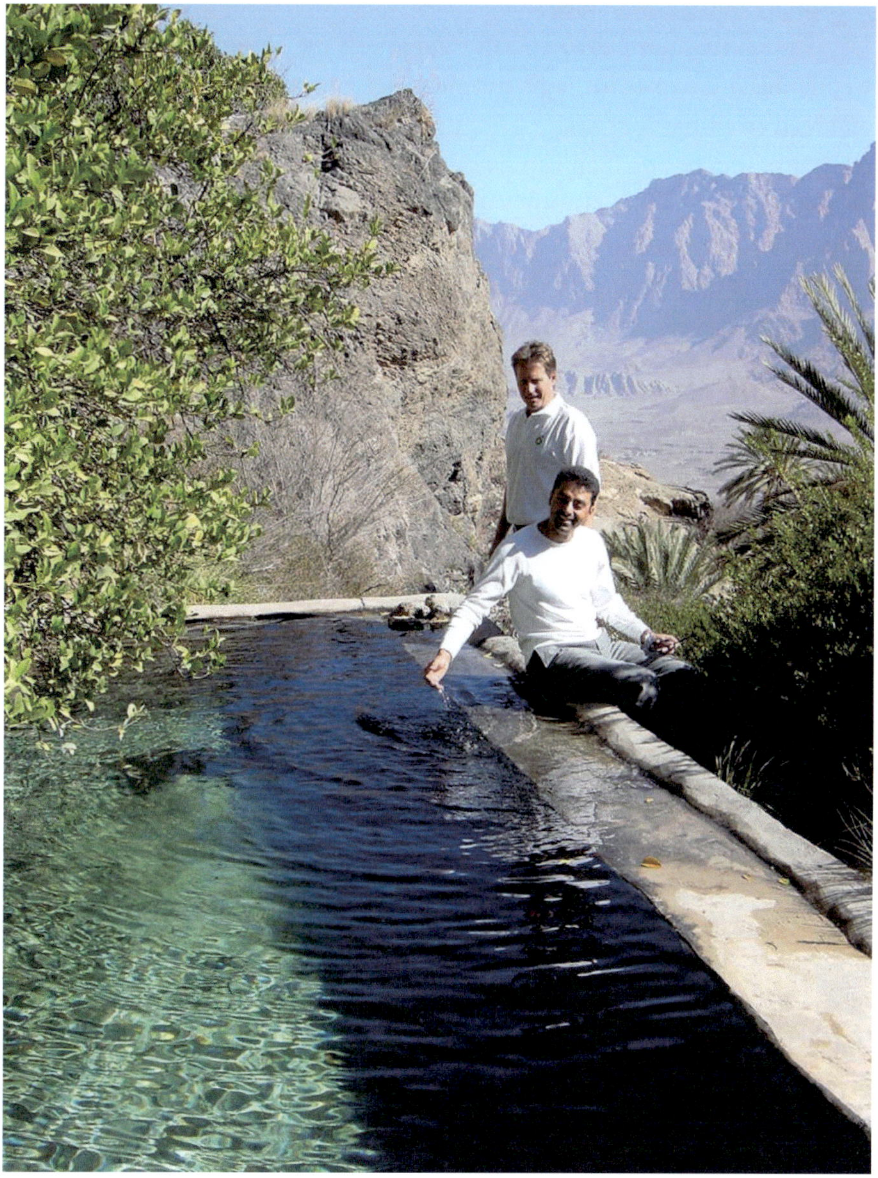

necessary, the ground is terraced with uncut stones built into retaining walls. The work forced upon these people's ancestors just to keep alive is incredible; the available space is no longer fully utilised, some of the plots seemingly being abandoned.

The cultivation ended and my guide left me to plod on upward, still beside the running falaj, until I came to a tank and a fall where the water emerged from the rock wall. After this, the path became less distinct, with grass growing beside it and a variety of shrubs and trees — more like Table Mountain than Arabia. To my right, there was the remains of a fortress of some sort, set high above the village on a bluff. The path to it seemed to run between the mountain and a great vertical slab of rock that had split away but remained upright. I considered following it up, but decided that getting up would be fine, but getting back down again would be hard on the knees so followed the path the other way, which I believe eventually winds its way up onto the plateau at two thousand four hundred metres. I stopped at a convenient rock with a foothold to climb up onto it and sat there to survey the bowl and the village below me.

I could then see another village, a little lower than the first, with a ruined mud-built palace, crenelated with massive steel-studded carved timber doors like those in Zanzibar. The view over the bowl was magnificent, and I sat on my rock for a quarter of an hour — looking; the wild distances counterpointed by the women below me working in their tiny plots; butterflies and martins, the smell of warm foliage and a stiff breeze to keep the temperature perfect.

If the geologists are right and the bowl was formed by the erosion of a dome a total of one thousand five hundred metres deep by fifteen thousand by ten thousand by, say, three tons per cubic metre = six hundred and seventy-five thousand million tons of rock all went out through the narrow wadi I came in by (the dredging contract at Salalah was thirty million dollars at three dollars a cubic metre, so they moved about three million tons). The Wadi floor is six hundred Ma = six hundred million-year-old conglomerates and the mountains are pre-Permian = two hundred and eighty-five million years old. So, shall we say, over the course of four hundred and fifty million years, one thousand five hundred tons of rock a year, every year, went through the gorge, carried by water. You would have to multiply that by at least ten thousand, on the basis of it needing ten thousand tons of water to carry a ton of rock, to get the water flow, or fifteen million cubic metres of water. The catchment being ten thousand by fifteen thousand means the rainfall would have to be one hundred mm per annum. I would like to see the wadi in flood if they ever got an inch of rain in a night. I confess that I started out wondering how it could be possible that all that rock got washed out of the one exit to the bowl. When you look at the amount of water flowing from the catchment area, it becomes more conceivable. Just by the way the ten thousand to one comes from some pretty rough calculations on silt deposition in Cochin.

The office is very quiet. A lot of people have left the company in the reorganisation, which was to have concentrated work in Cork. They hired two hundred people in Cork in the summer and they have just been told they will all be made redundant in January, as they have now decided not to do the Cork thing at all. Brilliant management! I am here for a few weeks then a short trip to Oman and back for Christmas.

22nd November 2003 — Shiel Bet, Gujerat

If you go to Pipavav, you will drive through miles of fields of cotton, maize, sorghum and some unidentifiable scruffy-looking crops. I believe they grow groundnuts, but I have not seen any. Just now the cotton is maturing; the flowers are still on some of the bushes and in among them the white cotton from the burst cotton bolls. They are growing GM varieties, but there is concern that the gene is becoming diluted and the pests, particularly bollworm, will develop resistance and start the cycle all over again.

After the farms, the salt pans and after the salt pans, the port and the cement works; it is not pretty. The salt pans have expanded behind the bunds built for access to the port and this has confused the water flow so that the roads are weakened and undermined and the car leaps from rut to rut in the bad patches. Tar-macadam is a poor substitute for a regularly graded dirt road if it is not maintained. Money is beginning to flow into the project, so these things are getting fixed, and the commitment is evident from the better organisation, cleaner aspect and the movement of trucks carrying cargo between the railhead, the godowns or warehouses and the quays.

As I was saying, there is nothing to Pipavav at first, and second, acquaintance. However, as you stand on the coal dust, eight hundred thousand tons of it a year, you can look across to Shiel Bet. Bet is an island and Shiel Bet has a fishing village on it of about a thousand people apparently, a little larger than West Meon. From the port, the details are rather indistinct, the more so because of the heat haze, and I had thought it might be diverting to at least go and look. Our consulting engineer, Murthy, had said he wanted to look at the lighthouse on the next Bet, Savai, so we booked a fishing boat to take us over.

The boat, when it came, was put together by someone without too much by way of tools and less by way of woodworking skills. However, it floated and the old truck engine didn't miss a beat. The tiller, part of a tree, was several feet long and needed to be from the apparent effort required to manoeuvre the vessel. The deck planking fitted where it touched, and the grapnel anchor was stowed by dropping its shank through a convenient gap, leaving the flukes for everyone to trip over.

Pilot launch

Country living

We, Vadya, our civil engineer, Murthy and Henrik, the port CEO, climbed down the side of the quay to get aboard and set off the few hundred yards to the shore the other side where the fishermen pulled the boats up the beach. The bay, with the houses coming to the high-water mark, is protected by a reef with a small gap for boats. There has been an ongoing argument, fuelled by competitor's rumour mongering, that we would have a problem with dredging outcropping rock. There is nothing a competitor likes to hear more than that your port is obstructed by diamond-hard basalt or granite; and if it's not there, well, it can be invented.

We alighted from our fishing boat and I and Murthy took a good look at the lime/coral that is the material of the aforesaid protective reef. It looked pretty hard to me, but a four thousand-horse motor can do a lot of munching in a cutter suction dredger. The ones I have seen have cutter heads six feet in diameter and teeth a foot long bolted to the head. Murthy was quite happy the stuff would give way in the face of such an assault.

The beach was clean and sandy, with a couple of defunct boats pulled well out of the water in front of an icing sugar-pastel pink and green Hindu temple with votive flags fluttering from poles lashed wildly to the roof. No one paid much attention to us as we walked up the beach, except for the proprietor of the tea shop on the beach, whose blandishments we declined. The fishing village turned out to be much larger than I had thought.

Fishing boats on the beach

The main village

The island just off the port from the approaches

The houses are built of dressed limestone, sandstone or coral; I think a calcified sandstone quite common in Indian ports and a real problem to the dredgers before the powerful machines we have now. I read an extract from a book written in the thirties by the then-port engineer for the Raj about his trip to Tuticorin. He described how the dredger had tried to break up the stone with a pile dropped over the side of a vessel but had only succeeded in punching holes in the strata. Much, much later, they had tried dynamite and left with the channel obstructed by another metre of broken rock and the effective depth reduced accordingly.

Each house is about the size of our sitting room, built of roughly-dressed stone, roofed with tiles and many of them locked up with thorn bushes placed to keep the goats off the verandas. Vadiya, our civil engineer, was with us and he speaks Gujerati, so he provided what information was available. The fishermen and their families were mostly away at sea for the nine months out of the monsoon season, during which they cannot fish at all. Someone remarked that they must get back often enough to keep up the population of small boys and girls being looked after by their grandparents in the occupied houses. Since everything comes over by boat and the families are not rich, there was little rubbish, unlike the rest of Gujerat.

The houses consist of one large room with a veranda at the front, to one side of which is an open fire, set in a niche in the wall. The verandas are often brightly decorated with geometrical designs.

Shei Bet House and decor

Some of the larger properties have a small walled courtyard. As we wandered through the village, someone spotted us from one of the courtyards and called to our fisherman guide, who imperiously shook his head. Long Imperial experience told me the lad was probably offering chai to the visitors, so I stopped the procession and said that if indeed chai was on offer, I, for one, was thirsty. Mats were brought out and placed on the charpoys, where I found myself a comfortable position against the wall to watch the Indians exchange pleasantries and the goats clearing up some of the garbage. Our host was the headman of the village but was not out fishing, as his licence had expired. Two of his eleven sons were employed in the port and the others were fishermen too. I asked whether any of the villagers had gone abroad, but it appeared not, they prefer to fish. In good years, they seemed to do quite well financially; they quoted incomes but what with lakhs and crores and rupees, you lose track of the zeros. Round Shial Bet, they catch a lot of Bombay duck, a small carnivorous fish, and some pomfret. My questions elicited an unlooked for result. The headman sent the lad in the baseball cap off and he came back with an old paraffin can full of dried fish, which was set down in front of the head man, who set about pulling the heads off, enough of them for a gift to us.

Bombay duck drying

Cows, goats, chickens and few, if any dogs, the odd cat. Parts of the island are quite green, but the wells are brackish after the residents dug them too deep and the sea water found its way in. We found a farm on a higher part of the island with a more recently constructed well that used to be used to irrigate some small fields, but the whole operation seemed to have been abandoned. Beside one of the wells, two little boys were washing and getting ready for school. I indicated that I would take their photograph, but I had to wait until hair was combed and they had arranged themselves for the camera. The digital camera has it's display on the back, so I was able to show them their pictures — then everyone wanted to see. Next stop, the school, and Henrik asked me to photograph it for his wife, who is a teacher. The children were just assembling, so I got them all standing on the veranda and then went over and sat on the step in the shade so they could all see the pictures. Magic!

The island school (children)

Later, we heard the school bell ring so perhaps one day we can go over and talk to the teacher, and I hope Henrik will find some money in his budget to support their efforts. The higher part of the island is largely uninhabited. As we walked in the sunshine along the path, we came to fields of aloes that Murthy told me were good for wounds. As children, if they hurt themselves, their father would break off a leaf and rub the sap in; they didn't like it much, he said. I remarked that in Europe, aloe juice is a very fashionable addition to women's make up. He rejoined with how wonderful it was that God had provided all these plants and animals for man's use. My Indian theology is a bit rusty, so I was not clear which simian, elephantine, blue or six-armed deity was responsible. Maybe all of them. I should have asked later.

The path dropped down from where we had been looking at our port from the top of low cliffs, and we found ourselves approaching what I had thought was a villa, but which turned out to be a shrine. Passing through a farmyard, we came to wrought iron gates which swung open, giving access to a courtyard with a well with a ficus tree growing in it. Murthy suggested we remove our shoes as a sign of respect, which we did, and ducked through a doorway into a small room with a bed in it and two fellows. The one on the bed was the sadhu and the one squatting cross-legged on the floor was his acolyte. We were invited, in good English, to take a place on the floor. It crossed my mind that his ex-Rotterdam colleagues would enjoy seeing Henrik, whose reputation is a bit Ghengis Khan, cross-legged on the floor in front of this toothless, bearded and not very clean sadhu. Something for the company magazine.

The gentleman on my left, in loin cloth and rather cleaner beard, volunteered to explain the sadhu's presence and purpose on a Bet in Gujerat and proceeded to take us through the religion of Naatism and its various saints, starting, if I remember, with Naat and his nine disciples. The sadhu had arrived ten years ago and relit the sacred fire, which had been allowed to die by the departure for better things of the last sadhu, I suppose. I wonder how many vacant sadhuships there are in India. Are they advertised? How did he know this one was vacant? There ensued a learned discussion about the differing nuances of Naatism, Brahminism and Jainism. I do know that the Jains have a rooted objection to squashing bugs — which, in India, must have its problems just for walking around. The port has a small jetty which is referred to as the pilgrim jetty, so I presumed this was the reason and asked whether the two of them had much custom. Mercifully not, apparently!

My neighbour on the mat then explained how he came to be able to speak such good English and how he came to be sitting there. He was a scion of one of the richer Bombay trading families, he said, and in the sixtiess had gone to the US to be educated. He had done a lot in the US, but not much of it was education. He had married an American girl and lived in America for fourteen years before returning with his family to Bombay, where he had taken up the reins of the family business. For reasons unexplained, after ten years in India, his wife had taken the children back to her country and he had dropped out of business and found himself in Shial Bet with his sadhu with the pierced ears and the endless succession of doubtful-looking cigarettes. While telling us this, he was idly twisting some raw cotton into an extended ear bud. I was not sure whether this had deep Ghandi-eque moral significance or whether ear buds were in short supply on Shial Bet. I saw no spinning whorls.

My friend's career plan was to study Naatism under the sadhu, until the old boy moved to a higher plane, then get his ears pierced and take over putting wood on the fire. His children were still in the US, and he had not seen them for many years. The boy had ambitions to become a rock star, as yet unfulfilled, and the daughter was studying religious Christian philosophy and both of them were in the pecuniary state to be expected of their positions in society — broke. He said he didn't miss seeing them too much and so long as they were all right, he was happy. We were invited to look over the shrine and the cave and take some ash from the fire to mark our foreheads. This, I felt, was not my scene, so I stayed on the mat while the others went to investigate. Murthy and Vadyia did their obeisance; what Henrik did, I don't know, but he came back with the ash in the right place.

Looking round the room, it was quite organised. Nails had been driven into the walls and things hung on them — two pairs of scissors, pictures of deities, that sort of thing — but among the household items were several bill spikes with a thick, faded accumulation of papers on them. I wondered what they could be for, ear piercing services, whacky tobacco, firewood… who knows. The cave part had been made over with Johnson's ceramic tiles (Johnson's Tiles, not just a tile, a Lifes-tile — Bombay commercial!).

The temple garden

We took our leave and walked out into the sunlight. In the yard outside, a tamarind tree with a trunk a foot thick grows horizontally for two or three yards before putting down a knee to be supported on three piled rocks and then proceeding onwards, refreshed. It gives shade to a small shrine with a marble carved bull couchant with a lily flower between its ears. There is a well with a stone trough from which you can drink the — probably — holyish water, if you don't mind the green soup in the well and the possibility of an unholy night in the loo. The shrine is on a slight rise, and below it, the valley contains two or three small fields with another well that might have been used for irrigation.

The well walls are constructed with a ramp on one side, indicating that it was used with oxen to pull the water up with a bucket on a rope over a pulley as they did in Arabia. The two or three cows, with the trees bordering the fields, leant an air of home counties peace to the scene.

We had completed our circuit of the island and made our way back to the landing staithe opposite the port. I photographed the fish drying on the beach and Henrik standing beside a derelict canoe-like boat with grown knees and copper fastenings. We boarded our vessel and headed northeast, following the channel between the islands and the mainland to get to Shiva Bet and the light house. A notch in the reef provided a short cut for our boat with the waves splashing around us and the deck hand keeping lookout in the bow.

We made it safely and were soon disembarking at another stone staithe leading to steps cut in the earth, with a mosque on our left hand and the lighthouse on our right. This island seemed to be Muslim, whilst the other was definitely Hindu. Through American insistence after 9/11, ports around the world have been forced to implement security measures governed by the locally appointed ISPS authority. They vary. The officer arrived at Pipavav to conduct his survey and make recommendations. He was very concerned that there was a small Muslim population among the fishermen which needed two measures implemented. We were to employ a spy to live on Shial Bet to keep an eye on the lads and we definitely needed a fast launch with a machine gun mounted on the bow with search lights. I had delightful visions of the spy arriving via the old lifeboats with a suitcase and disguised in a pointed hat and black cloak. It didn't happen.

Declining invitations to the mosque for now, we climbed out of the bay and across the shoulder of the hill to the few houses of more fishermen close to the lighthouse enclosure. We were invited for tea but pressed on through groves of aloes to the lighthouse compound gate. The keeper's boy let us in, and the keeper emerged, yawning and stretching, from his bungalow to shout greetings to Vadyia. The light itself, the optics and the mechanism, was built by a French company. I would have photographed the notice board with all the details on it, but these things are strategically important and secret. The fact that they are all available in published documents like the Admiralty charts is neither here nor there. The last lighthouse I was in was Dinas Head, which was designed for an oil lamp with the associated one ton of glass and mechanism. This one is electrically powered, but the reason for the green shaft running down beside the stairs became apparent on closer inspection. The fallback mechanism is weight driven, and the weight falls the full height of the tower. I wonder when it was last tested and what they use for a light source when they need the weight.

Henrik was getting edgy, so we declined tea again, this time from the lighthouse keeper, and set off back for the boat. On the way, however, we found that the small Muslim community, the part not mending their nets, had prepared tea and cold water. It seemed churlish to decline the water,

The view from the lighthouse, port cranes

which tasted smoky and a bit brackish. Sitting on the veranda in the shade and looking up, I noticed that the ceilings were constructed of heavy short beams supporting dressed stone slabs about a foot by nine inches wide. It must be a good construction to even out the heat of the day with the cooler night, as they seem to have a tiled roof above it as well. Maybe the tiles came later. Funnily, and I suppose logically, they are exactly the same roof tiles design as we had in Uganda — after all, the architects were Indian there too, as well as the builders. Above the door of one of the buildings, someone had written "Power House". Inside were the tools, parts and detritus of a repair shop to keep the pumps and fishing boat engines alive in a corrosive and difficult environment. Back in the boat, we headed home, stopping on the way to buy Bombay duck from a fishing boat. We had it for dinner.

The cement works berth from the island and Henrik